FELIX FRANKFURTER REMINISCES

Felix Frankfurter Reminisces

RECORDED IN TALKS

WITH

DR. HARLAN B. PHILLIPS

REYNAL & COMPANY / NEW YORK

To
"the granite tenderness of Hope"

SECOND PRINTING MAY 1960
THIRD PRINTING JUNE 1960
FOURTH PRINTING JULY 1960
FIFTH PRINTING SEPTEMBER 1960
SIXTH PRINTING SEPTEMBER 1960

Published by Reynal & Company, Inc.

Library of Congress catalog card number: 60-9777

Printed in the United States of America by
The American Book-Stratford Press, Inc.

Contents

Foreword

When Boswell wrote his life of Dr. Johnson he demonstrated how important it is in portraying the varied qualities of his subject to record in detail conversations with him. The Dr. Johnson, who emerges, however, had to be filtered through Boswell's memory, that line officer in the service of his personality which commanded a subjective view Boswell could not wholly avoid. In these memories of Justice Frankfurter I had the benefit of modern recording equipment and thus was able to capture the words of my subject without the multiple handicaps under which Boswell labored.

The recordings were begun in 1953, when I was a member of Columbia University's Oral History Research Office, an archival endeavor established under the direction of a Columbia University Committee in 1949 to accumulate reminiscences by tape-recorded interviews and to file the resultant manuscripts together with supporting papers in a special collection for the use of future scholars. By providing the means whereby a subject, his memory, his accumulated papers, and a trained historian are united in a joint enterprise—the creation of a memoir—invaluable elements of human history which might otherwise perish are preserved. Indeed, this process makes available for the future the kind of material relevant to a man's life which is not available in any other form, either in his written work, his diaries, or other working papers and which, by its very nature, cannot be reconstructed second hand by some future biographer.

Justice Frankfurter was reluctant to embark upon this recorded journey. He was not unaware that history had its rightful claim, but he manifested a convincing lack of interest in himself and was properly jealous of his time and wanted to spend it as and with whom he wished. When he finally did agree to subject his time to my intrusions, I sought and obtained access to his files up to the time he went on the Supreme Court in 1939, so that I might place before him during our conversations such of his papers as might help spur his memory and provide him with the contemporary demonstration necessary for more accurate recall. I was enabled to soak myself thoroughly in the detail of his past as revealed by his papers so that when we did meet I was able to strike the match which set off the intellectual fire-works, and these in turn illuminated the extraordinarily vivid and meaningful recollections this volume contains.

If the reader has ever had the general flavor of his own extemporaneous talk recorded, undoubtedly he has been shocked beyond measure to discover that his conversation is a seemingly endless parade of loose constructions, unfinished sentences, and undeveloped thoughts. This was not the case with Justice Frankfurter, though he was somewhat disturbing with his penchant for digressions—disturbing in the sense that a parenthetical thought bursting for expression would interrupt him in the midst of a sentence, and he would pursue the thought, amplifying it for full clarity, relevance, and appreciation, and then unerringly return and complete the interrupted sentence. I don't know which was the more maddening to a trained listener—the digression, or the surefooted return to the very point where the digression occurred.

For many years Justice Frankfurter was a teacher, still is in many ways, and when that essential fact was coupled to the realization that before him sat fresh, teachable material, the requisite ingredients for instructive talk were present. Our sessions usually ran about an hour, and while the time always seemed stolen from other pressing interests, once the topic was posed the Justice warmed to the telling and recalled his experiences and their consequent wisdom for my education in a manner at once spontaneous, witty, vivid, and alive.

During our sessions as we talked our way through his life to his appointment to the Court in 1939, no thought was given to the possibility of publication. The Justice certainly never had any expectation of its appearance during his lifetime. It was only when the recordings were completed and ready to be filed away for future researchers that a re-reading made it clear that these recorded memories were a contribution to the understanding of certainly one of the most versatile, incisive, even controversial intellects and personalities of our day, for me that rare combination of Puck and the angels. Editing has been done in the interest of providing unity and flow to the work as a whole with relatively few retrospective changes in wording and phraseology. Judgments on people relevant to a given topic are those which spontaneously bubbled in talk, and this is at once partly an explanation of what will be found within and partly a caution in its use. In no sense do these judgments represent final evaluations. They are no less real for not being final, but they are limited to and by the context in which they emerged. The presentation follows in more or less chronological order, though no attempt has been made to give a consecutive review of all the events in the Justice's life. In no sense is this to be deemed an autobiography. For the Justice it was just talk.

At this point I want to express my gratitude to Justice Frankfurter for his patience, his understanding, and most of all, his many, many kindnesses. It was the rarest of privileges to sit and chat with him. From here on his own words will speak for themselves.

Mattituck, N.Y.

HARLAN B. PHILLIPS

FELIX FRANKFURTER REMINISCES

1. *Opening*

MR. JUSTICE, *what of your emergence here in the City of New York? We might begin with newspapers—the difference from Austria, and the fact that one was available continuously to you in New York.*

If you read Dr. Jones's life of Freud, as you should, you will get a picture of Vienna much earlier than my period. Freud's portrait was in the seventies and still earlier. But what I want to say is about the cafe life of Vienna, the male member of the family going to the cafe, to the coffee house, and really drinking coffee, maybe playing cards, reading the papers which were on a rack the way we have them in our clubs here. One's father would then come home and tell the news. That's roughly speaking. If you say, "Well, didn't any newspapers come to your house?" I can't tell, but that is not my recollection. Certainly I have no recollection comparable to the recollection of very soon after we came here, when I could for a penny or two cents—certainly not more than two cents—buy a paper. I bought a paper. It was my paper. That opened up the world, or projected one into it.

Then, right near where we lived I discovered Cooper Union, the first of the common forums which are now scattered around the country, which was a kind of education for working people on the whole, like the Workers' Educational Alliance, except there it was localized. Cooper Union was a very important part of my education. There were classes. There were courses over the week—courses in history, in geography, and in the natural sciences. Downstairs was the famous red-chaired hall in which Lincoln made one of his great addresses. In that same hall Friday night there was always some public topic under discussion with an admirable moderator, Charles Sprague Smith. It was an eager, but disciplined audience. They knew this was intended to be a fair battle between opposing views. The meeting lasted from eight to ten, and at ten o'clock sharp the lights went out the way they do in an army outfit. Then the discussion would continue outside, sort of late night Hyde Park stuff. I mean there would be little circles of people.

Then I discovered that upstairs on the top floor was a reading room where they had on the rack all the daily papers of the United States, state by state. That was exciting. I could read not only a New York paper, but others. Or I would go buy my paper and then read the papers I didn't buy.

I never had heard a word of English spoken and never had spoken an English word when we arrived here in August 1894—not one word! There's a funny story. I came home one day and said, "This man Laundry must be a very rich man because he has so many stores."

School opened very shortly after I came here, Public School 25 on Fifth Street, still going I think. I used to tell C. C. Burlingham that he was responsible for whatever failings and inadequacies I may have, because when I graduated from Public School 25, my diploma was signed, "C. C. Burlingham, Acting President of the Board of Education," the only public job he ever held.

I was pitched into a class. I was in a daze. I don't know where they put me originally, but finally I ended up in the first class. Even that was intellectually much below my knowledge content, but English, of course, was a great barrier. We had a teacher, a middle-aged Irish woman, named Miss Hogan. I suppose she was one of my greatest benefactors in life because she was a lady of the old school. She believed in corporal punishment—I was going to say capital punishment. She evidently saw this ardent kid who by that time had picked up some English—I'm not a linguist and haven't got a good ear for languages—but she told the boys that if anybody was caught speaking German with me, she would punish him. She would give gentle uppercuts to the boys. It was wonderful for me that speaking English was enforced upon my environment in school, all thanks to Miss Hogan.

The neighborhood was one a lot of German-speaking people moved into. It was the district of which William Sulzer, that strange creature, was the Representative. I cannot tell you much because my memory of those things is almost empty. I had such a good time, I was so extrovertishly busy, that I wasn't thrown in upon myself to reflect upon things. Every day was full, and at the end of the day there was no subjective deposit.

I suppose early I was more bookish than others in my family, although I came in part from a bookish family—not bookish so much as intellectual. My uncle, my father's brother, was a vastly, oppressively learned man. He was the librarian-in-chief of the great library of the University of Vienna, and he was also an archaeologist. Unlike me, he was a linguist. He spoke I don't know how many languages and wrote more. So there was that vivid example. But I know next to nothing, and take very little stock in biological tracings or sequences of causalities. Doubtless if I lay on a couch for the next five years a Freud would be able to dig out of me some facts as a basis of speculation, but so far as I'm conscious of it, I know next to nothing about all this. Just as Fritz Kreisler began to play the violin when he was very young, and Mozart composed when he was four, to make irrelevant comparisons, and John Stuart Mill read Greek when he was four, in me there was no such precocious gift, but early, certainly in the early teens, it became manifest that I was interested in the world of affairs. Why that shouldn't be as pronounced a predilection as playing the fiddle or reading Greek I don't know. Anyhow, in my case it was. It began very early, and there's a good deal of justification for a witty remark by Joseph Alsop apropos of my great interest in the doings of the press and the frequent forays of Mr. Arthur Krock of the *New York Times* into jurisprudence. Joe Alsop said, "Arthur Krock is a frustrated jurist, and Justice Frankfurter is a frustrated journalist."

I don't know about Krock, but I do know that's a fair crack about me.

I find that one of your early heroes was William Jennings Bryan. What was the attraction there?

That was the most natural thing in the world. Bryan appeared on the scene in 1896. I was then in my fourteenth year. The atmospheric phenomena of Bryan has to be recreated. If you recall the kind of excitement that tousled-hair Wendell Willkie stirred, suddenly somebody emerged, William Jennings Bryan emerged that way for me. Youth, a golden voice, aspirations of humanity—what more do you want? Compound those and why wouldn't an ardent nature be fired by them?

I should tell you that my devotion to Bryan was not well received at home. The sympathy of my household was all for McKinley. My father tried to explain to me why McKinley was sound and Bryan was unsound. What did I know about 16-to-1? Nothing. And fundamentally speaking that wasn't the real significance of Bryan. His real significance was that he was a spokesman for the farmers, represented relief to the farmers' plight. He was the golden voice of the Middle West beginning to feel that eastern capitalism was exploiting it. It was the cumulative effect of the Granger Movement. Here was a fellow who could entrance people by the quality of his voice, the beauty of his speech. It was all so fresh and romantic and the voice of hope.

Of course, his influence waned. He had a certain naïveté, and a very parochial outlook, no sense of the forces he was fighting, except those forces immediately about him. He made a terrible break when he came East. He said, "I'm now entering the enemy's country." You don't tell an audience whom you want to woo that you regard them as your enemies, and therefore, by implication you're their enemy.

But he was an excitement. Bryan was for me with reference to public affairs what some actor or actress is to an adolescent girl. There was a wonderful Viennese singer who died not so many years ago whose records I like to hear played because he sings songs that are familiar to me—Richard Tauber. I've known about young women who followed him in his concert tours. They heard him in a recital in London, had to hear him in Paris, and in his native heath in Vienna. When I heard that Bryan was coming East, the newspapers having said that he would arrive at Hoboken on such and such a train, I played hookey. Instead of going to school I took the ferry over to Hoboken and waited at the train. I was a little bit of a shaver—not that I'm tall now, but I was smaller and sprightlier and a sparse little kid—so I could move around with great agility. I went over there to greet my hero and came back with him on the boat and stood very near him. I worked my way through those big men that were around. It was a very lovely day. I see him now with the chairman of the Democratic National Committee, James K. Jones, a Senator from Arkansas. There were other party leaders there also. That night Bryan was to speak at Tammany Hall. You may be sure I was there, found my way through the crowd, and was right near the platform. Well, that day was quite exciting.

Did you see anything of Bryan later on in Wilson's time?

No, but I did later on between his campaigns when he wasn't running. When he was just a lecturer he came on to New York and spoke at Carnegie Hall. His theme was "Pending Problems." You had to pay admission, from fifty cents to two dollars. The hall was packed. That fellow spoke for two hours. At the end of two hours he was as fresh as he was at the beginning, and the words just poured out of him to the delight of his hearers—at least this hearer.

I would also hear the opposition speakers. I remember in 1900 when Bryan ran again, and the paramount issue was imperialism; namely, the acquisition of the Philippines as a result of the Spanish War, and what to do about the Philippines. There sticks in my mind a reply to Bryan I heard at Cooper Union in the hall downstairs. The chief speaker was Jacob Gould Schurman, then president of Cornell. He was a Republican, and he made a speech in support of the administration, exposing the weaknesses of the anti-imperialists, Bryan, Moorfield Storey, Gamaliel Bradford, Carl Schurz, all that crowd in American history. I remember Schurman's speech, rather I remember one phrase of it—"The issue of imperialism is a tissue of etherealism." You know, I wouldn't think it was wonderful now, but I did as a kid. The sibilance seemed to me very impressive—"The issue of imperialism is a tissue of etherealism." I mention it to show that I did hear the opposition which is not too surprising because I've never been a party man. I've been that most disliked and wooed of all voters, a mugwump.

I don't know how long after I first entered school, how long after I first heard the English language spoken and spoke it, my first public appearance was. I think it was at graduation from school two years later, or some such function. I had to do a recitation. What do you suppose it was? I had to pick it. How I ever survived! Because despite the experience I've since had, it's exactly the same, not much change in agitation prior to actually facing the public for a performance. I remember with what relief I sat down then, just as I'm relieved when I'm through here on the Court. "If I were an American, as I am an Englishman, I never would lay down my arms—never, never, never!" It was Pitt's address, his speech on conciliation with America.

I began to read Dickens. My education must have been very bad, or rather the inducements to education, because there are some awful gaps in my education. Why in heaven's name did nobody throw me in the path of Mark Twain? *Huck Finn* I haven't read to this day. When I say I haven't read it, I don't mean to say I haven't read into it. I've read a lot of Mark Twain by now, but other things. I missed *Tom Sawyer,* and *Alice in Wonderland* is a reading of late life. There are gaps.

Then, every once in a while there is a commonplace word that comes to me with the excitement and revelation of first experience. Partly it shows what life in New York City is as against life in the country. To illustrate, it was very late that I met the word "andiron," which meant that if one lived in an apartment house in New York, one didn't have any andirons. I didn't come across that word. There are other simple things, certain gaps, but I must have read a lot because I browsed in the library very near us very soon. There was the Ottendorfer Branch of the New York Public Library which I discovered somewhere near where we lived. I used to go there, just as I do now, to see what new stuff had come in.

So far as you and your family were concerned, did they take an active interest in your education?

If you were to ask me what I think as I sit here, without any analysis, without having me stretched out on a couch behind you, the picture in my mind of me and my family is that my father and mother somehow or other saw that they didn't have to bother about this kid, that he was doing all right, and why bother about him. I was a sociable creature. I didn't give them any trouble, but please don't infer that I was goody-goody. I've said, and I've said this when I was nearer in time and feeling to my youth and my relations to my family, that the greatest debt I owe my parents is that they left me alone almost completely.

There were in New York Pulitzer Scholarships. Joseph Pulitzer left a lot of money for various things, or gave money before he died to Columbia for scholarships to the Horace Mann School which was a progressive school, though that isn't what they called it in those days. It was a teaching laboratory for Columbia people for which one took a competitive examination. I took such an examination within two years after I landed on these shores. One day I had a letter from Virgil Prettyman, the principal of the Horace Mann School, asking me to see him in his office. I went up there. He said that I came very, very close to being one of the winners in this contest throughout all the public schools in New York. I came so close to it that they would very much like to have me as a pupil. They would take me for the first year as a pupil at half the tuition fee, I think $100 then. The promise of my examination was such that there was a good chance that I would get a scholarship for the other years.

I said I, of course, would have to take that up with my parents. So there was a family council. Horace Mann seemed a little sweller than something else. Horace Mann sort of led to Columbia. I'm quite sure I said, "No, why should you spend $100 on me? It would be nice if I had had a scholarship."

That was that. Now, if I'd done that, you wouldn't be sitting where you are face to face with me. Everything would have been different—everything.

Since I assume the decision to make the try was your own, what was your purpose in going, or attempting to go, to Horace Mann?

After you're through with public school you go to high school. Purpose? You damned sociologists, you historians who want to get it all nice and fine on paper, you haven't learned how much in this world is determined by non-syllogistic reasoning, or without conscious exploration of a problem with a view to reaching a logical conclusion. You fellows haven't learned that. You think that we're just rationalistic—not merely reasonable, but rationalistic—automata of a logical process.

Horace Mann was supposed to be a better, a flossier high school. Maybe without thinking there entered into it a bit of social snobbery. I may be an intellectual snob, but I know I'm not a social snob. But an uncritical analysis is that Horace Mann is something better than one of the city public schools which is one of the moving reasons many parents send their boys to Andover, and Groton, etcetera. It was just supposed to be a very good school. Want any more "purpose" than that? I went up to see the principal because he wrote me asking me to see him. If we'd stop and reflect on the wisdom of every act we take, if we really stopped and thought about it carefully, if, when somebody says, "Come on and do this and that," we said, "Now, let's see. The advantages of doing that are thus and so. The disadvantages are so and so," life would be different.

City schools were good enough. I have very little doubt, although I wouldn't say I know, or am confident, that I said, "Well, these thousands and thousands of boys don't go to Horace Mann. Why should I fuss around? Why should I see if we can't scrape together $100 to give this boy the advantages that Horace Mann might bring?"

But if I had gone to Horace Mann, I would doubtless have gone to Columbia, and beyond that I don't know—Columbia Law I suppose. I'm not saying that I might not have gone on. I'm not saying that whatever would have happened wouldn't have given me as much pleasure and happiness and fullness of life as the course that my life has taken. All I'm saying is that it would have been bound to be completely different. I speak of that because I have such a deep feeling about the importance of contingency in life. These people who plan their careers—I have so little respect for them. You know what Holmes says? Somebody boasted of being a self-made man, and Holmes said, "Well, a self-made man usually hasn't made much."

In those days City College was an intensive course which crowded into five years high school and college. It is now being discovered that you can do in two years what isn't being done in four years in college. That was acted upon in the old days in City College. It was a fantastic thing really. For five days a week, four hours a day, there was classroom work. It was called sub-freshman. It combined senior high school and college. It was then on Twenty-third Street and Lexington Avenue, and it was a great institution for the acquisition of disciplined habits of work. I don't know that most colleges could claim that result in a large body of their students.

I made friends there particularly with one fellow who was a loquacious talker and a gluttonous reader of everything. It was through him that I saw a good deal of the intellectual, revolutionary, anti-czarist Russia. I'd sit hours and hours and hours in East Side teashops, coffee rooms, and drink highball glasses of tea with some rum in it, or lemon, and a piece of cake, and jaw into the morning about everything under the sun.

There were several fellows on the faculty who were very congenial to me. There was a most stimulating teacher, a scholarly professor of Latin named Charles G. Herbermann, the editor of the *Catholic Encyclopedia.* I had a course in Horace with him. He was wonderful, a great, big, beer-barrelly German with a beard, and very considerable histrionic talents. He would first read Horace in Latin and then translate it into whimsical, colloquial English—very exciting. He was a free spirit, except when anything came near his devout attachment to Catholicism.

At the college you took either the classical or the scientific course. There were no electives at all. The result is that I didn't have even a smattering of science, except that in the freshman year we all had to take a course in rudimentary chemistry of which not a scratch is left on my memory or understanding. The fellow who taught this course was R. Ogden "Pop" Doremus, a very distinguished chemist, I believe, but he was also a great teacher, a great classroom performer, and he was fun.

I started out much excited by Greek, an excitement which has never left me. But the weakness of my character is such that I allowed a pedant to put me to sleep with the result that I've had a lifelong wish that I had been properly taught, that the flame of my interest had not been snuffed out. The Greek language made an appeal to me. I had a feel for its nuances, its delicacies, that I have for no other language. I like to hear French spoken, but no other language so insinuated its way into my sensuous feeling about words as did the Greek language.

I also read a good deal of history. I read a lot, a terrible lot. At college I discovered what was the Lenox Library which is now the Frick. It was one of the foundations that has made the New York Public Library on Forty-second Street. I used to go to the Astor Library on Astor Place near Cooper Union. Then we moved uptown to Seventy-first Street in what is now a terribly opulent neighborhood—112 East Seventy-first Street. That's where the Lenox was. The reading room there was quite unfrequented. It was such a cool, quiet place—serene rather than cool. There were specialties there. I would just look at everything on the open shelves, commentaries on Shakespeare, and so on. I was a browser, and there you could browse.

Here's a line from a letter of yours, "Morals are three-quarters manners." What do you mean by that?

Since you throw back at me that phrase, "Morals are three-quarters manners," I had always attributed it to something I got from Matthew Arnold. A friend of mine who is a great authority on Matthew Arnold says he doesn't believe Arnold said anything like it, and I said, "Very well, if he didn't, then I'll appropriate it as my own."

I think he did say something like, "Conduct is three-fourths of life." I don't know what that means, but I do believe that what I mean by manners—courtesy, regard for the other fellow, considerateness, the opposite of aggressive self-assertion; all these things I call manners—if they are not morals, produce the same result. I suppose I have a general predilection against pedantic, didactic, formalized, so-called ethical principles. I distrust, I certainly distrust people who are preoccupied with their own nobility.

My wife says there can be few people who know as little about themselves as I do. There can be still fewer people who reflect about themselves as little as I have in the past. Therefore, when you ask me how to account for myself, you're asking me, as it were, suddenly to speak a foreign language I haven't been instructed in. I suppose that if I took a year off and did some self-analysis, such as Freud did on himself, I might come up with —that lovely phrase—I might come up with something. But to try to answer candidly your searching question produces so little that you think I'm reticent. I'm not reticent. I'm just ignorant. Or, in the language of my profession, when the sheriff is sent out to enforce a judgment, to seize the goods of a judgment debtor, he often comes back and endorses the writ *nulla bona,* meaning "nothing doing. There are no goods." And so I have to say *nulla bona.*

Certainly I was brought up in what might be called an ethical tradition. You were decent. You were respectful. You believed in certain verities. You were supposed to be truthful. Now, where I got these from: I might say my mother's milk, except I know damn well that milk carries no ethical instruction. But my definition of education is the air you breathe, what is in the atmosphere. That's the education that matters! What kinds of things instinctively, unconsciously enter your being. I suppose there entered into my being certain standards of sobriety, a certain purposefulness in life, and that's that.

When the time came to choose a law school, had you had any experience in a commercial way?

Well, about that I can tell you. When it was decided that I was going to study law I cannot tell you. I do not remember the time when I did not know I was going to be a lawyer. Now why that should be so I do not know, because that is the first appearance of any lawyer in my family—the first and last appearance. I graduated, or as the pedants say, was graduated in 1902 from the College of the City of New York. I knew that you had to have a little money to go to law school, so I thought I would stay out a year and make money in order to go. There was just then established the Tenement House Department of the City of New York. I took a civil service examination as a clerk in the Tenement House Department.

I got a job working with a very interesting fellow who was the superintendent, a man named G. H. Darwin. I remember him as the utterer of one of the profoundest observations that ever fell to my ears to hear. I've often recalled it, and it has often enlightened situations. Darwin was a bristling, red-bearded, red-headed, technical man. He had a secretary—not a young blonde, but as a Virgin Island cook of ours once said in trying to describe a man who was no longer very young, "He was a settled feller." Darwin had a very good secretary, and she was a "settled feller." He had a grievance against the deputy commissioner, a man named Lawrence Veiller, a very, very able public official with very rude manners. Darwin was balked in something he shouldn't have been balked in. His secretary who was a great admirer of his and devoted to him said that he oughtn't to stand for this and ought to have threatened them with resignation. I shall always remember Mr. Darwin for the wise remark, "Miss Williams, nobody is indispensable to nothing in this world."

A very profound observation on affairs. Winston Churchill's father didn't know that when he resigned as Chancellor of the Exchequer. He thought he couldn't be replaced. Do you remember that episode in English history? He forgot Goschen, a financial man they could take, and it changed the whole course of British politics for a time.

Well, I earned money there, and I also did some private tutoring. What a funny ordeal that was! I had to tutor a very stupid boy who was living with a very old maiden aunt. I had to teach this kid, who was preparing for college, Latin and geometry in the presence of his maiden aunt—a stupid boy and a fluttering aunt, a wonderful combination!

Then I thought I would go to night law school. I first started in the New York Law School, and that was so bad I couldn't stand it. Then I went over to the New York University Law School, and that was pretty bad too. I knew what bad law schools were. So I quit. I worked very hard that year doing all these things. One day I started to go up to Morningside Heights to matriculate in the Columbia Law School for the next year. I was making, I think it was, $1,080. That was a lot of money in 1902-1903. There it was, and with that I could get a legal education for the next three years. So I started to walk up to Morningside Heights on a nice spring day with ten dollars in my pocket with which to matriculate. On the way up I ran into a buddy of mine, a classmate from City College. He said, "Where are you going? What are you doing?"

I told him I was going to Columbia to matriculate. "Oh," he said, "you can do that some other day. It's a lovely day. Let's go to Coney Island. If you're going to matriculate, you must have some money on you."

So we went to Coney Island. The whole course of my life was changed by that diversion. I blew in the ten dollars. I wasn't matriculated. He was quite right—I could do it later.

In the meantime I guess I got a bug. In those days they hadn't invented viruses. I had a bad flu. I was run down. The doctor of our family, a terribly nice man, Dr. Goodall, examined me, and he said that if I didn't look out, I'd get t.b. Why he said that I don't know. I don't think he knew either. I was just run down. He asked me what I planned to do, and I told him I was going to study law at Columbia. He advised me strongly, if I possibly could, not to study law in the City of New York, but to go somewhere where there was a law school in the country, because he said if I stayed in New York, I'd be doing what I was then doing. I would not only be going to Columbia Law School, but would be trying to earn money as a tutor. That gave me a new thought. What I knew about law schools in those days was next to nothing. But I did know that Michigan was supposed to be a good law school. That was not in a bustling city, but in Ann Arbor, and to a fellow who was born in Vienna and lived in New York almost anything that wasn't a great big metropolis was the country.

I had a friend in the Tenement House Department named Meyer

Rosensohn. He became a very distinguished doctor. I had not known up to that time that he had a brother who went to the Harvard Law School. I told him what the doctor had said, and he said, "Well, have you thought about going to Harvard?"

I said, "No, I haven't thought about that because I couldn't possibly afford it."

My ebullient friend said, "Oh, don't be silly. My brother Sam goes there. The notion that only rich men go to Harvard is not true. Why don't you talk to my brother about it?"

I did talk to his brother. He was coming home for Easter, I think. I went to where they lived, somewhere in Jersey, met his brother, who afterwards became one of my dearest friends and a roommate, and he persuaded me to go to Harvard. I thought Cambridge was the country, or my notion of the country. Anything that wasn't New York, or Vienna, or Chicago, or London was the country—you know, the narrow-mindedness of a big-city fellow.

I told my parents that I was going to go to Cambridge, to Harvard. I don't remember any discussion about it. I had enough money to go. The tuition fee was $150. It's now $800 or thereabouts. You could live on very little. Sam Rosensohn was a first-year man. He would next year be a second-year man, and he said that next year we could live together. It was fixed up like that. I don't agonize over things. I don't consult a thousand people. I don't dramatize life. You know, you just go.

All that was the result of bumping into my friend and blowing the ten dollars at Coney Island.

2. *Harvard Law School*

It seemed Harvard was a good place to go, and off I went. I couldn't be there when law school opened because I wanted to finish my work at the Tenement House Department, and incidentally, to draw a full month's salary. I arrived several days after the school was underway. My new friend, Sam Rosensohn, picked me up and took me to the room we shared in Cambridge. He asked me whether I had brought this or that. I said, "I don't know. My mother packed my trunk for me."

He just howled. He told me afterwards that he said to himself, "My God, have I got a Mama's boy on my hands?"

That's very interesting because now I let nobody pack my bag. I am a very good packer. One of the few things I can do with my hands is to pack well, so that when the clothes come out they need no pressing. The art of packing literally is a very interesting one. Everybody isn't a born practitioner of that art. I remember Mrs. Holmes once quoting a book by James Stephens called *The Crock of Gold* in which there are wise Irish remarks about life. He says, "The art of life consists of skillful packing," or something to that effect.

I had never seen Cambridge or Boston before. We walked out, and I remember vividly that as we walked along there was a fellow who seemed small in stature ahead of us. My new friend, my roommate, whispered to me in an awed breath, "That's the editor of the *Harvard Law Review.*"

If he'd said, "That's the Archangel Gabriel," he couldn't have been more awed. "My God," I said to myself, "the head of the *Harvard Law Review*. He must be a giant."

The first day I went to my classrooms I had one of the most intense frights of my life. I looked about me. Everybody was taller. I wasn't as tall as I am now. That is a joke. I was a little fellow. I was much thinner. There were a lot of big fellows, tall fellows, robust fellows, self-confident creatures around. They had been there a week or so before. I remember the first classroom was that of Professor Samuel Williston with whom I became at once *en rapport*. He was the greatest artist as a teacher I ever encountered, not the most stimulating teacher, but the greatest virtuoso in conducting a class, a wonderful person. I thought at once, "This is a fellow I understand. This is a fellow who appeals to me."

He asked questions. He was a great exponent and practitioner of the Socratic method. He asked fellows questions that tangled them up. There was one fellow sitting more or less in front of me. Everything about him was unpleasant for me, but I remember everything about him because he struck terror into me. He spoke out, spoke up, butted in. I said, "My God, this is a place for giants, not for a little minnow like me." I wanted to leave and go back to Mama probably—you know, psychoanalytically—to return to the womb. I said, "This is too fast a crowd for me."

Then there was another fellow, a tall, handsome fellow, more like a race horse in the Derby. I remember him too. These two fellows seemed to know everything. I didn't know anything myself. Well, the fact of the matter is that both of them flunked out at the end of the year. One of them was a famous football player, a great hero at Harvard, but he was no good in the law. He thought a classroom was like a football field. You take the ball and run with it, but he didn't have the ball.

In no time I revelled in the place. I ate up not only the law, but attended lectures of other people, went to concerts. My roommate was by this time a second-year man and a great shark. At the end of the first year he got a very high mark and was recognized as one of the best brains in his class. He thought I wasn't studying law hard enough, which I didn't in the first few months at the Harvard Law School because I was rejoicing in its freedom. That was still when Eliot was president of Harvard, and, you know, it was still a free lunch counter. Nothing was prescribed. I went to this and that, went to the library, read, roamed all around, and just satisfied a gluttonous appetite for lectures, exhibitions, concerts. My roommate thought I wasn't attending to business and would disgrace, in the first place, him, and my college—he was also a City College man—and myself. He was terribly worried. He would lecture to me. I said, "Well, I don't think law requires that I stifle all other interests."

In those days, at the half year you had sort of a test that didn't count, except to let you know what you were doing, or what your relation to the law was. The faculty would give optionals. You didn't have to take them if you didn't want to. It was just a way of enabling you to find out what you had been taking in for the year. I didn't do very well on those optionals. That was the necessary jolt. I buckled down and ended up by being first in the class, which I continued to be the three years that I was there, but which I did not know about at the time. I knew I had a high mark because I was made one of the editors of the *Law Review*.

I have a quasi-religious feeling about the Harvard Law School. I regard it as the most democratic institution I know anything about. By "democratic," I mean regard for the intrinsic and for nothing else. There weren't any courses on ethics, but the place was permeated by ethical presuppositions and assumptions and standards. On the whole, to this day I am rather leery of explicit ethical instruction. It is something that you ought to breathe in. It was the quality of the feeling that dominated the place largely because of the dean, James Barr Ames. We had no course in ethics, but his course on the law of trusts and fiduciary relations was so much more compelling as a course in ethics than any formal course in ethics that I think ill of most courses in ethics. The delight he took in finding again and again and again the law had much higher standards than the businessmen who prate about it! This rancid talk about "public service" these days. Everything is a public service. When they break in on a Beethoven symphony with advertisements about some cheap gewgaws, or awful stuff, it's always as "a public service."

But if ever there was a scholar and a gentleman, it was James Barr Ames. He was a wonderful teacher, an original mind, and he illustrated, to a degree unexcelled by anybody I ever knew anything about, the conception by Socrates of a teacher, that of a midwife. Ames was the midwife of minds. I remember when he died I said something that struck Morris Cohen as exaggerated about Ames. Morris Cohen and I were roommates in my third year. He took his philosophy when I took my last year in law school. He said, "After all, what is the deposit Ames left behind him? He hardly wrote anything."

This aroused my fierce loyalty, and I said, "What he left behind him is that which Pericles says in his funeral oration is the most important thing. His deposit is in the minds of men. He excited and touched more first-rate minds in the profession of the law, I suppose, than any man who ever had pupils. Dean Ames would rather spend hours with a student than write a legal essay that would immortalize him."

He never was too tired or too weary to give a student all the time he wanted. In those days the professors didn't have offices. They had a desk in the stacks. You would go in there and talk with them. You would sort of walk off on clouds as a result of a talk with Ames. Or in the classroom he would try to find the kernel of truth in a heap of sand of nonsense, error and foolishness. Classes are conducted in the Socratic method, at least the best of them are at the Harvard Law School. Anybody would chip in and break in. If the question wasn't very clear, Ames had a way of holding his elbow on the desk and resting his chin in the palm of his hand, and he would then think a little bit. Then he would say, "If I understand what you mean, you're asking whether so-and-so."

The fellow would always say, "Yes, that's what I mean."

Ames would always make beautiful and penetrating sense out of a jumble of words. It was a standing procedure. There was a fellow in my class, a man named Williamson from Iowa, a great big husky, a kitchen knife of a mind. One day he got off some stuff. We thought it was stuff. Dean Ames thought hard over that

one. He said, "Mr. Williamson, I suppose what you have in mind is a case of an equitable easement."

That's a very abstruse conception in the law. Williamson said, "That isn't what I meant, but I'm ready to adopt it."

Well, the whole class just roared with joy that at least here was one man who for once was honest, which none of us had been theretofore, and recognized what Jimmy Ames was doing. I have a reverent feeling about him, but no more so than all the most notable contributors to the function of law as the instrument of reason and justice. Anybody who thinks the Harvard Law School was a stick-in-the-mud place and new light has come out of the East, or New Haven, is just ignorant of American legal education, that's all.

Then there was Joseph H. Beale who was the most versatile of the lot. He was all over the place. He was stimulating because of the antibodies he aroused. He didn't propose to do that, but he was so dogmatic and so logically versatile. He could straighten out the greatest confusion. Everything had to fall in its place. He didn't allow for any untidiness, and of course the law is as untidy as life with which it deals, though it is the business of people to bring some kind of order out of the chaos of the world, if only as a working hypothesis, and thereby to make it less chaotic. Beale was a stimulating fellow, a wonderful creature in his way. He was what a teacher ought to be—a helper to those who walk the steep heights after them. He was fierce in class. He was casuistic. He was a theologian, as somebody once said, rather than a lawyer—"a legal theologian."

Grenville Clark, a great citizen, and I were in the same class. He was one of these deep, but slow minds. He was always a little behind the most active minds in the class. Joey Beale would get off these funny theories of his. Some of us who were more agile than Grenny—not deeper, but more agile; they're very different things—would give Joey Beale a run for his money. After a while everybody would know where everybody was, and we would quit. Beale one day got off a most preposterous theory, trying to reconcile the irreconcilable. The hunt was on. After a while the hunt stopped, but Grenny Clark was still reflecting on this thing when everybody was through with it. He intervened and said, "But Mr.

Beale"—professors in these days at the Harvard Law School were called Mister, as a much more honorable, ordinary designation than Professor. As one of them once said, "Don't call me Professor, it reminds me of a boot black." Grenny Clark said, "But Mr. Beale, the rule that you've formulated is very difficult to apply."

Beale almost jumped across the table and beat him with one of his outrageous bits of casuistic repartee, "Mr. Clark, I haven't advertised this as a cinch course."

That is a perfect illustration of the chief necessity of repartee, which is to cover the hole of the moment and then move on before you get out of the hole and see that nothing's happened. Then there was the dear old soul, Professor Jeremiah Smith of New Hampshire. He had been a judge on the Supreme Court of New Hampshire, but had lung trouble, retired at an early age, and became a teacher. He was very different from the others whom I have mentioned. Indeed, anybody who is any good is different from anybody else. That is the point about being good—you're different. He indulged in the lecture system a little more than the case system, the Socratic method, but he, as was true of Williston, true of Ames, not true of Beale, instilled in one a sense of passionate regard for truth-seeking. That is the great thing about the Harvard Law School. It doesn't make disciples. Nothing pleased Dean Ames more than to have you disagree with him, or to have you make him re-think his thinking. He didn't want followers. He wanted thinkers, independent ones. Judge Smith was a wonderful example of self-searching, a wonderful example of what Professor Whitehead once said was one of the requirements of a teacher, that of truth-speaking. He said, "That's much more difficult than you realize"; namely, not to appear to know more than you know, not to be surer than you have a right to be, to be more tentative than most people are, etcetera, etcetera. Smith was a great preceptor, a great embodiment of that.

He was born when his father was seventy, or seventy-one, and his father was born when his father was seventy-odd. I think three generations of Smiths, four of them, almost spanned the history of this continent from the time that Columbus landed. He was the child of a second marriage. This really happened. One day he said in class, "Gentlemen, I hope you'll forgive me if I am somewhat"—what was his word, overwrought, or distraught, or forgetful—"because this is a sad day for me. A hundred years ago today my little brother died."

You have to figure that out.

Then there was John C. Gray. He was a man of the world, tall, handsome, with a beard and spoke into a beard. It's through John Chipman Gray that I came to know Justice Holmes. They were great friends. Gray was a practitioner. He was the only man on the faculty who also practiced law. They said of him that he made a million and married a million. He was the greatest property lawyer of his day. He was the most felicitous speaker, a gifted scholar, the acknowledged master of his profession; namely, the law of property. His word, his opinion, his writings were authoritative as few men's are in any branch of law. He was a wonderful creature, and I have a lovely story about him. Mr. Gray sat outside in the main reading room so that you didn't have to go to the stacks. He just sat where the rest of us did. In my third year Mr. Gray came to the table where I usually worked in the library of old Austin Hall. I stood up. He said, stroking his beard, "Frankfurter, what are you going to do when you leave the school?"

I said, "I'm going to Hornblower, Byrne, Miller and Potter in New York."

"You're going there right after graduation?"

"No, I'm starting in in September"—or whenever it was.

"Well, what are you doing this summer?"

"Nothing in particular."

"How would you like to work a month with me on volumes five and six of my casebook on Property?"

Well, it was like asking a fiddler, "How would you like to be the first fiddler under Toscanini?" or "How would you like to enter the Elysian Fields?"

"Oh," I said, "I'd be delighted."

I spent a month working with him on volumes five and six of his famous six-volume law of Property. I have strayed far from those technical fields of law, but in those days my specialties were the law of property and the law of partnership. I apparently got a whale of a big mark in each of those courses. They have as little to do with what I am doing now as the binomial theorem has, which isn't true because somebody said, "Culture is the deposit of things forgotten." I worked with Mr. Gray, had a wonderful time, and then went to New York. One day I had a little note from him thanking me very much for the help I had been and enclosing a cheque for $100. A hundred dollars in 1906 was a good deal of money. I wrote him back a note saying what a wonderful thing it was for me to have done for a month and that was ample compensation for me, and sent him back the cheque. I got back a short note from him, "Oh, you mustn't do that. Yours truly, John C. Gray."

I sat down and wrote another note. I said, "No, I really mean this. I don't want to accept a cheque for something that I am so amply rewarded for already."

Then came the note that closed the matter, "Dear Frankfurter: Don't be a damn fool. Yours cordially, John C. Gray," returning his cheque.

Those are the men whom I had the great good fortune, with hundreds of others, to have been brought up by, or through whom we were made to feel what law is, what its purposes are, what its exactions are, what its possibilities may be. Giants they were, and I revere their memory because they seem to me to represent the best products of civilization—dedication of lives of great powers to the pursuit of truth, and nothing else, complete indifference to all the shoddiness, pettiness and silliness that occupies the concern of most people who are deemed to be important or big.

That is why I have so little patience with all this talk about method, pedagogic methods, curricula. It's all the bunk unless you have men of stature and depth and quality in great things. Because, as Holmes said somewhere, "If you believe in great things, you may make other people believe in them."

3. *Student Body*

You defined education as "the air you breathe." While giants were able to impart a sense of direction, surely those you rubbed shoulders with, sharpened your tools on, were your classmates. Since you came to the "country" in Cambridge armed with the parochial view of New York City life, and met there students from all over the nation, perhaps you might indicate what your class was like.

That's a most congenial and provocative theme for you to stir in me, and the important thing to say by way of generalization is that which my beloved Dean Ames said, "The strength of the Harvard Law School is its student body." That is only a partial truth because the real strength of an institution is the interaction between teachers and students, both teachers of quality and students of quality. But I think it is particularly true of the Harvard Law School that its student body plays a very dominant role, plays the very significant role it has played in the history of that great institution. I suppose the reputation of a school for great teachers draws students of high quality because there is something happily in a man that is sufficiently compelling as a magnet for excellence, and when you have a faculty of excellent teachers it gradually gets noised about like Emerson's mousetrap. They attracted eager, adventurous and high-spirited minds that were drawn to the law. Because very good men came out of the law school, younger men were drawn hither, and so until relatively recent times the Harvard Law School was an institution all by itself, certainly in the law-school world, and was a model for other professional schools to follow insofar as the work, standards and techniques, what they now call skills, of one professional school are adaptable for other professions.

The student body was a very superior lot. When I eagerly turn each year to the register of the school to discover the diverse educational institutions the students came from and the diverse geographical ingredients represented in the Harvard Law School, I find a diversity that I suppose is not excelled, and I doubt whether equalled, in any educational institution in this country. Let's look at the Harvard Law School register. There are forty-eight states and the District of Columbia mentioned here. There are also fifty-six students from United States possessions and foreign countries, and those are all broken down. That representation was substantially true in my days. The total student body for 1902-1903 was 640. It's more than doubled since my days, but proportionately that representation held true. It was a national law school. The students came from everywhere. They were rich and poor. They were sons of obscure workingmen and of cabinet officers. Take Chester McLain, a partner of Cravath & Henderson, perhaps the biggest law firm in New York. His father was a brakeman. Another fellow's father insisted on taking his car out of the barn at five o'clock every morning long after his son was a prosperous lawyer. The notion that rich men only went to Harvard Law School is just not true at all. Naturally enough, if they were poor and if they came from far—meaning North Dakota, or the Southwest, or the Pacific Coast—they were likely to be topnotchers in their respective colleges. That is the other thing about the Harvard Law School. It drew not only the wonderful, myriad-like variety that this country produces, but it was the best of this. There were always fellows from Oberlin, from Antioch, and from some little Methodist college in the Southwest.

You very quickly got into the atmosphere. There was a dominating atmosphere, first, of professionalism, and what I think is an indispensable quality of true professionalism, the democratic spirit. What mattered was excellence in your profession to which your father or your face was equally irrelevant. And so rich man, poor man were just irrelevant titles to the equation of human relations. The thing that mattered was what you did professionally. If a man was respected, it was because he was very good either because he showed up very well in the classroom or in private discussion, or, after the first year, which was the novitiate year, the very good men were defined by the fact that they got on the *Harvard Law Review*. This was determined entirely on the basis of your work as a student by examinations at the end of the year. Election to the *Harvard Law Review* followed academic rank, an automatic affair. All this big talk about "leadership" and character, and all the other things that are non-ascertainable, but usually are high-falutin' expressions for personal likes and dislikes, or class, or color, or religious partialities or antipathies—they were all out. These incommensurable things give too much room for personal preferences and on the whole make room for unworthy and irrelevant biases. And so I say, as I've said often in talking to the young, the *Harvard Law Review* in particular and the Harvard Law School in general are to me the most complete practices in democracy that I have ever known anything about.

If one fellow got 76 and another 76.5, there's no use saying, "The 76 man is better." Maybe so, but how do you know he's better? If somebody whom the rest of the fellows may dislike has shown the mettle that is his in an open competition, that's that. If he hasn't shown it, it doesn't matter whether he is one of the nicest fellows in the world and that his father is Secretary of State. In those days you were taken on the *Law Review* at the end of the first year, and at the end of the second year it was a standing rule that if you didn't keep up your high rank, you resigned. It didn't matter who you were. In my day it happened that two sons of men of distinction and high influence in the country fell below the rank of excellence. They just resigned. That is all there was to it. It wasn't a question, not a problem. There was never a problem whether a Jew or a Negro should get on the *Law Review*. If they excelled academically, they would just go on automatically.

This system doesn't measure whether you can get clients after you get out, or by the good fortune of getting into one law office rather than another you marry the boss's daughter and thereby get a good footing for the profession. It doesn't measure certain things, but what it measures in the open field, it measures. I'm not saying that a fellow who gets A is going to make a mark, as against a fellow who gets B, in after life, nor am I saying that some fellows who get C aren't intellectually as good as some men who get A, or may not forge to the front by ten or fifteen years after they're out. But I am saying that it is true of the marking system at the law school what someone said was true of philosophies: "They're true insofar as they affirm; false insofar as they deny." A fellow who gets A gets it for something. He might be a grind. Well, that's important in the practice of the law. The charming fellow who catches things on the fly, or who steals bases, has that help in life as in baseball games, but the fellow who gets A's has a certain solid quality, and that's important in after life. I am not suggesting that the fellow who leads his class at the Harvard Law School should be Secretary of State, or a judge of the New York Court of Appeals. I'm saying that this system, the objectivity of the marking, and the other considerations—no kissage by favors has always been the slogan there—creates an atmosphere and habits of objectivity and disinterestedness, respect for professional excellence, and a zest for being very good at this business which is the law. The law, you know, is a profession of books. I know lots of fellows who are very successful at the law because they make clients on the golf course. That's part of life, but that isn't what a school is for.

Would you have had the same regard for this system had you been a C-man?

A relevant reply is that the C-men feel the way they do because of the respect they have for the A-men. There's no feeling that anybody is hobbled in this race, or that it's hard on the C-man, or that it gives the A-man more than he should get. I think the dominant preoccupation is to do the best you can. Of course, there is no *apartheid* between the A-men and the C-men. They are in the same law clubs. They mingle. They review together. They're buddies. You know, in the first year almost everybody is wondering if he'll survive the examination, and you aren't thinking of getting on the *Law Review*. There may be some foolish fellow who thinks, "I'm going to make the *Law Review*," but as often as not he's the fellow who falls by the wayside. This isn't really like entering a marathon race. The first year there's a preoccupation with survival, and you don't know, nobody knows how good he's going to be at anything in a contest in which he hasn't been tested. It isn't a contest really, except with himself.

Then after the first year this show has been going so long a time that it has behind it the weight of an accredited past. A fellow who gets an A just takes that in his stride the way a fellow takes a C. The fellow who misses getting an A by a narrow squeak, of course he's disappointed, but "maybe I'll make it next year," and there are other recognitions of men who aren't the top notchers —the Legal Aid Society, the Board of Student Advisers for the first-year men, and other outlets for appropriate intellectual and professional ambition.

I should say of the students what Holmes says. He belonged to the society of jobbists—that is, "Do your job!" He said the fellow who tries to shoot a bird on the wing is neither an altruist nor an egotist. He wants to shoot that bird on the wing. Well, all life is a bird on the wing. A fellow who is trying to pass an examination isn't thinking, "Gee, am I going to win out over somebody?" He wants to pass that exam with as good a mark as he can.

In the first place, I suppose predominately a man does not live alone. On the whole I should say a decisive part of the education at the Harvard Law School comes from the interplay of students chewing the rag at breakfast, lunch, dinner, in walks, on the street corner—you know, rowing about it. They're like medieval students. There's a great deal of chewing the rag, and there are very few anchorites in the school. Study groups form spontaneously the way human beings coagulate. There's always some fellow saying, "Could I join your review group?" It's a process of human association which enables you to review collectively what you have individually prepared. There was a fellow in my group who was one of the brightest of the lot, but he was a loafer. He would be a valuable addition to any group because he would stick his knife right into the jugular. He would ask embarrassing questions, not smarty questions. You don't want a fellow who is a smarty, a fellow who doesn't take this seriously. But if you've got a fellow who's awfully industrious, but oh so slow! You don't want to be mean, but life is too difficult to have him wait around all the time—you know, you make a contribution to the Community Chest, but you don't starve your own children in the process.

The fellow who sometimes asks the simple question that everybody else feels he would appear too stupid to ask is the fellow who may be of the greatest possible help to the group. They used to say that Lord Halifax during the war was one of the best elicitors of good talk, particularly with professional people. I remember a dinner and an admiral who was in charge of the western approaches —that is the waters nearest Ireland. Everybody was so scared stiff to appear ignorant and stupid. A lot of us said, "I wish I knew what western approaches meant," but you wouldn't ask. But Lord Halifax said, "Admiral, I don't quite know what that is." Sometimes the honest, simple question is a very useful elucidator.

I'll tell you an experience of mine. I was living in a boarding house or rooming house. One day there was a knock at the door. I said, "Come in," and in came a tall, gangling, six-foot-three fellow whom I had seen around. There were only 212 in my class. I think he said, "I'm Howard Brown, and I'm in your class." He was a well-to-do fellow, and he said, "For one reason or another, I haven't been tending to business. Will you tutor me for the exams?"

I said, "Let's talk about it."

We talked, and I found him an attractive fellow, had a good time with him. I agreed to go over stuff with him. We became friends quickly. I said, "I will do it on one condition. I'm not engaged in this as a commercial enterprise. I'd be delighted to do this just on the basis of one classmate to another."

I don't know why I said that. I was as poor as a churchmouse. He joined a small group of mine, and he was as bright as could be. We became very close friends and remained such until his death, much too young. He had a checkered career. I don't know what kind of mark he had. He just scraped through, but he had natively great intelligence and acuteness of mind. Well, I got a good deal out of him.

You know, you mustn't see this as though it's a horse mart. I made friends, great friends, with two men in my class. One of them came from Fargo, North Dakota. I don't suppose I had known anyone from there, or heard of Fargo, until I went to Harvard. As you say, when I came there I was a parochial New Yorker. We were great buddies, and are to this day. We had good times together, but he never drank. Well, having been brought up continentally I didn't recall a time when I didn't drink wine or beer. But he wouldn't touch any alcohol. One day I said, "Bill, tell me about this. Why don't you drink?"

For the first time I became acquainted with the whole Prohibition Movement. Then he expounded. He had been brought up in a place where "gut rot" was the liquor, not Rhine wine, Pilsner beer, or *Hofbrau,* but "gut rot." I had never heard the word. He went into the terrible social consequences of excessive drinking in the Middle West and the Far West. He gave me a kind of Bret Harte picture. I learned American history there, as much as you ever did in seminars.

There was another fellow from Maine, Colby College, Julius Fogg. He was a red-head, a down easter and all that, and we became good friends. We used to go walking. One day he said to me, "I think I ought to tell you something. Do you realize—you probably don't—that you're the first Jew I ever met in my life who wasn't a village peddler in my little village up in Maine. It was through him that I had notions about Jews—unclean," and so on. This grand fellow gave me as good a glimpse as I would get from those big-worded, sociological, jargonized books on some aspects of anti-Semitism. There you had it all in a roll. All he knew about a Jew was that he was a fellow who, if he could beat him out of a nickel, would because he needed a few nickels to sleep that night and was not dandily dressed. He was telling me what it meant to meet a Jew—he said so in so many words—who was clean, who was a nice lad and who was respected by the students at the Harvard Law School. He said that was a terrific experience for him.

Was there anything in the course of the three years that softened the steady diet of law?

I just luxuriated in what is called "culture." I listened to music. I'm ignorant about music, but I'm dependent on it. I went to the Germanic museum, and I read a lot of German literature in the library attached to it. I went to the Boston Museum of Fine Arts, and I attended, to my great satisfaction and with lasting gratitude for Professor Copeland, a debating class he had for law students on Friday afternoon. He made a criticism of me then which I have never adequately observed; namely, "You go off like an alarm clock. Don't talk so fast."

Copey and I became great friends. He was a wonderful teacher —not a scholar, but a teacher, a stimulating fellow. I also went to some of his readings, and he was a beautiful reader of every sort of literature. When I went back to teach in 1914, very early he had me up in those old rooms of his on top of Hollis. He was a Maine man, a down easter all right, with very shriveled, ascetic-looking cheeks, a little body. He sort of tip-toed along. In the early days he was a loud dresser, rather stagey. Friday evenings he invited undergraduate boys, and they sat all over the place. He used to call it "making the lions roar," and I used to be up there frequently. He was a witty fellow. In those Czarist days we were very sympathetic to the rebellious creatures in Russia. Not infrequently fellows came over here who had assassinated governors and so on. There was a famous anarchist named Tschaikowsky who had killed I don't know how many governors of the various provinces. The newspapers were full of this Russian hero. Copey told the boys, "At the next meeting I shall have for you Tschaikowsky."

A lad said, "You mean the composer?"

Copey said, "No, the decomposer!"

A wonderful pun! Well, Friday night he had people in on the condition that they could only smoke cigarettes which they must supply themselves. No pipes or cigars were allowed. He was a fussy person. He died at ninety-odd as an old bachelor.

How did your family react to your achievements at the school?

I stand on one of my deepest convictions in life; namely, the importance of luck, contingency. Certainly I have narrated on that subject. I came home for summer vacation after my first year. It was the middle of August or around there I got word I was elected to the *Law Review*. That was a kind of achievement my family were proud of. One day I was in the next room doing something when my mother had a visitor. I tell you this because it gives me great pleasure to tell you what a wise mother I had. She had a visitor, a lady, who was telling her what a wonderful son she had, what a wonderful man her son would be, etcetera, etcetera. My mother said, "Felix himself says there are brighter men in the class than he is. He just happened to have luck in doing well. He says 'so-and-so' is much brighter than he is, has a much better brain than he has, but he just hasn't had luck."

I regard that as a very important communication—you know, to have a mother who was wise enough not to say, "Oh yes, my little boy, he's the smartest boy that ever was."

It is rigorous stuff at the law school, and the tradition is immersion in the work, but you can come and go. It's the opposite of regimentation, the opposite of the iron rod in any of its forms. You don't have to attend a class. Nobody takes attendance. You're just sucked into the law by the very atmosphere of the place, and on the whole it's fun. People work like hell because the atmosphere in the school is exciting. I know this sounds awfully idealistic, romantic, unreal, and un-American, this intensity of intellectual interest. Suspicion of and on the whole disrespect for the intellectual is an old American tendency, much commented on by foreign writers as you well know, but somehow or other this is serious business. When men get to the law school they're sucked into the serious business of equipping themselves, as most of them overwhelmingly are training themselves, to practice the profession to make a living for themselves and the expected family and to make a living in a profession that has a great and ancient glory, giving the men who are in it, on the whole, a feeling of great satisfaction. A lawyer's life touches life at so many points. It's satisfying because if a lawyer is any good, he isn't the fellow the layman sees going into court on a pettifogging enterprise. A lawyer comes nearer being a priest and a psychiatrist in combination than any other profession. Like a family solicitor in England he not only attends to the business affairs of the family, but if there is domestic difficulty, or rows with a partner, he's a family adviser, and in the big cities he's a composer of difficulties and not just a wrangler in the Old Bailey or in the Essex Market police courts.

4. *Job Hunting*

What did you do senior year with regard to what would happen after you left the Harvard Law School—what were your plans? What did you want to do with the tools you had developed?

It's very important, at least in the meager knowledge I have of myself, to bear in mind that I am not a fellow who projects himself much into the future. I've got a kind of healthy, live-in-the-moment disposition. I became a lawyer because I always assumed I would be a lawyer. I always knew that I wanted to be a lawyer from the time I have any recollection. I also didn't think I'd want to practice law. I wanted to be a lawyer, but I didn't want to have clients. I didn't think much about what I was going to do when I got out. You float with the tide. I have always been of the view that what you want to do is to have a general direction and then somehow or other chance takes care of you. You want to put yourself in a position where a good chance can take care of you, but it's chance that takes care of you. I had evidence that evidently I had some aptitude in the calling of the law. And so I assumed that when I finished I would do what others do—go into a law office. If you study medicine, you practice medicine. If you study law, you practice law. It was as naïve, simple, and unsophisticated as that—indeed, almost as unsophisticated as life, mostly.

In those days, unlike later days, the New York law offices didn't send their junior members with their sample trunks of inducements and wonderful attractions and dangle them before young men, making them feel that they're the cock of the walk. They soon get rid of that feeling once they're caught, but I'm talking about 1906, close to the era when men went to law offices and either got nothing, or sometimes even paid a little for the privilege. This was a wholly irrelevant American manifestation of the English system of a fellow going into a barrister's office, being a pupil, and really getting his legal training there. 1906 was close to the era when New York offices paid a kind of a salary that you could live on—$100 a month, some of them $50 a month. This was 1906 and $750 was $750, and $1000 was $1000.

The students at the Harvard Law School didn't begin to stir, trying to get a job, until the Easter recess in April. When the time for Easter came I went to Dean Ames and asked him if he'd give me some notes of recommendation to the New York law offices which he did with great warmth and charm. In these days the marks were not given to the students. If you got on the *Law Review,* you knew that you were way up in the class, but you didn't know what your mark was, nor did you know what your rank was. I didn't know, but I did know that I must have had a very high mark—in the way you know things like that. My classmates made me aware of the fact that what I thought was important. I was called on in a way that indicated, "Well, let's see what this fellow who's supposed to be pretty good has to say." But I didn't know what my mark was. I'm saying all these things because they are relevant to my trying to get a job in New York. I didn't know that I had led my class each of the three years, and it was just as well I didn't.

These notes Dean Ames wrote for me in his own small handwriting to half a dozen of the leading lawyers who were products of the Harvard Law School commended me to them in very strong terms. I was such a shy and sensitive kid—there are those who find it difficult to believe that at any time in my life I was shy and sensitive, and I won't let them into the secret of what the present state of affairs is—that I was a little ashamed to hand out letters that put me in such a favorable light.

Well, I went from office to office, and it was not a pleasant experience because I was made to feel as though I was some worm going around begging for a job. One experience was not only not pleasant, it was extremely unpleasant. Indeed, as I've looked back upon it from time to time when there was occasion for telling it, I can hardly believe that it happened. Yet I can give no explanation other than that it did happen. This was an introduction to a leading lawyer, a very leading lawyer who was a product of the Harvard Law School. I presented my letter. We talked. I think he took the letter and put it down. As the talk went on, in fact, when I was almost to be dismissed by him and the interview was over, he picked up this letter and said to himself so I could hear it, "Yes, that's his signature."

When I got outside I said, "Gee, what does this mean? It can't mean anything except that he wondered whether I'd forged this excessively complimentary recommendation."

Dean James Barr Ames always understated. Unlike Dean Pound, all of whose geese were swans, Ames never had a swan, so this letter was out of the ordinary.

Then there was another eminent lawyer from one of the biggest firms who was a nice enough man, but intellect was not his specialty, so he thought evidently that he had to take me down. He said, "Of course, you know that the life of a lawyer in New York is not an intellectual life. You know that books are the easiest things to hire and generate."

He induced me to feel that the fact that I did very well at the Harvard Law School really didn't amount to much, because, I can assure you, he had not done very well at the Harvard Law School. The one happy memory that I have of going from office to office in New York for two days, which vindicated all this, was a fellow named Dwight Morrow. It was the first time I laid eyes on him, and my experience with him endeared him to me forever afterwards. We became friends. Not long before he died I had a telephone call from him from Mexico about his boy. When he got through talking with me on my rounds—he was a buoyant, vivid kind of a fellow—he said, "Well, I don't know whether we'll have room for you in our office, but just remember that a good office needs a good man just as much as a good man needs a good office."

That was a revelation from heaven. That put the thing in proper perspective, that I wasn't a mendicant, that I had something they wanted as much as they something I wanted. There was one office, Hornblower, Byrne, Miller & Potter, that was one of the best offices at the time. Lots of Harvard people were in there. I'd heard that they had never taken a Jew and wouldn't take a Jew. I decided that that was the office I wanted to get into not for any reason of truculence, but I was very early infused with, had inculcated in me, a very profoundly wise attitude toward the whole fact that I was a Jew, the essence of which is that you should be a biped and walk on the two legs that man has. To me as a philosophy of action, as an attitude, it's as simple as saying you should neither be truculent nor subservient. You should just be a biped. You should take that ultimate fact that you were born of these parents instead of some other parents as much for granted as the fact that you've got green-brown eyes instead of blue eyes.

An uncle of mine said to me when I was a boy, "You'll encounter a great deal of anti-Semitism in your life, but don't go around sniffing anti-Semitism."

Some of the lads at the Harvard Law School occasionally—a Jewish lad who failed and then thought there might be reasons for that—were soon made to realize that I was not a Jewish professor at the Harvard Law School, but I was a Harvard Law School professor who happened to be a Jew. In fact, I know that I exacted higher standards from Jews than from other people, and perhaps that was on the whole a good thing for Jews who have any capacity.

But this is partly a result of the way you're made. I have evidently a great deal of vivacity and buoyancy. I don't have much hate in my composition, and I'm a great believer in reason. I have a romantic view about reason. You've got nothing else except that poor reed of reason to lean on in order to get away as far as possible from the jungle and the earth from whence we all come and a good deal of which we have in us. So I thought that a rule like that, not to take a Jew into a law office, was just born of ignorance, stupidity and ignorance. I thought it would be interesting just to go there and have them realize that this was just an artifact of theirs, that a Jew was something different. That's where I wanted to go.

Well, I was so highly recommended, particularly to the junior partner who was hiring the people, that I went in there to get a job. This fellow, who was a distinguished younger product of the Harvard Law School, evidently took a kind of shine to me. He was a bachelor, and he sort of thought he'd be my patron. He talked to me, as he said, like a warm friend. He said that now that I had started life, as it were that life was beginning, "this is a good time to change your name. Frankfurter—you know, there's nothing the matter with it, but it's odd, fun-making."

That's the way to begin life. Up to this time I hadn't lived, and since I was going to begin living, he suggested, "Give yourself an appropriate name."

I said, "Thank you very much," but I thought I'd better get along with what circumstances had given me, and he thought that was very foolish. Anyhow I began at Hornblower, Byrne, Miller & Potter for $1000 a year. I wasn't with them very long before I had a call from the United States Attorney's Office that the United States Attorney wanted to see me. I use those words because that's what I was going up to see—the United States Attorney. He had no name for me. I didn't know his name. I didn't know anything about him. This was around August. I remember thinking that TR had put a lot of new regulatory measures on the statutes, such as the Pure Food and Drug Act, some animal disease act, and I wondered if I had committed any offense unwittingly. Well, the United States Attorney, of course, was Mr. Henry L. Stimson. He had recently become United States Attorney and had inherited an office which by tradition up to that time was, with negligible exceptions, manned by hacks, jobholders. Until relatively recently the United States Attorney was paid by fee, and it was a very fat job for politicians who were also lawyers. It had been put on a salary basis when Stimson became United States Attorney, and he accepted the job from President Theodore Roosevelt on the strong urging of his great adviser, friend, senior partner and idol, Elihu Root, subject to two conditions: that whatever legal business arose in the Southern District of New York would be handled by him and not, as had been the custom, have the government hire special counsel whenever there was an important case; and that he would have a free hand in the selection of his staff. Instead of handing out the appropriations which were given to that office whereby six hack lawyers would get $4000, $5000, or $6000—grand political plums or sinecures—he would be free to use the appropriations in running his office and organizing it the way he'd run his big law office. What he did was to write to the deans of the Harvard Law School of which he was an alumnus, Yale, Columbia and Cornell, I think, asking the deans what promising young men had recently come out of their schools. He was going to do what he did in his private law office—pick the best brains there were fresh from the law schools. He had a few seniors, but he mostly went in for young men.

In organizing his office he saw and interviewed I don't know how many suggestions that had come to him from Dean Ames at Harvard and from whoever was dean at Yale, Columbia and Cornell. There I found myself sitting at the table with Mr. Stimson who told me what I've just told you in substance. He asked me questions about myself, and asked if I'd come over. He was sorry that he was only able to pay $750—as you'll see in a moment, it was important—which was $250 less than I was getting. I said I'd have to think about it.

I knew at once I wanted to do that, because that solved my problem. I could practice law without having a client. There it was. Perfect. But I was in torture because I had said to Hornblower, Byrne, Miller & Potter that I'd be their slave. I wanted to leave, but I felt like an indentured servant who was running away from his master. I put my anguish on paper to Dean Ames in the hope of getting help from him. I received a note from him. I remember it verbatim: "Dear Frankfurter: I suggest you follow the dominant impulses of your nature. I am confident that if you were to go with Mr. Stimson he would like you and you would like him. Cordially yours, J. B. Ames."

That didn't help me to a solution. You just somehow or other go into executive session with yourself. You look inside and listen to the sounds that are usually drowned by raucous voices, and they'll tell you what to do. He couldn't have given me better advice. My situation was complicated by the fact that my buddy in the office was a classmate of mine, Elihu Root, Jr., an interesting, brilliant fellow, who was thinking of going over with Mr. Stimson too. Mr. Stimson was his father's great friend and disciple. If anyone wrote young Root's career I should think on the title page he'd put, *Der Geist der stets Verneint,* "the spirit that always denies." So often in his life he teetered on doing something and then said, "No." Well, we debated the ethics of leaving the firm having only got in there a few months before. I forget now what I said, but it was something like leaving the firm for the United States Attorney's Office couldn't be regarded as so-and-so, and I remember his saying, "No, and it isn't adultery."

That sort of made me feel like a fool. Well, the upshot was that I wrestled with my soul and then knew that was the call for me, that was what I wanted to do. I saw two senior partners to tell them about it. One was a man who was violent on the subject. He thought I was doing a very reprehensible thing. I mumbled, "I'm not doing it for any personal advantage. I didn't plan it that way, but I was glad that my salary would be less than I am getting here."

I remember his saying, "I don't think it's any different than if you told me Cravath was giving you five dollars more a week."

Years after I told Mr. Stimson about this. It's a memorable colloquy I had with him because in all the years of my intimacy with him there are only four people who ever received from him the accolade of "son-of-a-bitch." That was a high distinction from him to call anybody that. He said, "Did he say that?"

I said, "Yes."

"The son-of-a-bitch. He left his partner in the cold when he got a chance to become a partner in a better firm."

I found out afterwards that the heat of that particular partner was due to the fact that I was to have been his special slave. But I went to another member of that firm, Mark W. Potter, who lifted all the clouds for me. He said, "I think you're doing the wrong thing, but I don't think you're doing any wrong. I think you're doing the wrong thing, but you go up there, and if at the end of the year you don't like it, you come back here and we'll make a place for you."

That was simply grand, but of course I never went back.

5. Junior to Mr. Stimson

I went over to the Stimson office. He was beginning a series of litigations which induced him to accept the United States Attorneyship, and they involved suits against the railroads for rebating and against some of the big shippers who clubbed the railroads into giving them rebates. There was a suit against the New York Central for rebates on sugar shipments and others. It's hard to believe but when finally that case came on to trial and the New York Central was convicted and had to pay a fine of something like $120,000, there were screaming headlines in the newspapers. People talked about this as though it were storming the Bastille.

Mr. Stimson was a big-game hunter, and he went out West to get a vacation. He left behind a number of questions on which he wanted memoranda by the time he was to get back. I remember his saying to me, "We have against us one of the ablest lawyers at the bar."

He put the fear of God into me that I mustn't overlook any point. The "ablest lawyer" at the bar was a man named Austen G. Fox who was the occasion of one of the two or three epigrams that I got off which I'm willing to own. He was a pompous, stuffed-shirt fellow with a great deal of atmosphere about him, top hat, moustache, fine voice, a kind of professional Harvard manner. He afterwards led the opposition against the confirmation of Brandeis. There's a portrait of him at the Harvard Club, life-size, heroic-size. A friend of mine once said, "Who's this fellow?"

I said, "That's a study in unbeaten brass."

Well, here was Stimson. He had never crossed swords with Fox, and Fox had this great reputation. Stimson very early instilled in me that you must prepare the other fellow's case at least as well as he prepares it, usually better, so that there are no surprises, no nothing. I began in the fall of 1906, and I had nothing but a wonderful time being Mr. Stimson's personal assistant in one important litigation after another. After a while and during one of the interludes between big cases, he said, "I'm going to throw you to the wolves. You ought to try a case all by yourself. You can argue a case before a court. You can do pretty well in persuading the mind. But you ought to be able to persuade twelve of your countrymen that the cause you represent is right. You better try a jury case."

I was scared stiff, would be now. I remember the case very vividly, *United States v. Emil Sonner*. Sonner was a fellow who made a comfortable living year after year by pretending to be a Secret Service man. Technically speaking, the Secret Service is the detective force which is attached to the Treasury and is most efficient, non-advertising, non-Hooverian, competent and self-effacing. They're concerned with counterfeiting laws, with protecting the President, and a few very limited things. Sonner had a relatively comfortable middle-class income by palming himself off as a Secret Service man. He'd operate in Yorkville, go to a small shopkeeper and say that he was on a case for the government, was sorry but he'd left his wallet at home, or changed clothes, or whatever the excuse was, and could they lend him twenty-five dollars, ten dollars, or whatever he thought the easy take would be. Of course, he had to accredit himself. How did he do that? By pulling out of his pocket two letters on that interesting green paper which is the very special paper of the White House. They read, "Dear Mr. Sonner: The President asked me to acknowledge your kind letter of the 27th and to say that he appreciated it. Very truly yours, William J. Loeb, Secretary to the President." Sonner had two letters just like that of which, I suppose, there are a million —you know, just acknowledgements, but that's something to people who have never seen the White House stationery.

He could improve on that. He also would pull out of his pocket a photograph of the recent bridal party of Alice Roosevelt and Nicholas Longworth outside the White House—the President, Mrs. Roosevelt, the bride, the bridegroom, the whole bridal party. I have told Mrs. Longworth that she is sort of responsible for my whole legal career. There was the bridal party, bridesmaids, everything, and in the back this cuss Sonner had interpolated himself. Way in the back was his photograph. He was in charge of the wedding presents! You couldn't get more compelling proof than that that he was a federal man. He'd been operating for some time, and finally they got him, and I tried his case before a jury. I remember that awful torture of summing up the case, making the closing speech to the jury on behalf of the prosecution. When I sat down and turned around, I saw Mr. Stimson sitting in the back. The notion that he'd heard!

Along came lots of professional excitement. It was really a very rich life. Professionally it couldn't have been better. There was great variety. In those days there came to the port of New York something like 100,000 immigrants a month. They landed at Ellis Island, and there were a good many cases of detentions for one reason or another and *habeas corpus* efforts to get them out. Here was this wise man, Mr. Stimson, who at one time said, "You better handle the *habeas corpus* immigration cases. You are likely to have more understanding of these problems than some of the other lads in the office." He was referring to the fact that I was brought to this country as an immigrant child, when I was not yet twelve.

Then there was a panic in 1907 and banks smashed, particularly a very important State financial institution, the Knickerbocker Trust Company, and the National Bank of North America. It soon became evident that the panic had something to do with the manipulations of a fellow named Charles W. Morse who was a Maine man of powerful mentality whose real difficulty was that he was born I don't know how many centuries out of his time. He was meant to be a Viking. He was an absolutely ruthless manipulator. It may seem funny nowadays that he wanted to corner the ice business, but he did and also coastwise shipping. He acquired controlling interests in banks in order to utilize the funds of the banks to finance his transactions. Well, the thing smashed in the panic of 1907 with great loss to a lot of small depositors and a lot of other people too.

An investigation was begun. The concern of the federal government was the national bank. A grand jury proceeding was undertaken by Mr. Stimson. He put on a wise old national-bank examiner named Edward P. Moxey. I got into the investigation with him, and it went on for weeks and weeks. It soon became evident that, in his endeavor to corner the market in these two industries, Morse's was a labyrinthine performance and ours a many-trailed and deceptively trailed inquiry. He did business through seventy-odd brokerage houses to cover up his trail of manipulations and this took months and months to unravel. Eventually he was indicted for false reports to the Comptroller of the Currency. The reports that were false were things that inevitably got into the reports that every national bank must render to the Comptroller of the Currency. They almost automatically had to be false because initially, way back, Morse indulged in some skulduggery. This then got on the books of the bank and through a long process finally became a report to the Comptroller. He was prosecuted for these "initial false entries," as they were called. Well, you can see that that was a gossamer performance, and it took a long time to unravel. When I think of what I then knew about brokerage accounts! But I know nothing now. A lawyer becomes an expert in so many fields for so short a time.

Not long after—some weeks, maybe some months, but long before the end of the trial and while we were still operating this grand jury investigation—Stimson got a telegram from the President of the United States saying, "I'm sending up Loeb," the President's private secretary, indicating that this was a very important mission. The President didn't want to put anything in writing. Loeb said the President sent him to tell Mr. Stimson that he was greatly concerned that there had been no action about the panic, the closing of these banks, as he was getting lots of complaints asking why the government wasn't doing anything about the bank failures that just didn't happen through an act of God, but which some fellow had made happen. The newspapers were talking about it, and the President wanted some action.

Mr. Stimson in his sober way explained the situation, laid it bare, told Loeb exactly what the investigation was, how he had been rigorously proceeding, how complicated the business was, what needed to be done in order to find out whether a crime was committed to warrant recommending to the grand jury that they should find an indictment, and to make an investigation of such thoroughness that if it should be found that an indictment was proper, a conviction would ensue. Stimson said, "I don't know how long that will take. I have no idea. It'll take a good long while. When the evidence is all in, if it warrants my so advising the grand jury, I shall advise them to find an indictment. Now that'll take I don't know how long. You tell the President that is the way I shall proceed, and if that seems too dilatory to him and he wants other action, then, of course, it's in his power to remove me and get some other United States Attorney."

I'll never forget the excitement in me to hear Mr. Stimson tell the President of the United States, "This is what I'm going to do. If you don't like it, you can do what you want to do."

For contrast, there was a fellow in New York who afterwards became governor named Charles S. Whitman. He was the antithesis to Stimson. He was a politically minded district attorney—one of the great curses of America. There was the Triangle Fire—that awful holocaust in which hundreds of young women lost their lives. A terrible thing. The question was whether the fire regulations had been disregarded. Whitman was district attorney, and his office was a few blocks up the street from the United States Attorney's Office. One of my closest friends, if not my closest friend at the bar, Emory Buckner, was there at the time as one of Whitman's senior assistants. He had been with us and then went over to Whitman. He didn't have anything to do with this particular state prosecution, but he told me, as we used to walk home together, "Whitman came in this morning mad as fury, and he called in the head of the homicide division and said, 'What's happening in the Triangle case?' "

This was only a few days after it happened. "Well, boss, we're not finished with the investigation, but very soon we'll have the case before the grand jury."

"Well, get an indictment! We can always *nol pros* it. Here, look at it!" and he held up an editorial in the Hearst New York *American*. "You go and get an indictment. We can *nol pros* it if we can't maintain it. You can always *nol pros.*"

Whitman was getting indictments because Hearst's *American* was shouting blue murder!

Why did you decide not to become a leading member of the bar of New York?

In 1906, in the heyday of the TR Administration, TR and the various agencies of government under him including the Interstate Commerce Commission went after combinations. This is the anti-trust period. There was then operating in the railroad industry a little Napoleon named E. H. Harriman, the father of this very nice and very gentle Averell Harriman of our day. E. H. Harriman was a powerful personality, and he was seeking to gobble up one railroad after another. The Interstate Commerce Commission began proceedings to inquire into the expansion and concentration of railroads into the hands of relatively few, and the most aspiring and expanding figure in the railroad world was E. H. Harriman who then was the controlling interest, the dominating interest, in the Union Pacific. The Interstate Commerce Commission on its own motion started an inquiry into the concentration of railroad interests. In the course of this inquiry they came to New York to hold hearings because the Union Pacific was trying to get control of the Illinois Central, etcetera, etcetera. The hearings were held in one of the courtrooms in the Post Office Building, and since proceedings might eventuate from the inquiry of the Interstate Commerce Commission, proceedings through the Department of Justice either on the civil side, or possibly on the criminal side for violation of the Sherman Law, I was assigned to sit in and what the British call "hold a watching brief."

This was 1907, I think. I was young and inexperienced. People who had great names were still deemed to be men who were great. There was the committee of the Interstate Commerce Commission, headed by a very powerful and very able man named Franklin K. Lane, a very distinguished lawyer from the Pacific Coast. He was a master of the English language and wrote some wonderful letters. He carried the laboring oar of examining Mr. Harriman on the witness stand in regard to his outlook and purposes and practices, and more particularly his ambitions. I remember very vividly Harriman, a powerful fellow who couldn't understand all this restrictive legislation of the Roosevelt Administration, made no bones about it. When he was asked in substance whether he wasn't interested in acquiring one railroad system after another, and would there be any limits to it, he was frank to say that if he were allowed, if he had a free hand, he would if he could acquire all the railroads in the United States, and he could run them pretty well. I have no doubt he could run them pretty well. He was a very masterful fellow. You couldn't listen to him without feeling that here you had a powerful mentality and a still more powerful will.

He had a retinue of lawyers. He was handling the matter himself. He knew more about his business than his lawyers did. There were the lawyers, some of the greatest of the day—John G. Milburn, Robert S. Lovett, and several others, half a dozen or so lawyers. From time to time as this duel, this intellectual duel between himself and Chairman Lane was going on, he would turn to his lawyers and ask them a question or two. The way Mr. Harriman spoke to his lawyers, and the boot-licking deference they paid to him! My observation of this interplay between the great man, the really powerful dominating tycoon, Harriman, and his servitors, the lawyers, led me to say to myself, "If it means that you should be that kind of a subservient creature to have the most desirable clients, the biggest clients in the country, if that's what it means to be a leader of the bar, I never want to be a leader of the bar. The price of admission is too high."

In all seriousness, that had a very determining effect. Well, to put it at its lowest, to my poor little eyes way down in the valley it was very influential in making me think how one wants to spend his life, what the profession of the law is and what it isn't, what one is ready to do and what one is ready not to do to climb to those dizzy heights at which Mr. John G. Milburn, Judge Lovett and all the rest were. That's the story of how I decided not to become a leader of the bar.

Mr. Harriman, in due course, refused to answer some questions. He thought they were none of the Commission's business, that if they were authorized by statute, the authority for investigation which the Commission had didn't extend to the inquiries they were making; and that if they did have the authority it was beyond the power of Congress to confer such powers on the Commission.

Judge Hough, one of my heroes, a fearless fellow, didn't give a damn about either plutocrats, or the proletariat, or the President of the United States. He was a self-reliant fellow. Upon refusal to answer, proceedings had to be begun to compel Harriman to answer. At that point I entered as Mr. Stimson's assistant. We had to defend the Commission's right to exact these answers. Judge Hough decided against Harriman and for the Commission. 157 *Federal Reporter* 432. Then his eminent counsel took the case up to the Supreme Court of the United States where it was manhandled for the government by a rather loose-thinking lawyer. Mr. Stimson by that time was out of it, except his name nominally appeared on the brief. The government had special counsel, Frank Kellogg who afterwards became Secretary of State. The Supreme Court of the United States in an opinion by Mr. Justice Holmes, over a dissent, a strong dissent, reversed Judge Hough and said that Mr. Harriman was within his rights to resist the inquiries which the Commission was making. That is the story of *Harriman v. the I. C. C.* 211 US 407.

Sure it was exciting—my years in the United States Attorney's Office. In the first place, having the government as a client you never have to defend a case that you don't believe in because in cases that had no merit, you'd say, "No, Uncle Sam doesn't do this." You don't indict people who oughtn't to be indicted when the United States Attorney was as scrupulous as Mr. Stimson was! I don't see how a young fellow coming to the bar could possibly have had a more desirable, more deepening, and altogether more precious influence during his formative years than to be junior to Henry L. Stimson. He was rather—austere is a little too strong. I'm sure he must have had a good deal of influence on the exactions I make of my young men, what my standards are. This was an incredibly effective and wholly scrupulous man. When he went out to raid a place with a search warrant—not only wouldn't he do it without a search warrant, but he'd send youngsters like me or Tom Thacher with whom I shared a room, later Judge Thacher, to see to it that the raiding officers kept within the limits of the search warrant. No wire-tapping was allowed during his whole regime. If you read some of my opinions with regard to criminal prosecutions, that's where it all comes from. In one opinion I actually said this, that maybe this was a bias derived from having served under a United States Attorney who observed these standards and won his cases.

6. *TR*

When March 4, 1909, came, TR went out of office. Mr. Stimson did too. He decided to return to private practice and asked me to go with him which I did for not quite a year, I think. Then I was asked to go back as a special assistant to the United States Attorney, Stimson's successor, in some appeals that were being argued of cases that had originated in the Stimson days. I resigned from there in 1910, after Mr. Stimson was nominated for governor, and I worked with him in his campaign. He was not addicted to the present tendency toward ghost writing. Whatever speech he made that mattered was his own, though of course people may have worked with him, as was the case with TR.

Mr. Stimson took me out to Sagamore Hill to read to the Colonel his speech of acceptance as candidate for governor. On that occasion the Colonel made a remark that has stuck with me. Mr. Stimson read this speech. It was very careful. It was very responsible. It was very weighty. But when he got through reading, this was the comment from TR, "Harry, it's all very good. The stuff is all there. But you must remember, a political speech should be a poster and not an etching."

I'll tell you about TR's sense of humor. The strategy of the campaign was that the candidate, Mr. Stimson, and the Colonel were to cover the state at different periods. When the Colonel was upstate, Stimson was to be in the city of New York. When the Colonel was in New York, Stimson was to be upstate. They were then to meet the Saturday preceding the last week of the campaign. The candidate, Mr. Stimson, and the Colonel were then to have a whirlwind campaign in Manhattan and the Bronx, each to speak at a dozen meetings. The Colonel was then to go upstate.

He sent word to Mr. Stimson that he wanted to see me as there were certain facts that he wanted to get the details of, and he knew that they were in my head because I had been with Stimson all through his public career. I was told to meet the Colonel at some hall up in Yorkville. He spoke to a lot of Poles at the Polish-American Republican League. The place was a sardine box, packed more closely than any sardine box was ever packed. TR with a Rough Rider's hat came in, and they went wild. He began with a history of Poland. I could follow him as far as Pulaski and Kosciusko, but he had ten more Polish heroes. They just went wild. It was a terrific affair.

Then I rode down Fifth Avenue with him. Although this was toward the very end of October, it was a very mild New York day. We drove down in an open car from uptown to Grand Central Station where he was to take the train for Buffalo. He was to make a very important speech the next night at Buffalo, a Republican center. After he asked me the questions he had on his mind pertaining to Stimson's work as United States Attorney, he then turned toward me—mind you, I was a kid of about twenty-seven then, and this was the ex-President of the United States talking, who was my hero—and he said, "Tell me, what do you hear about my speeches? Are they all right? Am I making the right kind of speeches for Harry?"

The newspaper men who had been covering the trains of Stimson and Roosevelt shifted. For a time they would go with Roosevelt and then go with Stimson, and vice versa. I had seen some of the newspaper people, and they'd talked to me about the Colonel's speeches. This was the day before radio. The New York *World,* that powerful sheet, began a box score of the number of times that Colonel Roosevelt used "I" in his speeches. On the front page there would be this box score—563, 877, 2079—whatever it was, and it began rolling up. Then there was a cartoon by the famous Homer Davenport which showed TR pulling the string to his little puppet Stimson. That was the background in my mind when the Colonel suddenly said, "Tell me what you hear about my speeches, and what you think about them."

To this day—not that I could get any more light, but I could get more speculation—I have not made up my mind what it was that made me answer as I did. Whether it was the candor of his question, or whether it was the dark night, and darkness is a great corkscrew for candor, or the fact that I was just a bumpish young man, or all three, or something else, but the fact is that when he said to me, "Tell me what you hear about my speeches and what you think of them," I said in substance this, "I think the speeches are very good, Colonel. They're just right. But perhaps there's one thing that I ought to tell you about. I don't know whether you've heard about this statistical appetite of the New York *World,* but they keep track of your speeches for one purpose—to count up the number of times that you employ the first person singular. It's now run to . . ."—whatever it was. "Of course the only point about this is that it has a slight tendency to subordinate the candidate."

"Oh," he said, "I'm so sorry. Oh, I mustn't do that. This is too bad. I must stop doing that. I must bear that in mind."

By that time we had arrived at Grand Central. I put him in his berth and off I went. Off he went to make a speech at Buffalo the next day. Before the week was up I saw a correspondent who had been with him and then came on our train. He said, "I must tell you something very funny that happened at Buffalo. The Colonel was speaking in the big hall there. He told all about Stimson—Stimson's record as United States Attorney, how he went after the sugar trust, rebating, all those major prosecutions. He walked up and down like a leaping lion. He said, 'That is the issue. The issue is do you want government by Stimson or government by Dix. That is the issue. Of course, I know they want to make you believe that other things are the issue. They even want to make you believe that I am the issue. It's got to such a point that I can't even say *My Country 'tis of Thee* without being accused of egotism.' "

Stimson was defeated in 1910. Then he went down as Secretary of War. I went with him. When he was asked to become Secretary of War by Taft, Stimson said, "I want to talk to two people. I

want to talk to the Colonel. I want to talk to Mrs. Stimson."

I know this at first hand. He went to Sagamore Hill. He told TR that Taft had invited him into the cabinet. TR said that he must accept. "Of course you must accept. You must do everything you can to throw the weight of the administration on the side of the progressive Republicans instead of the reactionaries."

Stimson said, "Well, Colonel, if I enter Mr. Taft's cabinet and he runs again next year, I would be in duty bound to support him."

TR said, "Of course you would have to support him no matter what the eventuality."

He bludgeoned Stimson after he supported Taft though. You know what that was due to? Like all great men he was surrounded by bootlicks and sycophants and people who fanned the weak sides of him. The fellow who was responsible for that, more than any one man, was Bainbridge Colby who then turned Democrat and afterwards became Woodrow Wilson's Secretary of State—one of the most humorous things in the history of the United States. It was Bainbridge Colby who just fed the flame, as I know, about this terrible man Stimson who owed everything to the Colonel and then turned and was an ingrate.

It always amuses me how I learned that TR announced his candidacy to the seven little governors. I was in the room of the Secretary of War in the building that is now occupied by the President's executive office. I was in with Secretary Stimson, doing some work with him, as I was then his law officer. Stimson's secretary came in and said, "Mr. Kent is outside."

Kent always gave Stimson great pleasure. William Kent was a Congressman-at-large from California and a great friend of TR. He was Stimson's contemporary at Yale. Billy Kent was a wonderful fellow with a kind of Emersonian quality about him. He was an original, as his sons are now. Well, in came Billy Kent. The door was half open, and he walked in. He would always come in that way. He said, "Well, Harry, Terrible Ted has gone and done it."

Stimson said, "What's happened now, Will?"

"Well," he said, "Teddy went with the girl so long he finally had to marry her."

That is a perfect description of what happened. There it was. TR threw his hat into the ring. I heard, through some friends, that once he declared his candidacy, once he went out to contest for the Presidency, he became the Ishmael of the Republican Party. Nobody came near him. A friend of mine—George Rublee, as a matter of fact—said, "I was up there. Poor old Teddy is as lonely as can be. People shy away from him as though he were Typhoid Mary."

I was so mad at that that I sent him a wire, "Can I come up and see you?"

He wired back, "Sure, come up."

I went up to the *Outlook* office. There wasn't a soul in sight. I spent a whole afternoon with him. He had nothing to do. He said a very interesting thing that day, and it tells a lot about him, and tells a lot about Taft too. TR was very autobiographic. He talked a great deal about himself. He talked about how he was sucked into this contest. I remember he said, "I've got no glory to get out of being President again. All the glory that can come to me, my family, my name, can't be enhanced by being there again." Then he said this: "I have no particular religious beliefs." He didn't use the word "agnostic," but he defined an agnostic. He said he had no sense of assurance about the hereafter, or anything. He was a skeptic about it all. He said, "The one thing I want to leave my children, my grandchildren and those who follow me, is an honorable name. They have that now."

That interested me a great deal. He was sitting there in a swivel chair. This was at 287 Fourth Avenue. Then he said, "Oh, if only Taft knew the joys of leadership!" He almost jumped onto a horse to ride off—"Oh, if only Taft knew the joys of leadership!"

After TR announced his candidacy and the Bull Moose campaign was on I wrote to Secretary Stimson who was out of town, "I'm Bull Moosing and therefore resign." He told me that he didn't think it was a very wise thing I was doing, but that he was authorized by the President to say that simply because I was supporting Colonel Roosevelt and not President Taft there was no reason why I should leave office, considering what I was doing on water-power matters. So I remained in office and unashamedly, though not offensively, but candidly supported Mr. Roosevelt.

A great friend of mine in those days whom I saw a good deal

of was Gutzon Borglum, the sculptor. He was a Bull Mooser, and in 1912 he and I Bull Moosed together. He was one of those artists who had delightful incapacities for running government, but knew exactly how to do it.

He was a gifted user of language, both by speech and on paper. He was eloquent. He had the eloquence and the attractiveness of not qualifying his speech, none of the whereases, aforesaids, and howevers—no buts in his speech. It was all clear, black and white, passionate, uncompromising. He'd write endless letters. He was a great admirer of TR. Gutzon was for war, for all sorts of war, six wars at a time. People weren't wrong; they were crooked. People didn't disagree with him; they cheated him. He was a powerful fellow with his jutting forehead, and he'd talk with his hands. They were very plastic hands of course. He had to move them, and his mind was very plastic.

I remember saying to my housemate when I went back to Washington after that afternoon in the *Outlook* office with TR that when a fellow was gifted like TR was gifted for public life, he had to do that, just as Gutzon had to sculpt, work with his hands. "Oh, if only Taft knew the joys of leadership!" You could see that he just sort of jumped out and was going to lead the armies for regeneration. All this about, "We stand at Armaggedon," wasn't just flapdoodle. That's the way he felt.

7. *Assistant to the Secretary of War*

Stimson was named Secretary of War in President Taft's cabinet, and he asked me to come down to Washington with him. What was he going to do with me in the War Department? He wanted me to be his special assistant on all sorts of things. There was a job, somehow or other, into which I could fit called the Law Officer of the Bureau of Insular Affairs which was technically a good job. The Bureau of Insular Affairs had charge of Puerto Rico, the Panama Canal, the Philippines, San Domingo where we had a kind of receivership, and the like. That was the nominal shell into which I fitted, but I worked with him mostly on water power because the War Department also had charge of water power on navigable streams. Generally I was his personal assistant. As a matter of fact, the first job I did for him was to work with him on a speech in support of the reciprocity treaty with Canada which is far away from insular affairs. Until he left the cabinet on March 4, 1913, I was with him as a junior partner to the Secretary of War which was really what my job was.

When I was appointed I accompanied Mr. Stimson in the U. S. *North Carolina* on a tour of the possessions, as it were—Cuba, Haiti, San Domingo. Then we went down to Panama to open the Panama Canal, to let the water in. That was a very exciting experience—the way those great doors of the locks moved like a ballerina pirouetting on the stage of the Metropolitan! Then we came north to Key West. There was an episode at Key West that's worth telling because it bears on that most difficult of all things in conveying history, namely, change of climate. I should think you historians—my talk so easily slips into an attack on historiography and journalism, the chief miseducators of people—but I should think you historians fail, as much as you fail in anything, in recapturing that impalpable thing, what was in the air. That's the most important thing in understanding events—the things that aren't written down because everybody takes them for granted. There was an episode at Key West which bears on that.

I was in the hotel upstairs with Secretary Stimson when a card was sent up by a bellboy. The card indicated that the visitor downstairs was president of the Key West Bar Association. Secretary Stimson was sort of tired and said, "Will you go down and give him my compliments, entertain him, and dispose of him?"

I went down, and there was a handsome, an overawing creature. He must have been six feet and more, a giant in Palm Beach white ducks, black boots, and a great big seven-gallon or nine-gallon hat. He seemed to be a nine-foot man, and so he had appropriately a nine-gallon hat. I made the necessary apologies for the Secretary of War. He at once interrupted me and made perfectly clear, "Ah didn' come heah to pay mah respects to the Yankee Secretary of War. Ah came heah as the president of the bar association to pay mah respects to a distinguished lawyer."

Here was the president of a bar association in 1911 who wanted to make it perfectly clear that he wasn't paying his respects to the Yankee Secretary of War. That shows how feelings linger far beyond the event. Public men forget that. Whoever it was said a wise thing when he said, apropos of the potato famine in Ireland in 1848, that he wished the Irish would forget it and the British remember it.

That was my introduction to my job in the War Department. Washington in 1911, and I saw it for the first time after we returned from Panama, was a charming, large, peaceful, equable, big town. Automobiles were still rarities. Connecticut Avenue had sidewalks twice the breadth of the sidewalks of the present Connecticut Avenue. They were cut in order to leave more room for the ungracious traffic that now is so densely in evidence on Connecticut Avenue. In order to do that they cut like vandals perfectly beautiful trees that then gave shade and beauty to that avenue, but on the whole Washington was a most agreeable, delightful place. Work wasn't feverish. We were still in the legal and social consequences of the Spanish-American War, but that wasn't really a very dislocating event to experience in the history of the United States. It wasn't then seen to be, although it floated the United States actively into the currents of world affairs.

Apart from my own chief, Secretary Stimson, the great friendship I formed with a person of an older generation was Mr. Justice Holmes. I had a note of introduction to him from a great friend of his who was a professor of mine at the Harvard Law School. We soon became fast friends, and I became a regular visitor at his house. A regular visitor at his house meant that you sat in front of the fire when there was a fire, and sat in his study when there wasn't a fire, and he did practically all of the talking. He was probably the best talker—not the greatest talking in volume, but you just didn't think of talking when he talked because it was such a wonderful stream of exciting flow of ideas in words.

You told me a very wise story some time ago—the conversation Holmes had with Emerson.

That was when his father finally persuaded him when he was in college, a junior, to go and see Mr. Emerson. He went to see him, and there was talk about this or that. Holmes said Emerson had a beautiful voice, and, of course, Holmes had one of the most beautiful voices the Lord ever put into a throat. Emerson said to him, "Young man, have you read Plato?"

Holmes said he hadn't. "You must. You must read Plato. But you must hold him at arm's length and say, 'Plato, you have delighted and edified mankind for two thousand years. What have you to say to me?' "

Holmes said, "That's the lesson of independence."

So off he went and read Plato for a few months or a year, and then wrote a piece doing in Mr. Plato in one of those ephemeral literary things at Harvard. He laid this, as it were, at the feet of Mr. Emerson and awaited the next morning's mail, hoping to get a warm appreciation from Emerson. And the next day and the next and the next—no sign of life. No acknowledgement from Mr. Emerson. Holmes didn't see him again for about a year. When he saw him, this, that, and the other thing was again talked about. Emerson said, "Oh, by the way, I read your piece on Plato. Holmes, when you strike at a king, you must kill him."

Holmes said, "That was the second great lesson—humility."

Well, I came to know the bureau chiefs and the Chief of Staff in the War Department. You must remember that I was just a kid. When Mr. Stimson brought me down I was this side of thirty, not only young in years, but not very impressive looking. I was a little fellow—you know, "What is this little civilian doing around here?" It took me some time to identify the insignia of rank so that finally I called everybody "General." That made it safe.

Mr. Stimson being the kind of man himself governed by the intrinsic, no ego about him, no concern about his dignity—he was just dignified; that was that—he would have me in on conferences with generals sitting all around. I, not being a fool, tried to make myself as inconspicuous as I could in addition to my native inconspicuousness. I kept my mouth shut so that I was not heard and, therefore, largely not seen. I remember very well that he had me in there with all the major generals sitting around the room. In those days a major general was something. Now—what's the phrase?—thirteen to the dozen! I forget what the subject was, but one by one Mr. Stimson asked all the generals what they thought about a statement he had prepared, something which was going up "on the Hill." All of them said that it was fine. They all thought very well of it. He finally dismissed them. He indicated to the generals that the interview was over, and they left, and he indicated to me that he wanted me to stay behind. I had said not a word. When they all left, he said, "Tell me what you think about this."

I told him some criticisms I had. It was the most natural thing in the world. The relation was such that he assumed I was for him so I didn't have to say, "Boss, Chief, this is wonderful!" or "God, you certainly. . . ."

My office adjoined the office of one of the best professional brains I've encountered in life, General Enoch H. Crowder, the

Judge Advocate General. He was a heroic character. He went to West Point because that was the only way he could get an education. Then he was sent to this army post, that army post, and while other people were loafing, playing cards, or polo, or nothing, or drinking, or whatnot—he was a studious temperament, he had an instinctive drive for books—he studied to get admitted to the bar. That's how eventually he got to the Judge Advocate General's corps. He was in battle too—in one of the late Indian fights. The poor man was operated on several times on his head. He often had to hold his head, squeeze the upper and lower part just to relieve the pain. He was in the Philippines where he became acquainted with Taft who was a great admirer of his. He then helped to run the military government of Puerto Rico and eventually became Judge Advocate General. He drew the Draft Act of the First World War. He was a first-class brain.

He was a bachelor and I was a bachelor—what was he, twenty years my senior—and we became acquainted and friends, close friends until he died. From time to time he got me to help him on matters. I worked on the Articles of War. That's how I have some sense of military law. I remember shocking him—the difference between a civilian and military tradition—when he came into my room and said, "Frankfurter, I want you to help me. I've just been over to the White House"—this was just after we had seized the customs house at Vera Cruz—"and I'm asked to write a memorandum whether that seizure should be treated as an act of war and what its status is in international law. Will you work with me on that?"

I said, "General, I'm going to ask to be excused. I don't have to work on that. I know the answer to that."

"You do?"

"Yes, I do."

"What is the answer?"

"It would be an act of war against a great nation; it isn't against a small nation."

"I can't give him that."

"I know you can't, but that's the answer."

I still think that's a good answer. Well, he and I became close friends, and we afterwards remained such. It was an intimate relationship.

The Bureau of Insular Affairs was headed by a man named Clarence R. Edwards who was a very charming phony, a great friend of Taft, and Mrs. Edwards was a great friend of Secretary Root. Edwards was a major general, and God only knows how he got to that rank. His deputy chief of the bureau was a man named Frank McIntyre, a very scholarly soldier who died after I came down here to the Court. He and I became great friends. He became chief later as a Brigadier General. He was a superior person, a man of learning and understanding. He knew about finance and about problems of revenue. He devised the currency system for the Philippines. With McIntyre I had business and had to write legal opinions for the bureau. That was an intimate and happy relation. My relations with Edwards were social. He spent a good deal of his time in the Metropolitan Club.

Leonard Wood was Chief of Staff. Of course, he was a powerful fellow. He was very unscrupulous, meaning by that that he would manufacture facts when he didn't have them. That's a hell of a thing to say about a distinguished person. Well, it's so. I remember once or twice Wood said something to Mr. Stimson, and Mr. Stimson said, "General, are you sure?"

Well, he'd say he would make sure. He was a very powerful personality, a doctor who had risen in the military to become Chief of Staff and who had an alert mind. He was a surgeon, a fellow who could operate on himself by looking in the mirror. He had about him a first-class corps in his staff, a number of young people who became great friends of mine; Frank McCloy, Major James Logan, and Winship who became Governor of Puerto Rico. These were very good people he attracted because he was a dynamic personality. Mr. Stimson had a very high regard for him. Then he was sent out as Governor General of the Philippines where he messed up things. He was a strong armed man, no fool, although I remember well—I don't know why I say, "although," wiser men than he said it—bumping into General Wood in the subway going out from Boston to Cambridge. This was in the fall of 1914, around October. War had broken out in August, and General Wood and I knew each other and had pleasant relations. On the subway I asked him how long the war would last. "Oh," he said "It won't last longer than six months."

"Why not?"

"Because financially the world couldn't stand it."

That was a very valuable lesson for me. Ever since then I have known that money had no relation to whether there is or isn't going to be a war.

Among my tasks was representing the government in the insular cases that came up to the Supreme Court of the United States. They came up from the Supreme Court of Puerto Rico and from the Supreme Court of the Philippines. I don't know how many cases I argued—six to eight—and of course that was very exciting for a youngster. That's how I came to know the Justices. Supreme Court Justices should be tall and broad and have a little bit of a bay window. They should look the way Stone looked. You know, they should be physically impressive! The cases I argued involved some very interesting questions implicating, or largely based on, Spanish civil law because while sovereignty had been transferred institutions aren't changed overnight, and the legal institutions that governed Puerto Rico as well as the Philippines were the institutions of the civil code and not of the Anglo-American common law.

I remember the first case I argued in the Court was a suit by the Philippine Government against the claim of the Catholic Church, a controversy over a large area of land, the Philippine Government claiming that it was a public plaza and belonged to the public, the Catholic Church claiming that it belonged to it. There were at that time two Catholics on the court, the Chief Justice and Mr. Justice McKenna. Frederic R. Coudert represented the Catholic Church and he argued very deftly and lightly while I had to make a technical argument. Coudert was a charming fellow who afterwards treated me with that respect with which a man treats a fellow who bests him in a game—that is, if he's any kind of a sport.

There was a question of the status of Puerto Rico, the doctrine that a sovereign is not suable except by consent. There were questions of when various laws came into effect. Then there was a case that really was interesting, *Tiaco v. Forbes*. W. Cameron Forbes was Governor General, the great pro-consul—the American Cromer without Cromer's brains. He was the grandson of Ralph Waldo Emerson, and he illustrates the principle that being disinterested and having a high sense of public duty doesn't mean that you promote the public good. That requires understanding and imagination. Forbes came on east, and we spent a day talking over Philippine problems, he, Secretary Stimson and I. Since I am talking I will tell you things about myself. That is the awful thing about these autobiographical seances—they're so damned egotistical! After a whole day with him, Forbes finally left, and Secretary Stimson and I were left alone. He asked me, "What do you think of him?"

I said, "I think Emerson passed through him without stopping."

Tiaco v. Forbes was a suit brought by some Chinese whom Forbes had picked up and deported. There was a Tong Warfare between two Chinese gangs in Manila. Forbes, the Governor General, directed that one lot be picked up and whisked away. They brought suit for false imprisonment. It was not a very pleasant case. I had to argue the inherent power of the executive to deal with such a situation. Somebody trotted that out against me in the *Youngstown Steel* case. I had to dig up a lot of Spanish law and I remember saying, "The mere transfer of sovereignty doesn't change the basic political institutions of the territory."

Little Mr. Justice Day, weighing about 99 pounds, said in his nasal voice, "What's that you say?"

I repeated what I had said, that institutions do not change their intrinsic characteristics simply because there is a change of sovereignty. He said, "I thought that was exactly what we did try to do by the Treaty of Paris."

He was chairman of our Peace Delegation which brought about peace with Spain in the Treaty of Paris and he was quite shocked that any remnant of brutal arbitrary power, such as was exercised by the Governors General under Castilian rule in the days of Ferdinand and Isabella, should be the legal position of the Governor General of the Philippines the transfer of which to this country he had secured through the Treaty of Paris, which, you will remember, Speaker Reed characterized as "buying 10,000,000 little brown men at two dollars a head."

That was a very tough case, and to my great surprise it was a unanimous opinion, even Day, sustaining the power on, as is often the case, some auxiliary mitigating circumstance. One of the subsidiary arguments was that Congress could have given the Governor General such power originally; therefore, it can ratify it, and it did ratify it in that the Governor General reported this, and the War Department reported it to the Congress who did nothing about it. They appropriated money.

It took some time to make the Puerto Ricans citizens of the United States. In the annual report of Mr. Stimson there were two things we recommended, one was to make them citizens and the other was to encourage diversification of economic enterprise so that they shouldn't put all their eggs in one basket, and more particularly, so that they wouldn't be growing just sugar with all its consequences. Puerto Rico is now called a Commonwealth. She has good reason for wanting to be tied to this country. The whole push, as you will read from this memorandum of mine on the Philippines, was more and more a push in the direction of autonomy. The Philippines very early pushed for independence. The fact of my memorandum I had completely forgotten until McGeorge Bundy sent it to me when he was working with Mr. Stimson on Mr. Stimson's memoirs, *On Active Service*. I was glad to read it and also sad to read it because I'm not sure at all that I would write as good a memorandum now. I'm quite ready to offer that up on Judgment Day and defend it.

Did Congress interest itself through its Committee on Insular Affairs in these matters? Did you have any function of appearing and defending some action taken by the War Department?

Certainly. You had to get legislation all the time before the Committee on Insular Affairs. That was handled by McIntyre. Of course in addition to the Philippines and Puerto Rico there was the Panama Canal Zone which was an autocratic rule, a rule by executive order. In my office in the War Department we wrote out the workmen's compensation laws and other laws, and they were just promulgated by General Goethals, a great man, really a great man. The mention of the Panama Canal Zone recalls an episode which, I think, goes far to illustrate why I think that Taft was such a poor President, the fundamental reason being that he wasn't interested in his job. He didn't care for it.

This very thing that I mentioned, the workmen's compensation law for the Canal Zone, wages, wage rates, fair labor standards act, all the things were done not legislatively, but by executive order because Congress had given the President full power to govern the Canal Zone with power to delegate it to whomever he was, the Governor of the Canal Zone, now a commission. We had drafted all these things, and they required presidential approval. Mr. Stimson said to me one day, "I have an appointment with the President to see us on these Panama executive orders tomorrow at nine o'clock at the White House. You'd better be there on time."

I'm a late fellow. I'm not an early bird. Mr. Stimson was. Then he thought and said, "No. You pick me up at my house at eight-forty-five"—he didn't trust me to get there on time—"and we'll walk down together."

I picked him up the following morning, and we walked down together. We got to the White House at nine o'clock. The usher recognized the Secretary and said that the President would be down shortly. He took us to the Blue Room, and Secretary Stimson and I talked about what was in the paper in the morning, about this and that, looked at that awful bad portrait of TR which is still there, and at nine-fifteen Mr. Stimson began to get restless. Stimson had to hoard his time for he was only good during the day; he couldn't work at night, he suffered from insomnia. We had exhausted the topics of the day, our esthetic comments on the portrait, and we had begun to manufacture topics for conversation. He would pull out his watch every once in a while—nine-thirty, nine-forty-five, and finally a little after ten past ten, one whole hour, in waddled—he weighed, God knows what he weighed!—President Taft, literally slapped Stimson on the shoulder, "Glad to see you, old man. Sorry to be late, but my tailor kept me."

Well, not only was he an hour late, but he didn't have the remotest recollection of why Secretary Stimson was there, "What have you got for me this morning, old man?"

I think that is as full a commentary as you want on Taft as a President. Of course, Mr. Stimson not long after he entered the cabinet, which I think in those days met on Friday at two o'clock, never left his office until two-thirty because he knew the President was always at least three-quarters of an hour late.

Now FDR would upset the schedule that he had given to Pa Watson. I've been present when he would go over with Pa Watson whom he would see, "Well, I'll give him ten minutes." "Fifteen minutes will do for him." "I think he can say what he has to say in ten minutes today." Then it might be Frances Perkins, it might be somebody his mother wanted him to see, it might be somebody just back from France who opens up a line of enquiry that interests him, and then he'd say, "Now, Pa, get out of here!"

That was a different thing. He was engaged. He didn't waste time. On the other hand, Wilson rationed time and kept within the rationing with cruel precision. If he said that he would see you for fifteen minutes, you were on the other side of the door when the fifty-ninth second of the fifteenth minute was reached. There was no "Let's chew it over." He was very precise.

My God! Is this six o'clock? Heavens! You get out of here!

8. *Holdover with Wilson*

The episode I'm about to give has no relation to my work in the War Department, either during Secretary Stimson's time or the one year I stayed on in the Wilson Administration under Secretary Lindley M. Garrison. It has, however, I think, a good deal to do with, or rather it sheds considerable light on President Wilson's way of doing business.

The year that I was in the Wilson Administration, 1913-1914, John Bassett Moore was, I think, counselor of the State Department, while Bryan was Secretary of State. Moore was supposed to be the great, technical, wise adviser of the Department. Of course, he had a great reputation as an international lawyer. He had been Assistant Secretary of State, he was the author of the great *Digest of International Law,* and he was Hamilton Fish Professor of International Law at Columbia University. I remember walking down the steps of the War Department, and Moore approaching me. I had known him respectfully. We walked down together. This was during the period when Mexican affairs were very much the concern of the Administration. I don't pretend to have the details in focus; there was that rascal Villa and so on. Anyhow, it was one of the big problems the State Department was concerned with, and one of the troublesome matters for President Wilson. As we got to the foot of the stairs, the newsboys were shouting out and hawking extras of the *Evening Star.* John Bassett

Moore bought a paper, and I bought a paper. There in big headlines appeared, PRESIDENT APPOINTS JOHN LIND FOR MEXICO. John Lind had been an ex-governor of Minnesota, an important figure in the Democratic Party at the time, and President Wilson sent him down as a special envoy, or commissioner to investigate, or look into, Mexican affairs.

I remember Moore exclaiming, "My God! This is the first I knew of that!"

Here was this important action taken in connection with the then most important problem in foreign relations, and the fellow who was in the State Department because he was this capacious brain in connection with matters of foreign relations had to learn of this action by paying three cents for the evening paper. I say that that was the "most important problem" because I cannot believe the record will show that in 1913, at that time, Wilson remotely thought that we might get involved in the imbroglios of European affairs.

There are many such episodes, but this one I knew first hand because I was there when it happened, that Moore had been turned purple by what he read in the paper. But other Presidents have done it before and since. And, of course, one knows that Wilson would act without any kind of respect for orderly consultation if that was what he wanted to do. I think it's common knowledge and I think it's true, that Wilson kept Walter Hines Page at London long after he lost confidence in him—Page was too much engaged in the allied cause in the First World War and would write these letters, confidential letters to the President, who, I believe it is a fact, never opened them because he didn't care any more what Page said, deeming Page too pro-British, but he kept him there as Ambassador because he didn't want to have the bother of supplanting him, or there were other reasons for not kicking up the difficulty of having as ambassador at the leading diplomatic post someone in whom he did have confidence.

That episode of John Bassett Moore discovering that an important step had been taken by the White House on affairs on which he was busy without any consultation made an impression on me. I say "without consultation," without asking Moore, "What do vou think about this?" "What do you think about having any special commissioner go down and spy out the land?" "What do you think of this man's qualifications?" I suppose Lind knew where Mexico was on the map. I don't believe he knew much more than that, but President Wilson didn't care much for consultation.

President Wilson also sent to the Philippines a special examiner as his personal inquirer, a former colleague of his at Princeton, Professor Henry Jones Ford, a very good man, and that was certainly one of the contributing causes of Lindley Garrison's final break with Wilson. He made the appointment without telling Secretary Garrison about it. That wasn't the only reason for the break. All I say is that that is a hell of a way to run a railroad.

Is it possible to get you to do adequate justice to Lindley M. Garrison? You had served under Secretary Stimson who was standard for you. By comparison, I suppose, Secretary Garrison paled, but in terms of the Wilson cabinet Mr. Garrison was not without substance.

Your question has an innuendo which is without warrant. Mr. Garrison lacked, I thought, appropriate qualifications for the post, but I had very high respect for him as a character and as a man. Would you like to know how he came to be appointed Secretary of War? He told me this himself, and Lindley M. Garrison was a man of great reliability. In the first place he was a man of limited imagination, and that always helps toward accuracy. He couldn't branch off much from what was pedantically registered on his mind and memory. Secondly, he was a man of disciplined conscientiousness. Thirdly and perhaps most important where reliability of speech is concerned where the man himself is involved, he was a modest man and therefore not in the service of an ego to make himself appear better, or bigger, or wiser, or nicer than he really was. This is what he told me, and I have some background of knowledge which helps to verify it.

President Wilson first designated as Secretary of War to succeed Mr. Stimson a Mr. Wallace who was the son-in-law of Chief Justice Fuller and was afterwards made our Ambassador to France. He was a very nice gentleman of some means—a Democrat of means which was not a commonplace phenomenon in Wilson's time. He was asked to be Secretary of War, and Mr. Stimson was advised of that, and he at once invited Mr. Wallace to come to the War Department so that he could brief him on the job before he should actually take hold of it. Wallace came and he spent some time with Mr. Stimson himself and then he was turned over to different bureau chiefs to become familiar with the personnel and the functions of the different bureaus. He spent, for all I know, a week in the War Department in this process of education.

The War Department in those days embodied within itself functions, which, certainly in England and in western countries generally, are distributed in three ministries. The War Department was the ministry of war, the colonial office, and the ministry of public works—meaning by that that of course it had responsibility for the armed service, but by virtue of the engineering corps it was concerned with river and harbor improvements, bridge building over interstate streams, dredging in waters where interstate and foreign commerce is or might be carried on. Then by virtue of the acquisitions which came to this country as a result of the Spanish American War, the administration of those acquisitions was originally military and was continued under the War Department when the military were displaced by a civilian group. The Secretary of War was concerned with the administration of the army and all matters affecting the army, all matters affecting our possessions and the construction of public works which grew out of various river and harbor bills, throughout the country. There was a vast amount of public work administration.

Mr. Wallace was a very nice and very conscientious man—perhaps a little leisurely man. Anyhow, after he had this indoctrination of what the business of the War Department involved and what his duties called for, he went back to the then Governor Wilson and said, "I'm very sorry. This is too big a job for me. I'm not the fellow who can do justice to it."

That, I suppose, is not a commonplace attitude on the part of people who are offered cabinet posts. Mr. Wilson had to look around and get another Secretary of War. This story of Wallace Mr. Garrison didn't tell me about. I knew it apart from him. I don't know whether he knew that Wallace had been designated and felt called upon to decline. What Garrison told me was this. He had a phone call from Trenton, from Wilson, then the Governor of New Jersey. Lindley M. Garrison at the time was Chancellor of New Jersey Equity. New Jersey in those days had the old English system, two systems of law, the so-called common law and equity, the head of one was the Chief Justice and of the other the Chancellor, a system which until very recently prevailed in New Jersey and does to this day in one or two southern states, Delaware for instance. The phone call asked whether Garrison could come and see the governor. Of course, he went, and Governor Wilson—this was a few days before March 4, 1913; I should say about a week before that date—at once pitched in *in medias res,* as we lawyers say, and said to Judge Garrison that he was much troubled by the requirements in filling the post of Secretary of War.

He didn't make this analysis that I made that the War Department is a triune affair; he gave Garrison the impression that the most important responsibility of the War Department was its administration of the Philippine Islands, it having oversight of the government there. Wilson said, "That is the most important, most far-reaching of the functions of the War Department, and one that makes the most exacting demands on the person to be Secretary of War because we are trustees for the Philippine people. Therefore, the Secretary of War having this responsibility should be a man with a very sensitive fiduciary equipment, a man with a very strong sense of responsibility as a trustee. He must have a sensitive conscience, a delicacy of feeling being the man who acts for nine million other people. What I need is a man whose conscience is very well informed, very alert."

Garrison, in telling me this, said that when the governor said that, Garrison thought to himself, "Hello. I now see why he wants to talk to me. He wants me to recommend him some very good equity lawyer. He evidently wants somebody from New Jersey and somebody who has shown high qualities of sensitive conscience as befits those who are concerned with equity, and since I'm the head of equity, I must know the lawyers who are well versed in this."

And so he began to turn over in his mind who the outstanding fellows were who, by virtue of their professional equipment, would be capable of overseeing the administration of the Philippine Islands—certainly a very complicated mode of reasoning which might bring very dire results. Governor Wilson went on to expound this and wound up by saying, "Is there any reason why you shouldn't accept the Secretaryship of War?"

Garrison was taken aback. He had no more thought of that than of flying to the moon in 1913—it would be different now; that is, flying to the moon would—and he did say, "This is very sudden, Governor, and I'll have to think about it."

Wilson pushed him, "How long will it take you to think about it because I have to have an answer very soon?"

I won't now give bail for my memory as to whether he gave him twenty-four or forty-eight hours—I think twenty-four—but in any event, a very short shrift. Garrison said that he would have to talk with his wife, anyhow, and in due course, he accepted. That is how Lindley M. Garrison became Secretary of War. He was a very nice man, very ill-equipped for this job.

I can't think of a better illustration of how doctrinaire Wilson's thinking was. The notion that a fellow who sat in chancery and dealt with fiduciary responsibilities toward property, or had a keen sense in detecting shenanigans by a trustee, or was very alert in protecting the interests of infants and widows, and all the other multitudinous aspects in which the notion of trustee comes before a Court of Chancery, an equity court, the notion that there is any relation between that and wisdom in when and how a subject people should be given increasing self-rule, perhaps eventually, as it turned out, given independence, is fantastic, is just riding a word to death. You know, trusteeship implies a sensitive conscience. Responsibility for other people calls for a sensitive conscience. Therefore, it is the same conscience for both. Fantastic!

Garrison was no fool. Garrison was like his colleague, Mr. Justice Pitney, who became a justice of the Supreme Court, a disciplined, narrow-minded—not narrow, there was a human largeness about both of them, but these were fellows who were dray horses, pulling the more or less simple, relatively unimportant, mass of cases that come before the Jersey court, predominantly involving rights between two private litigants with very little infusion of that vague, impalpable but all-controlling consideration, the public interest. They were much guided by precedent. They didn't have many questions on constitutional law when they came to their respective jobs. I'm bringing this in because in connection with the river and harbor administration there were involved the powers of the federal government as against the states. Garrison didn't have his mind opened to those questions either by experience or doctrinaire, abstract intellectual curiosity and reading. The constitutional law that was in his head was what he had in law school when he read law thirty years before, and it stuck. Ditto Pitney—though both of them were very conscientious. The notion that this kind of careful, precedent-following habit of mind was fitted to deal with large public issues! Of course, this was silly!

Each was what he was, I suppose, because his forebears were Democrats or Republicans. But they were both men of honor, and I have the greatest esteem for Garrison. When finally he disagreed with Wilson on two important issues, one was the Philippines and the other was the organization of the army, he quit. He was one of those rare people for whom self-respect on what he deemed principles was more important than public office.

The reason why I stayed over after Mr. Stimson left and there was a change of administration was that they asked me to stay. Garrison said the President wanted me to stay, instead of going to New York and practicing law with Mr. Stimson. The chief reason was that in Mr. Stimson's regime there was the beginning of what is now the Federal Power Commission; namely, an attempt at systematic regulation of the power generated on streams that are within federal authority by virtue of the commerce clause, by virtue of the fact that commerce plied on those streams. It wasn't until Theodore Roosevelt's time that there was an awareness of the vast national interest here, the potential power in various falls on the streams throughout the country. Licenses had to be given to people to build dams and so on, and they were given just for nothing—gratis. Thus private power interests built up. A bill for each dam, the Black River dam in Alabama, the Connecticut River dam in Connecticut, a private bill had to be passed. The Senators and Congressmen would present a private bill, and it would go through like greased lightning because there were rivers in almost every state, and everybody had an interest in getting his people's bill through. This continued until TR came along and said, "Oh, no! We're giving away valuable natural resources, the power you're going to churn through those locks and dams through control of the water of these various rivers doesn't belong to anybody. It belongs to everybody. It belongs to the people, and therefore, you shouldn't turn it all to profit."

Various proposals were made from time to time to license these things, to get a return, to give short terms that provided that at the end of whatever the license period was it should revert to the public. That was done episodically during TR's time, and when Stimson came along, he was a conservationist, a great friend of Gifford Pinchot, and he alertly lived through all this row about conservation during Teddy's time. When he became Secretary of War—you will find this in his reports—he had formulated systematic inquiries to find out about every bill affecting harbor improvement. Any construction on every river over which interstate commerce may pass would go to the War Department down to the Engineering Corps for their comment. The engineers just had no sense of social implications. They were just concerned with whether in case of war this might be an obstruction or not, and they'd say, "O.K." We worked on this matter, and the upshot was that we drew up inquiries, questions which the engineers had to answer about each one of those projects all to the end that it wasn't enough that at present there was no commerce on this stream, there might be, so something that isn't navigable now might become a navigable stream by a little dredging, or a little diversion of the water, or what not. Also the potentialities of the stream for water power had to be assessed so that obstructing works couldn't be built. This eventually led to the passage in 1920 of the first Federal Power Act, as an Act instead of individual bills, piece by piece. A Power Commission was set up consisting of three members of the cabinet, and that wasn't any good because they wouldn't give enough time until, whenever it was in the thirties, the Federal Power Commission was established which is now operating. What it does of course depends on who the commissioners are. You can strangle a policy by administration, something the political scientists do not always know, or at least, little heed. Of course, to find out what really happens in administration requires a lot of digging. It's so much easier to think than to dig, but thinking without digging isn't very good thinking.

One of these matters came up, and Stimson said, "You stay

behind and get this new administration to put this thing you've been working on through. It's too important."

I stayed behind when they asked me to. I remember my first conference with Secretary Garrison on this subject. He said, "The federal government has no constitutional power."

Talking constitutionality is a professional disease, not only among lawyers, but it is also a kind of magical field of ignorance that attracts the laity. Everybody likes to talk about constitutionality. I thought to myself, "Oh, my heavens! This fellow is still living in the past."

I tried to educate him, and I remember saying one Saturday after a long discussion, "Mr. Secretary, please keep your mind open until we have another chance to talk about this."

"Very well, I shall, but I can assure you that once my mind is closed, it's closed!"

The following Monday the Supreme Court of the United States handed down a very important decision which I had forecast in what I was trying to make clear to Mr. Garrison, and he recognized that as authority, though he thought the world had come to an end, the extension of federal power announced in the famous Chandler-Dunbar decision, 229 U.S.

But the explanation is very simple. He had never had this problem or anything like it before him. He had read Cooley's *Constitutional Limitations,* and he had never thought about it for thirty years. He hadn't thought about it then. He just came to it cold. He was an honorable, modest, nice man, and when he left, he left. He didn't attack. He had a high-minded code. I believe that is called "Victorian," but I hope one of these days that it will be restored.

Is there something to the thought that by training and experience both Wilson and Garrison shared this "when my mind is closed, it's closed!"?

They were both dogmatic temperaments. Wilson was very dogmatic. That was his great limitation, and he didn't believe in debating. He used phrases like "laying mind against mind" and "consulting the common council of the nation," but he didn't carry that out in practice at all—quite the opposite. I always thought that he was one of those people whom people fatigued. He had limited vitality. That is why he wanted you to put things on paper. Wilson didn't believe in what he would call discursive argument. They were temperaments bound to clash, and since Garrison was a man of high self-respect, he wouldn't just stick around the way Walter Page did in London even after he knew Wilson had lost confidence in him. I'm not suggesting that Page should have resigned. All I'm saying is that he knew Wilson didn't pay any attention to him. Garrison quit and went to practice law.

With his background and experience how did he come to really understand and fight for the national army concept? He put that right on the line.

Yes he did. I do think that all his natural flow of feeling was for the allies—the war was on—and the chance, the likelihood that we might get involved was a contingency he could understand, and the very unsophisticated simplicity of his mind was against the kind of compromise that Wilson was working out. I think behind Wilson's attitude toward the National Guard and all that was a resistance to the thought that we might get into the war. He was sure that he would keep us out of war. That was a big slogan in the 1916 campaign, "He kept us out of war, and he'll keep us out of war!"

Now, I think FDR too hoped that we wouldn't get into the war, but at the same time he illustrated what Morris Cohen calls the principle of polarity. I don't suppose Morris invented it, but you've got to do the opposite at the same time. You've got to do your damnedest to keep out of war, but not forget that it might be beyond your control, and therefore, you don't want to be left with your pants down when the occasion arises. That's not an edifying position.

To do the contradictory is a tough problem; namely, with might and main to try to prevent from coming to pass the very situation in relation to which you're making preparations. That's what we have to do in life so much. You build a fire-proof house and nevertheless take out fire insurance.

9. *The Call to Harvard*

I should like to deal with the call to Harvard to join the faculty there, how it came to you, what you thought about it. I got the impression that with the departure of Mr. Stimson and the advent of the Wilson Administration perhaps the character of men around you had lessened your own excitement, if not your interest, in government service.

This is a perfect illustration of how one misconveys by trying to be too pithy. Wilson didn't appeal to me man to man. I didn't warm in his presence. I recognized then as I do now his great qualities, but he was not sympatico to me as a man. He was cold, dogmatic. I had seen something of him before he became President, and all the qualities that came out so strikingly in the tragic year of 1919 and earlier, but particularly 1919. Old age and sickness bring out the essential characteristics of a man, just as they bring it out in dogs, or so I'm told, as they grow older. Their basic psyche dominates. A gentle dog grows gentler, and a dog that is not gentle, though he might cover up his ungentleness, in his old age becomes a bad, mad dog. And so, as these conscious or unconscious, mostly unconscious, brakes on these undesirable and unattractive qualities in us are withdrawn by age or sickness when we haven't got as much energy, the native qualities break forth. He was dogmatic, intolerant; fundamentally didn't like his kind.

He believed in democracy in the abstract, but didn't care for people. That's true! And he'd cut off their heads with equanimity. But it isn't true that I didn't care much for him.

There isn't any doubt that in the normal course of affairs I would have left with Mr. Stimson when he left the Taft Administration. I wouldn't have left because the Taft Administration terminated—I was not of that suasion particularly, or still less generally, but I was with Mr. Stimson, came down to Washington with him, and I suppose that in the ordinary course of affairs, if I hadn't been mid-stream working on questions of the regulation of water power, I would have gone back to New York and practiced law with him. He wanted me to stay when Secretary Garrison asked me to stay. He said, "I think you ought to stay."

I don't know just when it was that out of a clear sky—a completely clear sky—I had a letter from Professor Edward H. Warren, writing for the Harvard Law School faculty, asking would I come up there and join the faculty. The reason doubtless why he wrote, why he was asked to write to me, was because he and I were great friends. He was a young teacher. He came to the school in my undergraduate days, and we became great buddies and had personal relations, so naturally he was the medium of communication. As I must have said at the time—it sticks in my memory—if I had received a letter from an Indian princess asking me to marry her, I wouldn't have been more surprised. My thoughts never turned to teaching. It never occurred to me. And what is much more important, I no more thought of myself as a member of the Harvard Law School faculty than I would have felt myself a member of the House of Lords—in fact, more easily, probably. considering the people who are in the House of Lords. I wrote back that this was so great a surprise that, "If you want me to answer in forty-eight hours, I will, but I prefer to just sleep on it for a few months."

My first concern was that I wasn't qualified. When I thought of Gray, Ames, Thayer, I couldn't think of myself in those terms. When I put that to Justice Brandeis he said, "I would let those who have the responsibilities for selecting you decide your qualifications and not have you decide that."

That is a piece of advice I have often, since then, given to others because it is very good. It works both ways. You're no good judge of yourself either of your fitness or your unfitness. I'm a disbeliever in asking many people about anything. That's a way of postponing decision and confusing your mind, but there were people with whom I wanted to talk over what they thought about this—Holmes who was then abroad, Brandeis, Stimson, Croly, TR, and the lady who thereafter became my wife. She was furious that I should ask her upon the theory that she was wholly incompetent to have a judgment on such a matter, and she thought it unfair of me to put such a question to her which shows her good sense. TR emphasized the thing that none of my other advisers emphasized. He said, "Of course, if you go up and become a professor, you want to bear in mind that your denominator will remain substantially static. Only your numerator is within your control."

He knew I had no money and his was a wise remark, "You'll have to adjust your wants. You'll have to have a wife who'll be content with a simple life. Your salary will substantially remain the same for the rest of your life. You'll have to work with that."

Holmes wrote me a remarkable letter pithily putting the dangers of the cloistered life as against thinking under fire; the dangers of academic life, the easy judgments, the irresponsibility of running the universe on paper. He didn't say what my mother said on a different occasion, "Paper is very patient." It's so much easier to tell people what to do if you only have to do it on paper as against persuading them. I always like the remark, "Paper is patient." You can write any damn thing on a clean sheet of paper and be sure about it too. Well, Holmes's advice was against it, very strong against it.

Mr. Stimson, I understand, engaged in a correspondence on the subject with the then dean of the law school, Ezra Thayer, who was a great friend of his and classmate at the Harvard Law School. I've always wished I could have seen their exchange of views. I don't know now whether it was through Mr. Stimson or through Mr. Thayer, who died within a year after I came there, that I learned that Stimson's point was that I was peculiarly fitted for public life, and that he thought there were very few people intrinsically fitted for public life. He thought it a very unwise thing for me to be withdrawn from activities in that realm, that you could get people for scholarship—that there were more people qualified for scholarship than for statesmanship. I believe Thayer replied, "Will you please name me a few?"

Well, they wrote back, "Take your time." As a matter of fact, they were going to found a professorship for me, and then events changed. One of the men retired, or was asked to leave, Bruce Wyman, an interesting episode in the history of the Harvard Law School. Without disclosing that he was under a retainer from the New Haven, Wyman made speeches on behalf of the New Haven in the famous row between the New Haven and Brandeis, and more particularly, Brandeis's attack in his book, *Other People's Money*. Since Wyman appeared to be speaking as a professor of the Harvard Law School and not under retainer, when that fact came out he was asked to resign the very next day. So there was a vacancy.

I did something that I've done rarely in life, namely, try to externalize, if not objectify, considerations pro and con by putting on paper what there was to be said for and against going to Harvard:

July 5, 1913

Speaking roughly, we have turned a corner, we have struck a new gait. There is a noticeably different demand in our national, in our community life. The exploiting, "manifest destiny" years following the Spanish War hastened the Rooseveltian decade of excoriating protest, of national arousing out of easy lethargy. That period is about over. Evangelicism has done its job. The social passions are alive and alert; they now want direction. The soil is pretty thoroughly fertilized; now for the seeds.

All along the line we propose, determine, legislate—without knowing enough. Empiricism of the worst sort is abroad —in administration and legislation of necessity. To be stable, to meet our realization of the need and capacity for conscious readjustments, requires adequate data, and correlated, persistent, prophetic thinking. Largely that cannot be done in office. It must be done from the outside and translated by those in office with all the risks and limitations of translation, or have been done before men come to office. There should be a constant source of thought for the guidance of public men and the education of public opinion, as well as a source of trained men for public life. The problems ahead are economic and sociological, and the added adjustments of a government under a written constitution, steeped in legalistic traditions, to the assumption of the right solution of such problems. To an important degree therefore, the problems are problems of jurisprudence,—not only the shaping of a jurisprudence to meet the social and industrial needs of the time, but the great procedural problems of administration and legislation, because of the inevitable link between law and legislation, the lawyer's natural relation to these issues, the close connection between all legislation and constitutional law, and the traditional, easily accountable dominance of the lawyer in our public affairs. In the synthesis of thinking that must shape the Great State, the lawyer is in many ways the coordinator, the mediator, between the various social sciences.

This organized thinking must be assumed by our law schools, and the most hopeful center, the rightful leader, is the Harvard Law School. As a matter of fact, it has been creatively stagnant for almost a generation. Since Langdell and Ames did their epoch-making work in the revolution of the *method* of law teaching, nothing has been done except the perfection of technique. Well, with Pound there, I think we could lug in a Trojan horse of what Hand calls our "heretical thinking." The resistance would be great, in atmosphere, colleagues, Higginson-Lowell University respectabilities, etc. etc., but I know it can be done. The student body would carry the day. I could keep my independence, or rather spread it, and say what thinking will lead me to say, and that, too, without any danger of having my thinking unconsciously softened or my underlying ardors impaired. It is a great big job that has to be done—to evolve a constructive jurisprudence going hand in hand with the pretty thoroughgoing overturning that we are in for.

I am not a scholar of the Langdell or Ames type, though Ames had a pretty lively sense of law's relation to life and affairs. I probably *do* have the needed spirit of scholarship for that line of work, and enough of the mere book scholarship—that is, the ability for it—needed to see what the past has to say in the work of tomorrow. How far my mind cuts, how deeply it can go—I rather suspect its scope. It's probably more incisive, illuminative, tough enough insofar as it goes, than profoundly creative, capable of powerful generalizations. However, it has hardly had a real go, and so far as it has been harnessed, it seems to do the job fairly well in the run of governmental problems. In any event, I shan't worry on that score. Perhaps I am overrating the demands, and if Pound and Brandeis, for two, think it adequate, there is a presumptive case.

The big thing, one of the big things, is that I would go in for about five years of thinking, not cloistered, but in the very current of the problems that are *the* national problems of greatest appeal to me. This intellectual hand-to-mouth living—well, it's like all hand-to-mouth living. It would not be cloistered, not if I did it as it should be done, and it would be well done only if I steered the boat in the current. For the first three years I would probably be pretty well tied up getting up the courses, *die Lehrjahre*. After that, I doubt whether law school would take more than half my time, leaving the rest for such activities as are on the main track. My "freshness," my "level-headedness,"—I don't believe Cambridge would spoil them. I agree, perhaps, with Val [Robert G. Valentine] that, at the root of any consideration of my job, is my gift of tapping people of all kinds, my coordinating faculties, the quality of productive sympathies. "To enlighten public selfishness and harmonize the public will"—that may be my job. It can hardly disqualify me for it to enlighten myself first and acquire a thorough foundation grip on the forces to be harmonized. It is against the nature of the beast for me to become academically sterilized, and there is some danger at the present game of spreading thin, of having done all too little self-wrestling, of being caught short in my thinks. On the other hand, at thirty-five I expect to be pretty much the same alive, contagious boy, with the advantage of definite, disciplined, stimulated thinking along the lines that will have to be tackled more and more with definiteness, concreteness, full knowledge of implications, etc. Thirty-five will be young enough to decide whether that is the forum, whether the danger there is toward softness, whether Boston does impose unnecessary limitations to usefulness.

Well, what are the alternatives?

(1) *The Valentine thing.* [Industrial relations] But I don't think I ought to give up the tools of the law for my stunt, for one thing, and to do this job I would have to, in effect. And I am not sure that my grip of men is for his kind of thing. So far as contact with these problems goes, big thinking them out, I can do more thinking at H.L. School, properly tied up with outside things.

(2) *Stay on here.* I don't find myself drawn to Wilson. There is an inscrutable secretiveness about him. His thinking, insofar as one can get it, isn't grippy, his aspirations appeal but his definitions of them are vague,—unthoughtoutly vague, not vague because big. He is largely drifting, and, I think, lacks the very robustness of equipment on these social-economic questions that I want so much to get. Then too, the atmosphere is Southern-Democrat—it's "party solidarity" feeling, they must live politically—shortsighted though that policy is for him. Garrison is a first-class mediocrity. Our relations are exceedingly pleasant, but he doesn't begin to know how to use me, and he couldn't because Wilson makes no such use of his Cabinet or other officials as T.R. did, or even as H.L. was enabled to serve Taft. Probably I should want to get out anyway by another year.

(3) That leaves *practice in New York.* Well, I could get fun out of it. But to do the things at the Bar that I want to do or could do with the best workman comfort and earn an income of, say, six thousand, would take practically all my time and leave only the odds and ends for the civic, social extras. Of course, I would get tied up with all sorts of things and all kinds of unexpected chances, but the main thing would have to be to peg away at the law. T.R. says he sometimes

> hoped for me a usefulness in New York as citizen-lawyer, like Brandeis in Boston. So likewise thinks Henry. Well, isn't Cambridge as hopeful a road towards that goal as New York, with irksomeness avoided and with the increased "bigness" that T.R. speaks of getting? Others think, above all, office for me. I have now no additional aim than the realization of ideas. But even *if*—I am not sure that Harvard isn't as good a ticket to draw in the lottery of chances for office as the other routes, either sticking it out here or New York practice. So far as one can tell, the trend is bound to be more and more towards drawing officials who are presumably thoroughly trained.
>
> Anyhow, the problem at its lowest terms is not an irrevocable choice of public as against private life. Cambridge, of course, for one thing, is very much public in itself. It leaves room for public work, say, on state commissions, (take the Wisconsin crowd), and a preparedness for it, if that's the way the die shall be finally cast. Even less is it academic as against public, because it isn't going to be academic, as I see what's to be done,—or rather, I can't become academic, unless forces are far less deep in me than I think, and then it doesn't matter.
>
> It is probably the best five years' investment ahead. Then is the time to take new stock, with more stock to take and better equipment for taking it.

I should think that the prevailing consideration was that I was unhappy about "the intellectual hand-to-mouth living" which had been my lot since leaving the law school, first as a lawyer in the United States Attorney's office and then in the government. You know, you had to do things quickly and you couldn't say, "What do I really think about this?" It wasn't so much the compulsions of partisanship because they weren't demanding, either during my years in the United States Attorney's Office, or with Mr. Stimson in the War Department. I mean I didn't have to talk to a brief—as the phrase runs. I didn't have to go in and fight for a client on a claim that I thought was no good. But I think "intellectual hand-to-mouth living," the fact that whatever was done had to be done within a given time, prevented one from sitting back and thinking long and hard, not writing anything, and then thinking some more. On the whole that was the attraction, and I was young enough not to think that this was a Roman Catholic marriage—you know, if you're in law and not completely incompetent, you've got a means of livelihood in the profession.

I suppose you might find evidence that life in the Wilson administration was not exciting for me, not absorbing. Of course, I didn't get any what is called "inspiration" out of President Taft, but Mr. Stimson was my generator of satisfaction, and my source of intellectual and spiritual nourishment was working with him. I didn't give a damn what happened over in the White House which didn't give Mr. Stimson and me any happiness. You couldn't get any happiness out of Taft as President, not because of his policies, but because of his ineptitudes. Robert Valentine once said something that tells one a great deal about TR and Taft as Presidents. He said that the difference was that when you left TR's presence "you were ready to eat bricks for lunch," and when you left Taft you thought, "What's the use."

I remember Mr. Justice Brandeis once saying to me after Taft became Chief Justice, in that way that he had when he was about to say something very intimate, putting his arm through yours, "Felix, do you still think that Taft was as bad a President as we thought he was?"

I said that I hadn't changed my mind on that subject; looking back on it I still thought that he was as bad a President as I thought he was contemporaneously. Then I said to him, "Why do you raise the question? Why are you ready to reconsider that judgment?"

Then he said, "It's very difficult for me to understand why a man who is so good as Chief Justice, in his function of presiding officer, could have been so bad as a President. How do you explain that?"

To which I replied, "The explanation is very simple. He loathed being President and being Chief Justice was all happiness for him. He fought against being President and yielded to the acceptance of that heritage because of the insistence of Mrs. Taft"—very ambitious in that direction. It always had been the ambition of his life to be on the Supreme Court. Taft once said that the Supreme Court was his notion of what heaven must be like. I must say that he had a very different notion of heaven than any I know anything about.

Well, these remarks were apropos of getting no satisfaction or no inspiration, no warmth out of Taft—nice a man as he was. But Mr. Stimson was all that was necessary for a young, ardent spirit such as I was. Garrison was a man I greatly respected, but he wasn't Stimson. Moreover, there wasn't the past association with Garrison that I had had with Stimson. It was easy enough to leave. There were no personal ties to break, and when this offer from Harvard came, after I slept with it, worried about it, thought about it, I disregarded all my advisers except one and went up there.

I went up there—not hard, you know. I was young enough to feel that nothing was hard. It may be irksome, but not hard. I left Washington in early summer of 1914 and spent the summer in the stacks trying to find out what had happened to the law generally since I left the school in 1906. You know more about the law the day you graduate from a law school than you ever again do the rest of your life. You may deepen, but you don't broaden your channels after you get out.

What impact did you feel from the students the first year?

I'm a bad man to whom to put such a question. As my wife rightly says I'm not a very reflective person. Dean Thayer, the son of James Bradley Thayer, when he came up from a class would dictate what took place. He'd say I should have answered this question this way, and I didn't handle this right. I don't mean to say that I'm an ass, or that I'm bovine—quite, but the notion of looking back and regurgitating what had taken place and going through a searching self-examination of where I could have done better never occurred to me. I'm no fool, and therefore some things give satisfaction, and some things don't, but to answer your question, I was thirty-one, and I felt at ease and at home with the boys—it wasn't a problem. I was scared stiff, of course. Anybody who isn't scared stiff might as well fold up to begin with. I told you that the greatest hesitation about going up there was a sense of inadequacy which I never shook off and haven't shaken off to this day. But to go and, having once plunged in, then each day to ask myself, "Am I fit to be here?"—you know, that way madness lies.

Anyway I'm not that kind of a temperament. I'm a spontaneous creature, and I like people, and it's a pleasure. I can listen as well as talk and delight in the well-doing of other people. I get great pleasure out of a performance, strangely enough, even when it isn't mine. To that extent, there was a quick rapport between myself and the students. It just wasn't a problem.

10. *The New Republic*

What in Herbert Croly, one so silent and mute, was attractive to you initially? Did you meet him in Washington?

I met him in New York through Judge Learned Hand. It was just about the time that he published his notable, seminal book I should call it, *The Promise of American Life*. Judge Learned Hand, who had recently come to the federal bench, while I was in the United States Attorney's Office, and I had become friends. He thought that Croly and I would be very sympathetic, one with another. He brought us together, and we hit it off right away. I being, as it were, a kind of loosener of other people's tongues, with a certain warming quality, thawed him out. Once that relationship was established we became intimate. Of course, while he was inhibited in company, he was a free talker *a deux*.

Croly was a noble creature. Learned Hand uses the word "noble" about him. He was noble, in the sense that to a rare degree he had a sense of justice. He was one of the most just-minded men I ever knew on or off the Supreme Court of the United States. His *Promise of American Life* made a very deep impression on TR. Contrariwise, TR's conception of the Presidency as an affirmative mechanism for society—the President as leader, which is very different from this miserable thing called Fuehrer, a recognition that the leader expresses the strength of the people, not that the leader paralyzes the intelligence of the people and puts it to sleep —was very congenial to Croly. They saw each other.

TR shifted from mere humanitarianism—being kind to people and not being oppressive, passing tenement-house laws, prohibiting the manufacture of cigars in a tenement house—to an understanding of the labor movement, namely, that you can't deal with masses of men by doling out kindness. The very essentials of our citizenship and our nation require that they should be self-respecting, self-determining individuals. That got his interest into labor unions. TR wanted to know more about the labor movement. By this time I had been called to the Harvard Law School. It was arranged that three of us, Herbert Croly, Walter Weyl and I, should spend a day with the Colonel at Sagamore Hill. The date was fixed. We were to go out, spend the day and have a day's talk with the Colonel on August 4, 1914. It happened to be that fateful day in the world's history. This had been arranged months or weeks before when nobody thought of a war. Needless to say, when we got out at Sagamore Hill, we didn't talk about the American labor movement, or American industrial problems, we talked about the war.

There was another guest there who had also been asked to talk about industrial matters. He was one of the men most competent in all the world to talk about them, Charles Booth, author of *The Poor of London,* the first comprehensive, detailed, and what may fairly be called scientific attempt to study quantitatively the condition of the poor in London. But Booth was also, and this is a phenomenon one finds, or did find, more frequently in England than in this country, chairman of the Cunard Steamship Line. He was a man of wealth and a man of social sensitiveness. He was an exquisite-looking creature—delicate, with a beautiful Van Dyke beard. He had the quality of an Arab steed, that delicacy. I remember well the difference between so boisterous a creature as TR was, a man with so much animal zest, so much horsepower, and the refined reticence and hesitation of thought of Booth. The contrast between them in physical appearance was enormous, but also in attitude, because here was TR in the comfort of Sagamore Hill in Oyster Bay shaking his fist at Mr. Booth, saying, "You've got to go in! You've got to go in!"

Here was Mr. Booth, head of the Cunard Line with God knows how many ships on the water, just sitting quietly. It was awfully easy for TR to say, "You've got to go in." We weren't going in. I'll never forget this beautiful creature Booth. There was TR doing a tomahawk war dance around Mr. Booth and this exquisite gentleman, who was seventy-four at the time, with Roosevelt shaking his fist at him and saying, "You've got to go in!," shook his head like one of these china mandarins, saying slowly, "I suppose we've got to go in."

While we were talking the English cabinet was sitting. I remember very vividly what TR said, though one can't be sure that one remembers anything unless there's contemporaneous demonstration, but that day at Oyster Bay Roosevelt was very outspoken. He had no doubt that the issue was very clear, that Germany was an aggressor and that you had to stop this. He said, "I say all this, though probably in a few years Germany will be an ally of ours in our fight against Japan."

We talked about the war. Here was the world on the edge of a world war. Anybody who knew anything, and certainly people like Herbert Croly, Walter Weyl, TR, Mr. Booth and I knew that this had implications that nobody could have any confidence wouldn't sweep us into the swirl. When we came back from Sagamore Hill we came out of the Long Island side of the Pennsylvania Station. We came back together, and then I went off by myself in a different direction. I crossed the street on Seventh Avenue. As I was walking uptown, Mr. Stimson was walking hastily to catch a Long Island train out to Huntington. We bumped into each other. I remember him with his intense voice saying, "I wish you'd get your damned friend Lloyd George to be a patriot!"

My damned friend! I didn't know Lloyd George, but Stimson knew my general sympathies were in that direction. Of course, "my damned friend" voted for war, and John Morley, Charles P. Trevelyan and John Burns who was a wonderful person left the cabinet on that issue. I remember that incident because it was so like Stimson. Well, that finished that memorable day.

You mentioned Walter Weyl. Didn't he and Croly write similar works within that same period?

Those general ideas were in the air. It was a seedbed time, if that expresses what I want to say, but I think Croly planted not a few of the seeds.

What brought the original group on the New Republic *together?*

I suppose the story is well known that Willard Straight and Dorothy Straight, the very sensitive, gentle being, responsive to spiritual interests and considerations, were on their honeymoon, when, I don't know how, or through whom, somebody put *The Promise of American Life* their way. She was the daughter of William C. Whitney a hardboiled fellow who made vast money in the days of piracy, in the days when the bases for big fortunes were laid and who left her part of that fortune. They read it, I think, in Japan or somewhere in the Far East. Their interest was aroused. Willard Straight was an ardent young fellow who was studying architecture and had lots of teeming ideas and who unfortunately died very young as the result of a flu epidemic at the Paris Peace Conference. They said, "We want to get hold of this fellow Croly. We wonder who he is." The book excited them, and when they came back they sought out Croly through the publishers. They learned where he was. Croly was at that time earning his living as editor of the *Architectural Record.* I think that was the paper, a weekly. Technically, professionally, Croly was a student of architecture, and was earning his livelihood that way.

Well, they met and they got to talking about things. One thing brought on another. He said, "What we lack in this country is some vehicle for expressing liberal ideas."

He had these ideas in his book, but ideas have to be kept alive. The tennis ball of ideas has to be played across the net of the human mind and human concern. They said, "Well, how could we get such a periodical going? What would it mean? Would you mind putting on paper your ideas of such a publication?"

Croly did, and that was the prospectus of the *New Republic.* They said they would finance it. And then the problem was to get editors. Croly got on to Walter Lippmann who had just recently published his first book, *A Preface to Politics,* and got hold of him. Francis Hackett was then editing the best book review page of any paper in the land, the Chicago *Evening Post.* Somebody knew about that. The editors were brought together the way a producer of a play looks around and asks for suggestions in filling the roles of a new play. It took Croly more than a year to bring the board together, and they were an unusual lot.

Francis Hackett was the most brilliant of conversationalists, and by long odds the most gifted of creatures. Holmes thought he was the only genius in the lot of the *New Republic*. As Holmes said, "Francis Hackett is one of those creatures who can express the inexpressible." He was a very gifted person. Philip Littell had a page in the *New Republic* after it got going entitled "Books and Things," under the initials of P.L. Walter Weyl was a wise, sensitive, cultivated and highly civilized social reformer. He didn't think you could save the world overnight, or that, at least, he could do it. He had purpose without being boring about it.

Croly was very anxious, terribly anxious, to have me join him. I suppose I was as close to him as anybody. We became more and more intimate and he, I think, found more and more comfort in my responses, perhaps because I was more expressive than others, and conveyed my feeling, my warmth of feeling, more articulately. He was most anxious that I join him and become one of the editors. But I resisted and went up to the Harvard Law School to become a professor. Croly, in a sour way, made the observation that the Lord meant me to be a journalist, but perversity took me into law. And here I am.

I knew Norman Angell well. Whenever he came here, he came here to lecture. That's another thing that was characteristic of the *New Republic*. Although Croly had no social gift at all, none—it was almost funny—there were regular luncheons at the *New Republic*. He had a keen sense of beauty. They fussed around for months before they got the format and the lettering of the paper right. If you look at it, you see how beautiful it was. He moved in a world of artists. The offices were in an old-fashioned house on Twenty-third Street, two houses knocked together, and there was a nice luncheon room. Croly cared about food. When he came to dinner he would always bring his own cigars because he had a special brand. And the coffee had to be just right. He was a fussy fellow that way which was another bond between us.

There were these luncheons. Croly was, of course, the representative host for these various English publicists, but he could hardly open his mouth. Somebody else had to do the inciting and the interchanges that keep a dinner table going, if it goes. If it had depended on Croly, there would have been an eternal frost. But he would then take his guests upstairs and talk to them tete-a-tete, and that was a very different story. Well, Norman Angell, H. N. Brailsford, Gilbert Murray, H. N. Nevinson would come over. Nevinson was the most exciting of them all, a wonderful creature, the author of my favorite autobiography.

He was a tall, handsome, six-feet-three or four, English with a distinguished-looking beard and a distinguished presence. He was a pacifist, and he had been a war correspondent in every war for the last forty years. He was a gentle creature, and he would have terrific passionate outbursts. He was a daily journalist, but wrote a very important book on Goethe, was soaked in classical and modern literature, mastering I don't know how many languages. He was the kind of a journalist of whom, so far as I know, there's no American counterpart. He could easily have been better than the head of the department of Romance Languages in most American universities, or professor of Greek and Classics, or in the German department. I say "exciting," and if I have to prove my case, I would put in evidence his autobiography with its three remarkable well-known titles, taken I believe from the *Common Prayer Book, Changes and Chances, More Changes and More Chances, Last Changes and Last Chances*. Read that if you want to read anything that's exciting!

Brailsford had none of the flaming gaiety, or ferocity of Nevinson. He's a much more steady person, a flame, but a steady flame, whereas Nevinson's flame was low and high. That kind of fluctuation of the human spirit of course is very exciting.

Norman Angell was a mousey kind of fellow with unrelenting logical powers—but mousey as a personality, with a mousey voice. It's hard to think of him in all the glamorous and adventuresome activities in which he was engaged, including his connection with Lord Northcliffe. What a bruiser he was! A powerful fellow!

I became associated with, though I was not an editor of, the *New Republic*. I was one of the trustees, technically speaking. I was with them and sat with the editorial board all through the early stages before the child was born. When the child was born, I was kind of a godfather, or perhaps godcousin is better.

11. *"Liberty of Contract"*

I do not know, and I haven't got the time now to search in my mind for what was the source of my interest in the general domain of social reform of which the minimum-wage law for women was one expression. I wrote an introduction to a book on Mrs. Florence Kelley, and that tells of the general direction of the influence exerted by the National Consumers' League of which she was not only the executive secretary, but the embodiment, the soul, and almost everything, in promoting social legislation that now is so taken as a matter of course that it seems almost unbelievable, and rather silly, that there ever should have been this mountainous opposition to such primitive legislation as maximum hours for women, minimum wages for women, etcetera. I suppose I was very early interested in those matters, partly through reading and reflection, and partly acting on the temperament that believed in elementary decencies, if I may put it that way.

When I came to the Harvard Law School in 1903 I was drawn by legal interest to some of these problems. One was the constitutionality of legislation copying what had long been in practice in England: measures, through legislation, against sub-standards in industry, and more particularly sweat-shop wages for women. Men, even before the New Deal, could exert the power that unionization gave. They had an economic club of more or less capacity for impact upon employers. But in the case of women it was very,

very difficult; indeed it is still difficult, I suppose, to unionize them because they are a much more mobile group than men. They drift in and out, go into the home, or most women marry, and so you haven't the stability that constant employment in a given industry enables men's unions to have. So there was devised this scheme of a board fixing what should be the minimum wage for women in particularly low-wage industries. There was an act passed in several states through force of imitation, or the force of common interest among the various states, for such a minimum wage for women. And in the Bull Moose days, to characterize the period when social reformers like U'ren, the elder La Follette, and a little later Norris, by common interest promoted legislation in various states, Oregon became a very so-called progressive state. It introduced the initiative and referendum, that horrendous radical measure! There also was passed in Oregon a minimum-wage law for women.

Legislation curtailing what was called "freedom of contract," or "liberty of contract" was very widely declared unconstitutional not only by the Supreme Court of the United States, but by state courts even more in cases before they reached the Supreme Court. Laws limiting the hours of work had been widely declared unconstitutional until Mrs. Kelley finally thought there ought to be some way by which the nature of that problem could be presented with power and persuasiveness to the Supreme Court. She tried one so-called eminent lawyer after another to argue the ten-hour law for women, the famous Muller case—*Muller v. Oregon* 208 US 412—and despairingly she found that no eminent lawyer would care to argue such a case. There was no money in it. From their point of view it was a dubious social policy. Legislation fifty years ago was deemed to be a kind of an interloper in the harmonious symmetry of the common law declared from time to time by pure reason, as represented by more or less inadequate and incompetent and unimaginative judges on the various state courts—at least incompetent with reference to understanding the nature of these problems.

I know Mrs. Kelley went to the great Joseph H. Choate, probably the most brilliant advocate at the bar, shortly after he returned from his ambassadorship at the Court of St. James's. She got an introduction to Mr. Choate who was a magnificent specimen—handsome, with a beautiful voice, charm of expression, a perfect illustration of a very charming gentleman blind to the significant events about him. She told Mr. Choate what this case was about, that this was a law limiting the hours of women in industry to no more than ten hours a day. Choate said that he wasn't going to argue in support of such a law—you know, "Why shouldn't a healthy Irish laundry woman work ten hours a day?"

That was Choate's conception of what was called the nature of our industrial society. Finally Mrs. Kelley went to Mr. C. C. Burlingham, that wise man in New York. He said, "The only first-class lawyer I know whom you might interest and who might be persuaded by you to undertake this is a fellow named Brandeis up in Boston—Louis D. Brandeis. Why don't you go to see him?"

She went up to see this Brandeis in Boston and put the case to him. He said that he would undertake to argue that case provided she would take the necessary steps to have prepared the essential stuff of a brief appropriate for such a case. This had very little to do with what are called questions of law. If the facts are compelling and there are some very good reasons why there should be such a law, then it isn't violative of due process. It doesn't take property without due process of law.

Brandeis had a sister-in-law, Miss Josephine Goldmark, a distinguished product of Bryn Mawr, a charming, handsome, sensitive creature with a literary and scientific bent of mind, a disciplined mind. I do not know whether Brandeis suggested her, or whether Mrs. Kelley knew about her otherwise. Anyhow, Josephine Goldmark became the research worker for Mrs. Kelley in the National Consumers' League, beginning with *Muller v. Oregon.* That case was argued on January 15, 1908 and decided on February 24, 1908, and it's the seminal case in the adjudication in the Supreme Court on matters of constitutional law because it broke away from an abstract way of arguing these questions in that Brandeis put to the Court not the abstraction—whether this was an abstract infringement of "liberty of contract" because that phrase isn't in the Constitution at all. It was sort of spun out of the phrase "life, liberty and property should not be taken without due process of law." "Liberty of contract" was thought to be one of the attributes of man, but it was forgotten that it was merely one of them which sometimes may be used not for the public weal, but for the public woe. It has limitations and counter-considerations, but it was treated as a dogma. Anything that interfered with "liberty of contract" had something the matter with it.

The brief submitted on the law was I forget what, five pages, six pages, and on the facts was whatever it was, 150 pages. Nobody disputed the general propositions of law and the question was the application of these to the myriad, complicated facts of life, the fact that most countries of the world had such limitations, the psychological consequences or tendencies of overwork, the nature of fatigue, the toxin that fatigue creates, etcetera, etcetera, etcetera. Well, Brandeis set the pace. This was a pioneer effort. This kind of brief has ever since then been called "a Brandeis brief." From questions involving hours, after arguing cases in various state courts, he went on to the minimum-wage law of Oregon. He was engaged in that preparation when he was named to the Supreme Court, eventually confirmed and took his seat in June, 1916. Accordingly, he could not argue the case.

Mrs. Kelley turned to me to take over which I did. There were three cases: *Stettler v. O'Hara* 69 Ore 519, 139 Pac 743 (1914), *Simpson v. O'Hara* 70 Ore 261, 141 Pac 158 (1914), and the other one was an hours case, *Bunting v. Oregon* 71 Ore 259. I worked with Miss Josephine Goldmark and argued the Bunting case, and in *Bunting v. Oregon* 243 US 426 the Court, following the *Muller* case, applied the Muller doctrine, or rather applied the Muller attitude to a limitation of hours of work for men. With women you could talk about maternity, motherhood, the next generation, and so on. Well, you couldn't talk about maternity in the case of men workers. Nevertheless, the Court by a majority of two, five-to-three—Brandeis didn't sit because he had been counsel in the case—held that in any mill, factory, manufacturing establishment, etcetera, men should not work more than ten hours a day, or at the least not without paying for overtime. The question was whether this was a wages' law, or a health law, and the Court sustained it. That's *Bunting v. Oregon,* the hours-of-labor-for-men case. That now is so accepted and such commonplace—it's one of those things that time has absorbed, and you go on from there.

Stettler v. O'Hara and *Simpson v. O'Hara* were both argued twice. They were first argued on December 16 and 17, 1914. The Court evidently was divided so they were restored to the docket for reargument on June 12, 1916, and the cases were re-argued on January 18 and 19, 1917 and were decided on April 9, 1917.

It required a good deal of contrivance on the part of Mrs. Kelley to get the state of Oregon to invite us to be of counsel because the litigation was in the hands of the attorney general of the state. The controlling counsel who was called the attorney of record was the attorney general. He's the fellow who would represent the state on the records of the Court, the responsible person on whom papers were to be served in the first place, and it required getting friends in the state to persuade the attorney general either to share the argument or to turn the argument over to Brandeis in the Muller case and later on to Professor Frankfurter in the Bunting and O'Hara cases. That was done. One day, looking as was my custom at one of the back pages of the *New York Times* for what had happened the day before in the Supreme Court—the Journal is printed in small type, as you may have noted—I noticed that the O'Hara cases were submitted on briefs by both sides. The attorney general without telling me about it, or consulting me, or informing me, or asking me, had agreed with counsel on the other side just to submit on briefs. When I read that I nearly passed out because the brief that he would submit would be just flimsy stuff. This was precisely the kind of a case in which you need, if anything can help, the impact of argument, of personality upon the Court to goad them into an awareness of what is involved.

When I saw that the attorney general of Oregon had submitted these cases I was in the doldrums and began to think what could I do about it. What could I do about it? I thought and thought. I thought of the two men I knew on the Court. Mr. Justice Holmes. Well, I didn't want to bother the old gentleman. I couldn't talk to Brandeis. He had been of counsel. I worried much about it. I assumed that the attorney general of the state wasn't unaffected by the fact that the counsel on the other side was a fellow named Fulton, a former United States Senator of considerable influence. I don't mean to suggest corruption or anything, but just good fellowship—you know, with Fulton saying, "Jim"—or whatever the name of the attorney general was—"Washington's a hell of a way off. Why don't we just leave it on the briefs?"

He had nothing to lose by that. The attorney general would say, "We'll save the fare to go to Washington."

I thought and thought and finally I concocted a night letter, a telegram, to the then Chief Justice whom I had known pleasantly, Chief Justice White who was a very gracious, charming Southern gentleman. He was a massive man, a charming gentleman and a devout Catholic. I forget whether I sent this telegram to the Supreme Court or to his house. He had a house on New Hampshire Avenue, a few blocks away from where the present Catholic Cathedral is, and I sent him the following telegram: MY DEAR MR. CHIEF JUSTICE I SHALL CALL AT YOUR HOUSE AT ABOUT NINE O'CLOCK SATURDAY MORNING NEXT IN THE HOPE THAT YOU'LL BE FREE TO SEE ME ON A MATTER OF CONSIDERABLE PUBLIC IMPORTANCE. RESPECTFULLY YOURS FELIX FRANKFURTER.

Knowing the kind of gentleman he was, I thought that that would at least arouse his curiosity—you know, why should I want to see him on "a matter of considerable public importance"? Well, I took the Federal from Boston and turned up at the house. His man at the door said, "Yes, the Chief Justice is waiting for you." He greeted me cordially. He hadn't seen me since I went up to Harvard. He asked me how I liked it and then said, "How many Southern students have you got, students from the South?"

Luckily I knew at that time with great particularity the composition of our student body and so I told him. He was perfectly delighted to hear that so large a percentage of our students came from the South. Then he spent a considerable time descanting on the ruin that the Civil War had wrought in the South. They were just about then emerging from all its devastation and the consequences of such a war. He tried to tell me what it would mean in terms of the North if all the railroad tracks were ripped up and so on, and so on. I'd give anything if that had been taken down. It was so eloquent. White came from Louisiana, and he was essentially an orator, eloquent and illuminating. As Holmes says somewhere, "His big frame was meant for politics rather than the law."

He had been a United States Senator and was an impressive fellow. Then he sort of moved his chair a little forward and said, "Well, son, tell me what brings you here. Tell me what's on your mind."

Then one of these special interventions, divine interventions if one must conceive it, put just the right thought into my head. It is more or less a habit of mine to let things stew around inside of me and trust to the moment to express it, having the right words come. It's my good fortune to believe in the moment instead of preparing rigidly. I prepare thoughts but not words. As he said, "My son, what brings you here?" the happy thought struck me to say, "Mr. Chief Justice, I am not at all sure that I have a right to be here. I am not at all clear that I should put to you the matter that I'm about to put to you, but I come to you as though in the confessional."

Well, that was a master stroke. I felt at once as though the whole church was enfolding me. He came nearer, more intimately, he said, "Tell me. Just speak freely."

Well, then I told him. There were these two cases on the calendar of the Court. I was to argue them. I was the counsel, but not the attorney of record. The attorney general of Oregon had exercised his prerogative of submitting them, by agreement with counsel on the other side, on briefs. As a student of the Court I was convinced these were precisely the kind of cases in which the Court should have the benefit of oral argument. I thought it very bad for the Court to be confronted with merely the briefs which were perhaps inadequate without the benefit of the give-and-take of argument and questions from the Court to bring out the difficulties of the cases.

"Well," he said, and there were briefs and records strewn all around his big living room, "now suppose—mind you, just supposin'—the Court were to hand down an order next Monday saying that in numbers so-and-so, whatever they are, the motion for leave to submit without oral argument is denied, and the case is set down for oral argument. Now, supposin'—now you see I'm just one of nine, just one of nine—but supposin' the Court were to do that, would that meet the situation?"

After the necessary moment of deliberation, deep thought led me to say very promptly, "I think that would absolutely deal with the situation just as it should be dealt with. I think that would take care of the situation entirely."

"Now, I'm supposin'. I'm just supposin'. I'm just one of nine, but supposin' the Court were to take that position would that meet the situation?"

"I think, Mr. Chief Justice, that would take care of the situation quite adequately."

I made my getaway as soon as I could in warm cordiality. He took me to the door and let me out. I climbed a telephone pole. On Monday that order came down. He was going to conference within an hour or so after I left him. I always regard that as my single most successful professional achievement. That's what is called *ex parte* practice.

You argued this case in the old courtroom where one was virtually surrounded by the Court. Do you have any impressions of the argument?

Certainly. It was a small room, you know. Mr. Justice McReynolds was a strange creature. He is a good illustration of my deep conviction that on the whole as good a dividing line as any between men is those who love and those who hate, with varying degrees. McReynolds was a hater. He had a very good head. He was also primitive. He had barbaric streaks in him. He was rude beyond words to that gentle, saintlike Cardozo. He had primitive anti-Semitism. A tough-skinned fellow like me could deal with him because I could be just as rude as he could be. Rude isn't the exact word. He was not rude really, but indifferent which is worse than being rude. He was handsome, able, and honest. I sort of respected him. My wife can't understand that in me. I said, "I despise McReynolds, but respect him." I respected that he refused to sign a letter when Brandeis left the Court. There was the usual letter of farewell to a colleague, and he wouldn't sign it. I respected that, because he did not remotely feel what the letter expressed, and I despise hypocrites even more than barbarians.

When I was arguing the ten-hour case, I dared to do something in that argument. With two Catholics on the bench I said to them that I thought that on the whole the problem of the due process clause is not where you're going to draw the line, but how you're going to draw the line. There isn't any line about it. That falsifies the problem. That makes it appear as though it's a problem in mensuration. But what is involved is attitudes of mind. What were the standards? That was the basis for judgment. I thought that as good a guiding line as any, as good a guiding consideration, a guiding mood, that should propel the Court in its reflections was that which was expressed by Cromwell. With two Catholics on the bench I dared to say, "The real attitude is one expressed by Cromwell in that famous scene when he said, 'Brethren, I shall think well on all ye have said. Ye may be right and I may be wrong. But by the bowels of Christ I suffer ye to conceive it possible that ye may be wrong.' If it's that kind of a situation, then you have no right to invalidate that which those who have the responsibility of legislation have done, because theirs is the final responsibility. The duty of this Court is merely to say that men charged with that responsibility have exceeded the speed limit."

During the course of the argument McReynolds said to me, "Ten hours! Ten hours! Ten! Why not four?" He was then the youngest member of the Court and was sitting to my extreme right. "If ten, why not four?" in his snarling, sneering way. I paused, synthetically, self-consciously, dramatically, just said nothing. Then I moved down towards him and said, "Your honor, if by chance I may make such a hypothesis, if your physician should find that you're eating too much meat, it isn't necessary for him to urge you to become a vegetarian."

Holmes said, "Good for you!" very embarrassingly right from the bench. He loathed these arguments that if you go this far you must go further. "Good for you!" Loud. Embarrassingly.

The first time I argued the *Stettler* case McReynolds plainly enough was bent on not enabling me to argue because he just interrupted every minute throughout. I just couldn't make a consecutive argument. That was his tactic. When I argued it the second time he did something else. The poor fellow thought that he would distress me more, and, in fact, he did quite the contrary. He leaned way back in his chair, way back, and at arm's length held up and read a brief. What was he reading all the time I was talking? The brief of the other side. A childish form of sadism. I was perfectly delighted because I thought, "Gee, this is swell. You're out. I don't have to pay any attention to you. I can't possibly reach your mind anyhow so you might as well leave the chair empty, and that suits me down to the ground."

The Court decided the *Bunting* case, the hours-of-work case, for the state, but in the *Stettler* case, the minimum-wage case, the court divided 4-4. Judgment was affirmed by an equally divided court. When you've got an equally divided court the lower-court judgment stands, and Oregon had sustained this statute.

The question was reopened when *Adkins v. Children's Hospital* came on, and in an opinion by Justice Sutherland expression was given to the most doctrinaire view about "liberty of contract" in that the Court said that presumptively every encroachment on "liberty of contract" is unconstitutional, and you had to show some very good reason why there should be a curtailment of the freedom of contract—freedom of contract between a great, big laundry and Bridget McGinty. They were at arm's length, etcetera, and therefore you shouldn't interfere with their contracting equality. That opinion struck the death knell not only of this legislation, but of kindred social legislation because it laid down as a constitutional principle that any kind of change by statute has to justify itself, not the other way around. Before you invalidate a legislative judgment you must show that there's no basis in reason for it.

In those days when almost everything was declared unconstitutional that a majority of judges on the Court didn't like, the defenders, the apologists for such decisions, said, "Well, numerically only relatively few cases knocked out legislation." That was a very shallow view of the matter and a very wrong calculus by which to determine the consequences and the meaning, because, in the first place, all legislation is not equally important. People constantly talk about cases as though they were fungible goods, like peas in a pod—every green pea is like every other green pea. Even that isn't wholly true, certainly not if you can taste the difference in green peas done by a French cook and green peas when you get them out of a can. But it's true enough. Not so of laws.

But secondly, a decision like the Adkins decision doesn't merely bring about the result in that case, but has very serious inhibiting influences on kindred legislation. Not only did the various state legislatures not pass minimum-wage laws, and the minimum-wage laws on the books of some eleven or twelve states were put to sleep, but any other social legislation would encounter the argument that it's unconstitutional within the principle, or the meaning, or implication of the Adkins case. And so, while there might be only one bomb, as it were, the radiation from it did lethal damage to kindred legislation. It prevented legislation from being introduced, and it made still-born legislation which was by way of being introduced.

Well, Sutherland was very nice, a thorough gentleman, but limited because his basic ideas came from a predominantly different social and economic society than was asserting itself in the twenties and certainly the thirties.

12. *"The House of Truth"*

When I first came down to Washington I lived in an apartment house for bachelors, but shortly thereafter I moved into what became known as the House of Truth. The house was at 1727 Nineteenth Street and was owned by Robert G. Valentine who was at that time Commissioner of Indian Affairs. He was a gifted, imaginative, poetical thinker. Indeed, he wrote a lot of poetry. I came to know him because he was a classmate of Winfred T. Denison, one of Mr. Stimson's assistants who was a colleague of mine in the United States Attorney's Office in New York, who had come down to Washington to be an Assistant Attorney General. He had been some years ahead of me at the Harvard Law School. Anyway, Valentine asked us to join him in his house when his wife and his child moved north. The child, a daughter, had an illness which made the climate of Washington insalubrious for her.

I cannot tell the origin of my association and friendship with Lord Eustace Percy who was the seventh son of the seventh Duke of Northumberland, one of the great magnates of the United Kingdom. Percy himself was much more of a dreamer and a mystic than the son of a great landowner. He was the seventh son and none of the money filtered down to him, but he was a most gifted person. He was at that time one of the chief assistants of the then British Ambassador, Lord Bryce. There soon joined us

Loring C. Christie who was a little after my time at the Harvard Law School. He had got into the government through Denison whose assistant he became in the Department of Justice. Christie's career, I suppose, is unique in the history of the United States because he was for a period Acting Solicitor General, though a Canadian citizen, and afterwards was Canadian minister in this country. Between those two periods and during the World War he was the legal adviser of the Canadian Prime Minister, Sir Robert Borden. At Harvard he was president of the *Harvard Law Review* which to us lawyers is a distinction.

That was the original group that lived in the House of Truth—Valentine, Winfred Denison, Eustace Percy, Loring Christie, and myself. The house continued as bachelors' quarters, and we lived an easy and gay life. The house was in charge of a colored housekeeper, but parties ran continuously. Life was then of course much cheaper. Even though our salaries were much less than the prevailing salaries, you could get more for the dollar, much more. It soon became a center of liveliness. How or why I can't recapture, but almost everybody who was interesting in Washington sooner or later passed through that house. The magnet of the house was exciting talk, and it was exciting because talk was free and provocative, intellectually provocative. We were all young, as it were, in our late twenties or early thirties, and all desirable, available young men for dinner parties where we met young women. So a gay time was had.

The house continued as successive members departed and others came in. It was still going when I went back to Washington during the First World War. Eustace Percy came back. He left in late 1913 or early 1914 and became the right-hand man of Sir Edward Grey in the Foreign Office. In 1917, after we entered the war and Prime Minister Lloyd George dispatched the so-called Balfour Mission to this country headed by A. J. Balfour, afterwards Lord Balfour, Eustace Percy was a natural to be sent with him in view of his great familiarity with Americans and his understanding of our situation. So he came to live again at the House of Truth. Successively other people joined us. With the exception of Eustace Percy they were all government officials. Louis G. Bissell joined us. He went to the Interstate Commerce Commission as one of the legal lads. Then there was Edward H. Hart who became the son-in-law of Frank Noyes, the president of the Associated Press and the owner and editor of the Washington *Star*. In short, it was an interesting group of people who managed to create an atmosphere of intellectual liveliness, governed by curiosity and free and high-spirited talk and lovely ladies.

I forget who dubbed it the House of Truth but the name stuck: namely, something about the fact that it was a place where truth was sought, and everybody knew it couldn't be found, but even trying to seek the truth conscientiously is a rare occupation in this world. The dominant quality of the house was that you were unafraid to talk about anything. That makes for an interesting society. When there are repressions, or inhibitions, or fears, or timidities, or prudences you can't have a good society. It started out in the most innocent fashion, but it became a fashionable thing. We didn't make it fashionable, but people would say, "Gee, we had a wonderful time last night at the House of Truth," and so, since most people are copycats, other people would regard it as a wonderful thing to be asked to the House of Truth. And, indeed, a good time was had.

You must remember that this was in 1911, 1912, 1913. One had high hopes that by the steady progress of free inquiry you could remake the world. It never dawned on anybody that a war like the great World War in 1914 was still possible—you know, "We've gotten beyond that. This is the age of reason." This was the period during which the Bull Moose Movement got underway. You remade society to deal with the great problems that the industrial revolution, the industrialization of society in the western world, had thrown up. Here was Teddy the Terrible himself, "We fought at Armageddon, and we battled for the Lord." The air was rife with intellectual enterprise and eagerness, intellectual eagerness. After a preoccupation with mere money-making, money-getting, money-keeping, opening up and despoiling the continent, the time had come for social movements, social reforms, putting an end to glaring and garish ruthlessness and inequalities. That's the kind of thing we talked about. We talked about all sorts of things. Of course, there was a lot of talk about personalities. Washington is a beehive of personalities. A presidential election is always around the corner. Four years pass soon. Election comes around quickly. A party is in, or a party goes out.

What quality did Mr. Denison contribute?

He was a very artistic advocate, a very good lawyer. Mr. Stimson had brought him into public service from a leading law firm, the firm that later was headed by John W. Davis. Denison argued numerous cases. He was an Assistant Attorney General, and in those days the Assistant Attorney General argued the cases. They don't do that now. They're so busy with administration. He made it a point of pride never to use the hour that he had for the argument of a case. He would do it sometimes in twenty minutes, or half an hour. He was extremely well read, a very cultivated person. A lovable character. A generous person—very charming, very successful socially. He once said of himself about going out often, perhaps too often, with a childlike innocence, "It's that damn charm of mine!"

I pause because he evokes very sad reflections. He had a very bad strain, a family strain, a bad inheritance, and he was a manic-depressive. He had fierce elations and fierce depressions. He ended his life by throwing himself in front of a subway engine in New York, but Denison was a very considerable personality. It was through him that I became intimately acquainted with John Lord O'Brian, one of the really, absolutely, first-class characters in Washington, and Joseph Cotton who was one of the most trenchant, original of minds. I'm very glad you caught me up on this. Denison was not a character you mention just in passing. He was a salient personality.

The traditions of the house persisted, and a lot of people were transient occupants of it. Stanley King who became president of Amherst College, and before that was secretary to Secretary Baker during the World War, was there. Walter Lippmann was there for a time. There were a lot of overnight visitors, but of the permanent people I think I haven't left out anybody that I should have included.

Excitement implies a sudden and a very unusual occasion, but this excitement had continuity about it. This was quite an aliveness.

It was exciting all the time and therefore perhaps one should say aliveness and vitality were the characteristics of the household.

We'd have all sorts of people come there for dinner. We'd take turns at the various duties. On one occasion it was my job to shake cocktails. In those days we shook cocktails in a shaker. During one month that was my task. In connection with that I remember how heart-searing . . . or how a compliment can have, what shall I say, unwarming ambiguity. I was shaking my cocktails one night when our guest was Mr. Justice Lurton, a Southern gentleman. I had shortly before that argued one or two cases before the Court. As I was pouring out the cocktails to Mr. Justice Lurton, he said to me, "I hope you mix drinks as well as you argue cases."

Well, to be praised by a justice of the Supreme Court for a kid like me was something! Wasn't I proud and happy! He sipped his cocktail and said, "You mix drinks even better than you argue cases."

If ever one compliment displaced the pleasure of another that was it, but that's typical of the kind of gaiety that reigned in that household. It had charm. We had all sorts of what are called important people, or prominent people, for dinner. They were delighted to come. There was hardly a public man who presumably had ideas, who wasn't there for political reasons, who didn't come —not that we didn't also have politicos there. All sorts of people met at that table. Any friend of any one of us who came to Washington came there. It was a free, open house kind of a place.

A great friend, a constant visitor, was the then Washington correspondent for the London *Times,* Arthur Willert. He became Sir Arthur Willert. His wife, Flo, was a Scotch woman, and she was much troubled at the looseness, the easygoing way, in which the house was run. She told me how I ought to exercise more control over our staff—a cook and a maid. She thought the house was being run much too expensively. I told her that the most we could save each was fifty dollars a month, and the fun we were getting in not running the house that way was worth the fifty dollars a month. I suppose if we had had wives and children to support it would have made a difference, but since we didn't,

I didn't see why we shouldn't have the luxury of carefreeness, very un-Scotch and un-New England doctrine.

Unimportant things were treated as unimportant which is always important in making possible an agreeable and a gay society. In the first place, it was a smallish house with I don't know how many bedrooms upstairs. Downstairs, on the entrance floor, there was a little entrance room that led to a small hall into a rather big room—that is, as small houses go, a big room. That room was dining room and sitting room combined. Near the entrance, in one corner of this biggish room, was the dining-room table. As you moved down the room there was a great big couch on which sometimes seven or eight people could sit, or crouch, or stretch themselves. Beyond there was a desk where one wrote a letter, if one wrote. That's where the guests found their way. Then when lunch or dinner was called we moved forward to the dining room, and sat around the dining-room table near the door. When you were through with the dinner, you moved, without the break of going from one room to another, with ladies going to one place and men going to another place. There was a continuity of whatever talk, whatever hares were chased at the table continued to be chased after you left the table.

Those are physical aspects, but physical aspects have some relation to the conversational success of a dinner party. You can't have too many at dinner to have "a party." If you have a big dinner, the party's bound to break up into little tete-a-tetes. I never could see why you should have twenty people for dinner, except for ceremonial purposes, if you wanted to have ten separate couples. General conversation, so-called, wasn't artificially contrived here. It just naturally blossomed and burgeoned because there were some good talkers at the table and some good listeners. And as often as not—in fact, it was contrived more often than not—there were some good lookers at the table. All sorts of people.

Then the informality extended itself to a spirit and atmosphere of liveliness, so that one remembered instances like a French General pushing his plate forward and drawing on our white tablecloth the line of battle during the World War. At another instance which I remember vividly, Mr. Justice and Mrs. Holmes were present, with Gutzon Borglum, the sculptor, who was expressing, formulating, his plan of doing the three great figures in American history on the Black Mountains. He excogitated that at our table. Justice Holmes became greatly interested and said, "Well, what do you mean?"

Gutzon said, "I'll tell you what I mean," and he pushed not only his plates, but his next-door neighbor's plates into the center of the table, and then began to draw on our white tablecloth, and soon the three heads were visible. He drew the first sketch at our dining-room table to the great excitement of Mr. Justice Holmes and everybody else.

Those were typical episodes. I don't mean to say we had Gutzon Borglum with his—what shall I say—exciting imagination at our board every day. But it was Gutzon Borglum, and it was General Requin who commanded the final army that made its stand during the Second World War on the French front against the Germans. Or it was John Galsworthy. There they were. I don't know how they got there. They got there by the natural attraction of a pleasant place. And various people had various friends, and various friends brought various friends, and, first and last, all sorts of people passed through that house.

Then another thing. My wife thinks it's very important in an understanding of the house and the spirit of it, its gaiety, the relaxed behavior of guests, etcetera, that it was run by men and there was no sticky woman around making it sticky—nobody who worried about things being just right. That's what I meant a little while ago when I said that unimportant things were unimportant. If something happened to the soup, so what? If the ice cream that was to have turned up for dessert didn't turn up, then so what. Nobody worried about it. One ate sufficiently well, nothing to write home about, but plenty of good food in an easy, devil-may-care sort of way.

All those things add up to great informality, great ease, free flow of talk. There were no sacred cows. You weren't afraid to express differences of opinions, which is the very life of good conversation. Men felt that what they said wasn't going to appear in a column, let alone appear in a distorted and untruthful fashion. Visitors weren't treated as though they were being cross-examined by some fierce prosecutor who treated them as though they had committed either arson or forged some checks which seems to be the current way of dealing with public men who meet the press—you know, they're there to stand up and surrender. Our inquiries were not directed toward getting copy, but we assumed that we were all friendly, truth-seeking and truth-speaking people. The friction of minds through the friction of tongues would make everybody have a good time, and in the second place it would make us see things a little bit more comprehensively than each man saw it alone in his own mind. The free spirit of man, in short, asserted itself and gave enjoyment in its exercise.

Of course, there was no radio throughout this business. There was no TV. People didn't fix their dinners so they wouldn't miss this or that show. They didn't stop conversation because they wanted to hear some morally larded voice over the TV expound something beyond the understanding of the speaker and to the disgust of the hearers. You had to roll your own in those days. You had to provide your own delight, and conversation is still the common basis for human intercourse.

Well, that formulates what was the spirit of the house. We didn't think about the spirit. It would have been obnoxious, it would have been poisonous if anybody had a consciousness that, "This is really an exciting place. We must keep it exciting by being exciting." In other words, it didn't suffer from pretension. It didn't suffer from pomposity. It didn't suffer from self-consciousness. There was just a spontaneous play of the human spirit and a diverse variety of people who enjoyed the process.

13. *Industrial Relations and World War I*

When the First World War finally broke out I wonder what alterations confronting this challenge were made in the atmosphere of Boston and in you.

The assassination of the Archduke Ferdinand at Sarajevo took place on June 28, 1914, and the war broke out officially on August 4. Because of my Austrian nativity this stirred more interest and had more meaning for me than for most anybody else that I saw in Cambridge or Boston, but we as a country, as a people, were out of it. I do not recall the date of Wilson's "neutral in thought and deed." That was a silly remark to make, that you should be neutral, that you should stop thinking, that you shouldn't analyze what were the contending forces and which ones you wanted to prevail. If that's what "neutral in thought" meant, it was silly. If it didn't mean that, it was a deception. That doesn't mean that I don't think Wilson was right in not hurling us into the war, or having us take governmental sides. On the whole he was right not to bring this country, to the extent that the President does which is a very great extent, into war until this country was educated. Up to that time broadly speaking there were only two inured convictions respecting international affairs on the part of the mass of American people who control what is called public opinion;

that we have nothing to do with Europe, and that Europe has nothing to do with us. Those were the dominant influences that made what is called public opinion.

Not only was Wilson right, but I haven't seen in his writings an awareness of the European problem. In fact, for a historian he was singularly ignorant and indifferent to the whole history of Europe. He might talk about it, but as he said himself, he thought that when he was elected in 1913 he would be concerned with domestic problems which he summarized by talking about the "New Freedom." He said to a friend of his that it was just luck that almost from the day he entered the White House, March 4, 1913, he began to have to deal with international problems. I am not critical of him for not at once jumping on a charger and saying, "The Western cause is our cause," or "The Allied Powers represent Western Civilization." "Terrible Ted" didn't say that either. Theodore Roosevelt also was for us keeping out of the war at the beginning. Only later did he discover that he was earlier for saving Belgium and France. But, as is true of so much of Wilson, he had to phrase and formulate what was a judgment on balance in terms of eternal truth and eternal morality. Every judgment on policy had to have a sanctified moral ring to it, and so "neutral in thought and deed" was—well, I've indicated what I think of it.

When the war broke out for us in 1917, I had a wire from Secretary Newton D. Baker asking me to come down for the weekend, if I could. I packed my suitcase, and the weekend didn't terminate until the fall of 1919. There was good reason why Baker should ask me to come down. I had been in the War Department from the summer of 1911 until the summer of 1914. Baker and I knew each other rather well. He was president of the National Consumers' League, and I was its counsel. I succeeded Brandeis as the lawyer to argue cases in which the Consumers' League was interested, and in that connection I had seen not a little of Baker, and we were sympathetic in outlook.

When I went up to Harvard in 1914 I became a major in the reserve corps in the Judge Advocate General's office. A great friend of mine, Judge Advocate General Enoch H. Crowder, asked me if I would become a member. I never came out of the reserves, as it were, never went into uniform, never had an active military commission. I strongly resisted it when Baker said, "What about it? You'll be assigned to my office."

The reason I didn't want to go into uniform was because I knew enough about the doings in the War Department to know that every pipsqueak Colonel would feel that he was more important than a Major, and from the point of view of being effective as Baker's assistant it was very important for me to remain a civilian. As a civilian I could get into the presence of a General without saluting, clicking my heels, and having the Colonel outside say, "You wait. He's got a Colonel in there." The matters for which Baker wanted me to stay were problems of minority groups, conscientious objectors, and industrial relations, because the War Department at once expanded its activities in ways that demanded a large labor force under its control. I thought this miscellaneous business which was before the War Department was entirely filled with civilian implications and considerations and would not be helped if I got into a uniform, and besides, I'd feel silly to wear a uniform.

Some labor troubles were stirring, particularly in the west to which the war came as quite an outside, unfamiliar thing. The Balkans and Germany, France and England were awfully far away from the workers in the copper mines of the southwest, or the forests of the northwest, or the oil fields of southern California. The war to them was most unreal. The copper mines of Arizona, I think, produced one third of the copper supply of the United States, and they were shut tight as a drum for three or four months. We were pretty close to the limit of our reserves. In those days one also heard emphasized that "this is a local affair" and "the state ought to settle it," but the copper situation became so acute that the suggestion was that the President send a commission of inquiry, investigation and mediation. Finally the President did name such a commission called the President's Mediation Commission, and at the head of it he put the then Secretary of Labor who was the first Secretary of Labor, William B. Wilson.

Billy Wilson was a most endearing creature. He had been the treasurer of the United Mine Workers. He was a coal digger from Pennsylvania who went into the breakers when he was a kid—I don't know what, eight. He had hardly any schooling, and I remember his telling me that when he went into the breakers with his dinner pail he was such a little shaver that as he walked along the tracks the dinner pail would click against the rails. Well, he was a dear, dear person, a good rich Scot with an accent, a clear head, wise, self-educated. He read books, but most of his education was thinking about things. He was totally devoid of any embitterment because of the hardships of his early days. He was a great believer in the goodness of this country, in its possibilities of goodness. He was extremely tolerant, extremely kind, strong minded, slow, ponderous, absolutely impossible as an administrator, no sense of the process of action between decision and execution. Papers would pile up. He was slow, and he'd take his time, but this to me was an enduring lesson in the fact that there are much more important things than administration.

Then there were people representing the employers and people representing the unions on the commission. The two union people were a fellow named Ernest P. March who was chairman of the State Federation of Labor in the State of Washington, and John H. Walker, another Scot, a wonderful creature, association with whom began a friendship that I cared a lot about. We corresponded for years afterward, indeed, until a few years ago when he died. Walker was then president of the Illinois Mine Workers, a witty, shrewd fellow, and I can illustrate that quality by a remark he made to me.

The last strike we dealt with at the President's direction was the Twin City Street Railway strike. The then president of the Street Railway was a man named Budd, and to him the union was the enemy. He made you realize what foolish ideas can become almost religious convictions. He thought a union took away men's liberty. The question for him was dealing with each individual man, and our problem was getting the union leaders and this fellow into the same room. We'd go to the sixth floor where he was and then go to the ninth floor where the union people were, and we'd try to get them into the same room. He held fast to the one deep conviction that under no circumstances must he recognize the union. We made various verbal assurances, not only that we would say, "This is not to be deemed recognition," but even saying, "Well, you'll be in one corner, and they'll be in another corner."

"No. To be in the same room would be recognition!"

Finally Jack Walker said, "This fellow reminds me of a girl I knew in Scotland who wouldn't dance with a man because she thought that if a man put his arms around her she'd have a baby."

The employer people were Jackson L. Spangler, a coal operator from Pennsylvania, and Verner Z. Reed, a silver-mine owner and a sheep rancher, a rich man from Colorado, an art connoisseur who had with him a spiritual adviser. He was in the process of joining the Roman Church, and he had with him a wonderful priest, Father O'Dwyer, with whom I became very great friends. In the course of the nights while we walked up and down these copper mines, particularly in Bisbee, Arizona, I suppose I talked to him more intimately about the mysteries and the issues that existence poses than with any other person in the world, except my own wife. Father O'Dwyer was a man of cultivation, a great delight.

Before we started on our trip to Arizona to get the copper mines open Sam Lewisohn got in touch with me. He was once an editor of the *Columbia Law Review,* a lawyer who then went over and conducted the Lewisohn vast personal interests. He was more or less a contemporary of mine, and I had come to know him through Eugene Meyer's younger brother Walter who was at the Harvard Law School with me. I had known Lewisohn in New York, and he thought I was—you know, "a doctrinaire professor." When the appointment of this commission was publicized, it was announced that I was to be secretary and counsel of the commission. I assume that the President talked with Secretary Baker about it. We went over to the White House and got our instructions from the President in about two words. When this announcement got into the papers I got a message from Sam saying that he would like to see me.

We saw each other, and he said, "We own, as you may or may not know by now, the great Inspiration Mine down near Phoenix, Arizona. It's a wonderful mine, has a complement of five thousand miners. When the strike began in a mine owned by the Phelps Dodge interests I communicated with our mine manager, and he said, 'Don't worry. Our men are loyal. They may strike at Phelps Dodge, but they won't touch us.' "

When they struck the Phelps Dodge properties, five thousand men, every mother's son in the Lewisohn mine, walked out. The mine manager broke down, had a mental collapse when his men struck. Sam said, and this shows his wisdom, "There must be something so wrong when that can happen. When a man who thought he knew his men can be one hundred percent wrong, probably something drastic needs to be done."

These aren't his words, but in substance he said, "You may be too idealistic, or may not understand the process of business, but I know that you will dig out the facts, that you have a sense of fairness, and that I trust you and believe in you. I can tell you now that whatever recommendations you give on the spot after your investigation we will support."

That was quite an ace in the hole to have, so off I went. When we got there we found that the origin of the strike was not money, or hours, or wages, but status. The single wisest thing I ever heard Roscoe Pound say was that "People want to be who's and not what's." Well, the strike originated in a most unbelievably incredible way. The Phelps Dodge people built a modern hospital, a very good hospital, and they assessed the men a dollar a month for hospital care. Needless to say, the dollar wasn't one to ten what the cost was for the maintenance of this hospital. That was all right. But the men said that if they contributed, they ought to have a representative on the Board of Trustees of the hospital. The company resisted this plea for minority representation like utter damn fools, and that led to the strike. As is true of family quarrels, you begin about a minor matter, and then it gets hot and then you say, "Your grandfather, after all, was in the China Trade, and he cheated the government, and your second cousin cheated at cards."

After you get started, the charges roll up, and grievances nobody thought anything about were a mile long. In the same way this labor controversy diverted into totally different aspects and problems. Not only did it go off into complaints about working conditions, but it took on a patriotic hue so far as the employers were concerned. By way of giving significance to their resistance to either minor complaints of the union, or more or less legitimate demands, they took the aggressive by saying that "the real issue is Americanism!"—that very definite and concrete subject matter of controversy! They grabbed the patriotic issue.

There soon developed strong insistence by the representatives of the copper people that what was involved was really "pro-Germanism." The basis for that, so far as it had any basis at all, was that a good many of the miners were southeast Europeans, some Hungarians, some Italians, but mostly from what we now call Yugoslavia. The managers took the position that they wanted nothing but American miners. Of course, you couldn't get American miners just by whistling for them, and indeed, one of the grievances of labor was that management had brought in "cheap Mexican labor." I got interested in this claim that these were pro-Germans who were making all the mischief—the "devil theory," the agitator theory. All labor controversies are so often attributed to the outsider coming in and disturbing the idyllic, paradise-like conditions. The agitator is the snake in the Garden of Eden. My assistant was Max Lowenthal, one of the keenest blades of the legal profession, and we went into this business to find out what the composition of this labor force was. They were natives of the so-called suppressed nationalities. In the course of the examination of witnesses and in the discussion of this aspect of the controversy, it gave me great pleasure to point out to the employers that those whom they called "un-American" were representatives from that part of the world where American boys were stationed with a view to vindicating their claims to freedom. Of course one has to see these things in context and the period during which the commission was at work was one in which the notion of unions as an indispensable factor in the industrial context was not yet accepted by the body of American businessmen, not accepted not merely eagerly, willingly and in a statesmanlike manner, but not even accepted as a necessary evil. The chief difficulty in this contest between management and labor was in the claim of the workers for status within a limited scope, that they weren't just "hands," but men.

It's worth noting that in the endeavor to bring the mines to some recognition of the claims of the men for status I had the good fortune to have the help of the then rector of the leading, most influential Protestant church in Phoenix, Arizona—William Scarlett. Later he became the Bishop of Missouri and is now retired. He was a young man, more or less a contemporary of mine, a product of Harvard College, and a very charming, persuasive man who preached to the unconverted because his church had among its parishioners many of the so-called substantial citizens, that meaning the well-to-do people of the Copper World. He was fearless, and he was persuasive, and he wasn't a rabble rouser. He had love in his heart so that the kind of sermons that he'd preach against their presuppositions and predispositions were so engagingly, persuasively and gently worded that they went down in a way that rougher talk wouldn't have gone down.

Thanks to the readiness of the Guggenheim people to yield, the upshot was what I venture to call a "rational and sensible settlement," the essence of which was the establishment of a process within the industry for the settlement of grievances, in many cases petty ones, before they should accumulate and gain a momentum and dimensions which eventually would lead to strong feeling on both sides and both sides digging in. This took a little while. For months we were living in what people thought at the time was a luxurious way on a siding in a private railroad car, and I can imagine few things more disagreeable than that.

The mine interests that held out longest against dealing with men, otherwise than giving them orders, were Scottish interests, a case of absentee ownership. The superintendent with whom I dined on more than one occasion was a Scot, still a citizen of the United Kingdom, and he was intransigent. He held out, and he held out. I began to inquire into who were his bosses. He was only the resident manager. When I found out that his bosses were British interests, I then bethought myself, "How can we get them to have as much sense in dealing with the management of their American properties as certainly, to a large measure, Britishers had at home?" Unions had progressed much more in Great Britain than they had in this country. It so happened that an old friend of mine, Lord Eustace Percy, was then an assistant of the British Foreign Secretary, Sir Edward Grey. I sent him a cable, telling him of the circumstances and the conditions and the British interests involved and responsible for the failure to have the necessary copper supply on which their lives depended and expressing the hope that he might exert the influence of reason. What went on on the other side I do not know, of course, but I do know the result. This obdurate Scot got orders from home. Eventually we got an agreement for all the four copper districts. It would have been difficult to say that there was a settlement in some and not in others, and that's the way it ended. The strike in the Arizona copper fields was settled.

These strikes in the west popped up successively. Naturally enough labor was in the condition to make demands. This period, as it were, was labor's market, the necessity of the war, and soon there was trouble in the oil fields of southern California and finally that was settled. Then we were told, "The lines are down." The Pacific Telephone and Telegraph Company had labor difficulty. The men went out on strike, and there was the breakdown of the telephone system on the Pacific Coast. Washington, Oregon, and California were involved. The issue there was a very different one. The men had been unionized. The Pacific Telephone and Telegraph Company had had years of collective bargaining relations with its men, but now the girl operators wanted to be unionized and to be recognized as the bargaining unit. While for a time the men were very indifferent to the status of women, eventually there came into power a more liberal contingent of the men's union, and the men took up the women's cause and struck when the company firmly refused to recognize or deal with the women as the Women's Telephone Operators Union. I believe that the company was quite sincere, quite serious in urging the differences between women employees and men employees, that women are a more or less impermanent employing force because of the marriage of the young women. Anyhow, the men struck, and there was a pretty how-dee-do.

We got to San Francisco and took up headquarters at the Palace Hotel. We invited the striking men to meet me, and they said, "No," that we should go up to Seattle where their headquarters were. Secretary Wilson was a very illish man; in fact, was in bed a good part of the time and practically turned over the responsibility of the commission's conduct of affairs to me. I was very strong in my urging on the commission that we should dig in in San Francisco and not go up to Seattle. I wasn't much of a baseball fan, but I knew enough about baseball to know that it's easier to play on your home grounds than it is to play on the other fellow's grounds, and therefore I said, "That is a concession that we must not make. We must not yield to their demand on the government to do what they want us to do."

We were the arbitral tribunal, as it were, and therefore "the demand of neither party should guide us in our determination of what is right," and we said that we would wait for them to come down. This was a battle of endurance, and I don't know how many days we spent—maybe as much as a week—just waiting for them to come down. In the meantime I was not wholly idle.

The Postmaster General was Albert S. Burleson, a Texas politician, a Congressman, who came into Wilson's cabinet, I think, on the urging of Democratic leaders that he ought to have somebody in his cabinet in whom the leaders of the House and the Senate had confidence and who could be a connecting link between the White House and the Hill. That was Burleson. Well, his outlook on economic problems was a little outmoded from my point of view. He understood the movements of the world, of industry and economics on a social and human side about as little as the copper operators in Arizona, and I had very little doubt that if the lines were taken over by the government, even during the duration of war, the situation for the workers would not only not be better but probably worse than they would be if they remained in the hands of the Pacific Telephone and Telegraph Company. I knew that was the short-sighted purpose of the leaders of the telephone unions, not to reach an agreement, but to have the government take over the lines.

I soon discovered that they were rather doctrinaire and thought that all ills would be cured and life would be very pleasant if only the government took over the lines. It was clear in my mind that Burleson had already shown bad tendencies. He was full of the notion that in war you didn't allow any freedom of speech, that everybody who lived in 1917 instead of 1817 was probably un-American. I was determined, if possible, to avoid the government taking over the lines, not only because of Burleson, but Washington was already taking in more than it could absorb. The general administrative conditions were not all that could be desired; indeed, far short of it, and should the government take over the telephone lines in addition to all else I didn't know who the people would be who were competent to have due regard for the needs of war, the needs of the government and also due regard to the human interests that were involved.

That was one aspect of the human situation. Another thing I thought about while waiting for the men to yield to our insistence that they should come to San Francisco for our negotiations, was how to bring reason to bear, if possible, on the executives of the Pacific Telephone and Telegraph Company. That awful situation in which people make important and immutable principles out of empirical and relative social and economic factors! I made inquiries and ascertained who the lawyers were for the Pacific Telephone and Telegraph Company and was happy to discover that the senior lawyer was a highly esteemed alumnus of the Harvard Law School. I was on leave from the Harvard Law School, so I got hold of him, had several talks, and found him to be a sensible fellow. We had friends in common and that gave a quick starting point of friendly talk. Moreover, we were products of the same kind of teaching at the Harvard Law School, the same rational way of trying to analyze a problem and see what the factors are in order to reach an accommodation. The upshot was that he saw that this wasn't a fight for immortal principles. This was a situation calling for the give-and-take of sensible people.

I had a good many friends in San Francisco and more particularly former students of mine, and San Francisco is to me a most exhilarating, in some ways the most exhilarating city in the United States. The air is so sparkling and so stimulating that somehow or other I could go with less sleep in San Francisco than anywhere else, and while waiting for these telephone union men to come down, I dined out every night with this friend or that. The days passed and one night I returned to the Palace Hotel past midnight to find the rather impatient, somewhat excitable assistant of mine, Max Lowenthal, waiting for me. He said, "The men have come down from the north, and the Secretary"—who was ill—"said that you should go into conference with them just as soon as you can."

I said, "Where are they?"

"They're in room . . ."—whatever it was, 657.

"Let's go straight up."

He said, with a fierce look in his eye, "You aren't going up like that!"

"Like what? I'm as sober as a Bishop."

"Oh, no. I know that, but you're not going up like that!"

I had some trouble getting him to explain, "Come on, don't waste any more time in your round about way."

"Well, you're not going up there in your dinner coat. You're dressed in your dinner coat."

"Max, you just told me that the Secretary wants me to go into conference with the men—you said they were waiting—just as soon as I got in. You know that while I do almost everything else in the world quickly, I'm a very slow dresser. If I have to go upstairs now and change my clothes, a lot of time will be wasted. Come on, let's go up."

"Really you can't—they're pretty wild men."

"Look, Max, if it were a question of reaching an agreement, or making an impression on these men tonight, why I couldn't do that no matter how I was dressed. I couldn't do that if I were dressed in dungarees, or calico, or whatever may be the most democratic of attire. I've got three strikes on me to start with so that I can't possibly make a dent on them tonight."

"What do you mean—three strikes?"

"I'm a professor. I'm a lawyer. I'm a Jew. Perhaps there's four strikes—three's plenty—for I'm alien born. What more do you want? What do you suppose these fellows think of me? This is just a beginning. We'll just meet each other and say, 'hello,' and each will look down the nose at the other fellow. Come on."

"Very well," he said, "I just want you to know that I protest."

So we went up to their room, and there they were. The leader was a tall, sparse, redheaded fellow who looked at me as though I were some really great enemy of mankind. We shook hands limply, and we talked—just how-do-you-do, when did you get in, all the sparring preliminaries, "How about a drink?" Well, they said that they would have a drink, and so we had a highball and chitchatted, talked about nothing in particular except when we should meet and what room. By this time it was about two o'clock.

We ended the preliminaries for that night, said goodnight and went to our room, Max and I.

We agreed that we'd meet at ten o'clock. We were on a lower floor, and we turned in for the night. About half-past nine we entered the elevator to go down and have breakfast, and in the elevator were these men who were coming from an upper story. I said, "Good morning, gentlemen."

This redheaded, firebrand of a leader sort of half-heartedly, sort of unconcessively, said, "Morning." Then he looked at me and said, "Professor, you looked handsomer in them clothes last night than you do this morning."

I said, "I couldn't very well wear it for breakfast, could I?" and the chatting went on, but I said to myself, "I guess this is going to come out all right if a fellow can make that remark."

By way of a digression, I utilized that story fifteen years later as I've utilized it since when occasion made it appropriate. On Christmas Eve in 1932 my wife and I were spending the night at the Executive Mansion in Albany with President-elect and Mrs. Roosevelt, and Governor Roosevelt talked about a lot of things and, quite unrelated to anything else that had preceded, he said, "I'd like to ask you a question. I'd like to find out what you think about a problem of mine. I ought to get away for two or three weeks before I go down to Washington and the only way that I can get for me the most refreshing vacation is on the water. In the first place it's invigorating and in the second place it's the only way I can get away from being hounded every minute by the press. The only feasible way for me to do that is to go off as I have been doing from time to time, on Vincent Astor's *Nourmahal.* The press can follow in another boat, but at least they're not on my neck all the time. I'm physically separated from them. What do you think about my going on Astor's yacht, the times being what they are?"

The "times being what they are" was when men who'd had wealth were selling apples on Wall Street, and farm mortgages were being burned in Iowa. "What do you say to my going off that way?"

I said, "Let me tell you a story," and I told him this story about my having a dinner coat and how the union negotiators took it in their stride. "It seemed perfectly natural that I should have a dinner coat. That's what you'd expect a Harvard professor to wear. I made no bones about it. That was the normal way of life for me, and in the course of negotiations that wasn't held against me. That was just part of being an eastern law professor. The moral of that for me is that if you want to make your dent on the American nation during the next few weeks, of course, you shouldn't do it. Any little thing that may hit some people's prejudices, or interests, would close the account, but if you have any kind of faith in the good sense and decency of people, no matter what anybody will say about this, it will be sufficiently well known that that's what you've been doing every year. You're not being indifferent to the hardships of people. You're not being callous because you do this, and I think that it's a short-sighted deference to short-lived prejudices to think that you now can't do what you've been doing every year since you've been governor."

"Well," said FDR, "would it interest you to know that you're the only person whom I've consulted who's given me that advice. The politicians are all up in arms. They say, 'I mustn't do that. I can't do that.' "

"I'm a professor, as you know, but I venture to say that it isn't the first time the politicians have given you bum advice."

To go back to San Francisco, we had these negotiations back and forth and back and forth, and finally thanks to the telephone company's lawyer, we worked out a plan for settlement. As is so often true of a strike and the consequences of trying to settle it, the fly in the ointment is that the conditions have changed. It isn't a case of a shutdown and negotiations open the plant to which all the striking employees return. The company tried to keep open the service through the hiring of new help, and so in various places they had what the workers called "scabs." You were in the position of having people help you out. Were you going to fire them? The problem of new loyalties came into play, a very difficult problem. Eventually by expansion the company could absorb not only the old, but keep the new, but the fact of the matter was that they couldn't, on the day of the settlement, take back all the older employees. The problem was to persuade the strikers in the various towns to yield, to go back to work, though they all wouldn't be taken back *en masse.* I agreed to visit the various towns and try to make the strikers agree to a settlement that involved a little hardship, at least for a short time, to a few of the girls in the larger interest.

I did go to several towns, but I remember in Aberdeen, Washington, having one of the great and also one of the most enjoyable failures of my life. I made my speech to these girls, tried to win them to seeing the margin of good over the disappointing disadvantage, and when I sat down the chairman recognized a young woman. She marched to the front. She was a striking beauty. She was a perfectly lovely-looking creature—tall, handsome, black-haired, charming voice, not at all a ranter, a very sober speaker. She was made to order for my discomfiture. She sought to appeal to reason as much as I did, but—gee, I didn't have a chance against her! Even if she hadn't had a good point, she would have been persuasive. She was a striking tribute to the persuasiveness of personality apart from reason, but I'll never forget the warm, appealing voice in which she said, "Do you think it's fair, professor, to have any of us return to work, if all of us can't return to work?"

She sat down amid cheers. Well, I wanted to say, "How can you fight beauty?"—but anyhow, that strike was settled in the broad way I've indicated without having the government take over the lines. As a matter of fact the government of the United States did take over the lines later for other reasons unrelated to this, and all that I had feared about Mr. Albert S. Burleson turned out to be true.

Well, from there we went north. There was a strike in the spruce industry, and spruce was then indispensable material in the manufacture of planes. We settled that strike. Before I leave the west coast I ought to say that it was there that I realized that the most radical labor leaders of the country were not East Europeans like Hillman, Dubinsky—not at all. The most radical labor leaders were Scotch-Irish. They were the old stock of Americans and not the newcomers. That realization did make me reflect on the unreliability of so much of the shallow thinking in regard to the industrial conflict. You know, people think, "Of course, people who come from Scotland are our kind of people. They must be solid and sound! But these East Europeans! Why do they talk a language that we can't understand? Their language is different so their thoughts must be different and their purposes must be different."

Then we got a telegram to go to Chicago. A strike had broken out in the stockyards. Some of our allies, particularly Belgium, depended not a little on our meat shipments, and the strike in the stockyards was something. Talk about smoke-filled rooms! That certainly was a smoke-filled room. We negotiated back and forth, and it wasn't 'til way into Christmas night that we reached a settlement with the stockyards. The leader of the men, then an A.F. of L. enterprise, was none other than William Z. Foster. That was my first glimpse of Foster. That negotiation was a long drawn out affair largely because the chief adviser of the stockyard people was nothing like the telephone company's lawyer in San Francisco. The stockyard lawyer was the head of one of the biggest, if not the biggest, law firms in Chicago, Levy Mayer. I had an amusing experience with him, and it partly confirmed my conviction of the responsibility of lawyers for many of the delayed reforms in the economic and industrial life of this nation. A great lawyer, Mr. James Byrne, said to me in 1936, "I haven't any doubts that most of President Roosevelt's legislation is inadequate, faulty, but who am I to complain. He's had to formulate measures in three or four years that should have been introduced piecemeal in this country over the last fifty years."

In my opinion, lawyers are much responsible for that in the sense that they didn't have the attitude Brandeis had when he was at the bar, that a lawyer is a counselor, an adviser. He isn't just a hired man to do the bidding of his clients, but he must exert the independence of his mind and understanding upon the conduct of his client's business. Instead of being advisers, lawyers were collaborators in their client's short-sightedness in large measure. I should say from the time that things got booming after the Civil War—from the Eighties on certainly—the legal profession's contribution was that of collaborators in the rampant, short-sighted, *laissez-faire* outlook. The lawyers did their clients' bidding instead of illuminating their minds to understanding something about the forces with which they were dealing.

All this by way of a side remark except that a particular episode with Mr. Levy Mayer of Chicago illustrated just what I've tried to convey in a striking way. I went up to his office. We had negotiation talks. He was a much older man than I was, and he was taking me out to lunch to his swell club. On the way out a young man greeted me whom I recognized and said, "Hello." Later I said to Mr. Mayer, "I'm ashamed of myself. He was a student of mine only two years ago, maybe only a year ago. Would you mind telling me his name in case I see him again?"

He was a little embarrassed for a moment. He said, "You know, we have so big a staff that I cannot remember the names of all the people who are on it."

I said, "Mr. Mayer, you can't remember the names of all the lawyers in your office, and yet you tell me day after day of the happy personal relations Armour and Swift have with their eighty thousand employees."

That illustrated deeply his imperceptiveness, his unimaginativeness, and of course it illustrated the wrong relations he had with his own staff. I suppose he had fifty or sixty lawyers, but the sense of his comment was, "You mustn't ask me to remember some petty lawyer on my staff."

14. *The Mooney Case and Other Experiences*

I've left untouched the dramatically most enduring episode of the task that was committed to the President's Mediation Commission. When we were at the White House President Wilson gave us a cold, short, high-minded few minutes' talk, which was the staple of his meetings with people on the whole. He got off some generality about the importance of industrial peace, all beautifully couched, perfect sentences. It could all be taken down. Even his speech was copper-plated like his handwriting. He said, "There's one more matter I want this commission to look into and, as the lawyer of the commission, Mr. Frankfurter, this will be particularly your concern. That is the Mooney case which is greatly disturbing to our Allies, Russia and Italy. When you get to California, I hope you will look into that and report to me about it."

That's all he said. That was the first I ever heard of the Mooney case. I had been abroad on some jobs for the War Department, and more particularly for Colonel House, and it was during the time I was abroad that the agitation about the Mooney case got going in our press. I'd never heard it. To such an extent was I ignorant that when he said "our Allies, Russia and Italy," I foolishly jumped to the assumption, "This fellow is either Russian or an Italian," and I asked somebody, "How do you spell Mooney—M-U-N-I?"

I quickly informed myself what the Mooney case was and was

about, and being a great believer in prepared improvisation I said to myself, "I want this case studied before we get to San Francisco." I didn't know how long we would be in Arizona. I assumed that we'd be there a few weeks. I didn't expect us to be there for three months, almost. I was wholly innocent of all the terrific feelings that the Mooney case had released and the state of mind of the community so that in my innocence I wired out to a classmate of mine, a very good lawyer, "Would you be good enough to get together for me all the documents, the record, and prepare a statement for me of the situation?"

I got back a telegram expressing great regret that professional duties would preclude his doing so. I thought, "He's a busy lawyer," and I then wired to another fellow and then another fellow. Morris Cohen taught me to be on the alert between what he called "the good reason people give and the real reason for their actions," and I soon realized that this was a ticklish subject. I finally persuaded George Arnold, a son-in-law of Congressman William Kent, an independent fellow, a lawyer, and he undertook to do this. I put it out of my mind until we got to California.

The chief witness against Mooney was a cattle rancher from Oregon, a man named Oxnam. He was the absolutely damning witness who saw the car, took the number plates and identified Mooney as the fellow who planted the bomb, or left a suitcase where the bomb exploded which killed many people at a Preparedness Parade in San Francisco on July 22, 1916. After conviction and after the case was in Supreme Court of California for review —Mooney was sentenced to death—it was established that Oxman was a perjurer, a liar, that his testimony was absolutely untrustworthy. Then there arose a succession of legal moves. They tried to get a new trial on the ground that the chief witness was found to be a perjurer, and the Trial Court said, "The case is now in the Supreme Court, and I am without power to grant a new trial."

It went before the California Supreme Court. It wasn't decided when we got there, but I soon was made aware by members of the bar, probably Arnold, who was the strong member of the court. He turned out to be Judge Henshaw who afterwards retired from the court lest he be exposed for having taken a great big, fat bribe in the Fair Will case. He was a wonderful kind of an Italian Renaissance character. He took me to luncheon in a swell club. My, how well he lived! I was invited to sit with the whole Supreme Court while they were discussing the matter. They said that they couldn't do anything about it because they could only go on the record before the trial judge. The trial judge couldn't do anything about it because the case had left him. The Supreme Court had no power to deal with disclosures that would undermine the reliability of a verdict.

The basis of presidential concern over this matter was what President Wilson had told us, the evil propaganda use that was being made of this alleged miscarriage of justice in seeking to weaken the war effort both in Russia and in Italy. As was written in the commission's report to the President:

> "War is fought with moral as well as material resources. We are in this war to vindicate the moral claims of unstained processes of law, however slow, at times, such processes may be. These claims must be tempered by the fire of our own devotion to them at home.
>
> "Your commission, therefore, respectfully recommends in case the Supreme Court of California should find it necessary (confined as it is by jurisdictional limitations) to sustain the conviction of Mooney on the record of the trial, that the President use his good offices to invoke action by the governor of California and the cooperation of its prosecuting officers to the end that a new trial may be had for Mooney whereby guilt or innocence may be put to the test of unquestionable justice. This result can easily be accomplished by postponing the execution of the sentence of Mooney to await the outcome of a new trial, based upon prosecution under one of the untried indictments against him."

This report was written by me. The President acted on his commission's recommendation and made that suggestion to Governor William D. Stephens of California. Governor Stephens didn't act on it, but just commuted the sentence to life which made no sense, none at all. Anyhow, Mooney was saved from the electric chair.

Later on there was an attack on the report by the then Solicitor

General James M. Beck, and the *New Republic* asked me to answer it. Beck's attack was in the form of a letter sent to the *New Republic.* Robert M. Lovett, the distinguished professor of the University of Chicago, was then an editor of the *New Republic,* and he came to Cambridge and told me the charges that Beck was making about the basis of the report and how I went about investigating, that I saw only Mooney and his adherents. These were charges by the second law officer of the nation—pretty serious stuff. Until Beck made this public charge, with one exception on July 26, 1918, when I sent a telegram to Governor Stephens and gave it out to the press associations to counteract an affidavit filed with the Governor by District Attorney Charles M. Fickert who prosecuted the case against Mooney, I never uttered a peep about the case. All sorts of people asked me questions. I was asked to comment on this and comment on that, "What do you have to say about this?" and so on, but I said, "No, this is a quasi-judicial report to the President of the United States. I follow the standards and attitudes of courts."

But when Beck came out with this allegedly detailed charge, I said, "This is grand. This really gives me a chance," and I said to the *New Republic,* "I will answer it, provided I can have all the space I deem necessary to lay bare the distortions, the mutilations in utter violation of the canons of decency and accuracy which Beck's communication conveyed. Evidently"—in the vernacular of the day—"somebody sold him a bill of goods. He couldn't have gone through the record. Somebody, some either purblind, or consciously intellectually corrupt person wrote this stuff for him, and I can just destroy it."

That issue of the *New Republic* aroused nation-wide interest because editorials from all over the United States came to me, a long editorial by Frank Cobb, the then editor of the New York *World,* which I remember particularly, but this was an opportunity of setting the record straight when the other fellow had absolutely disrespected truth and accuracy. Croly told me that their circulation rose, and he had a kind of a strangely naïve and generous letter from Beck asking, "Would he care to tell him how many letters the *New Republic* had and what the effect had been on their circulation," and he thought it was the better part of valor to shut up and not do any more about it. Beck really destroyed himself.

One of the charges that he made against me was that I only saw partisans of Mooney, not personal Mooney partisans, but those who were ready to believe in any cause to the "left." One of the chief informers I had about Mooney was a kind of a saintly man, Archbishop Hanna, a most influential, most important Catholic prelate. I found out about his great influence in the community on the coast and in the whole Catholic world outside. The Archbishop was good enough to ask me to dine with him at his palace. His sister was there that night, but there were monsignors, bishops, priests—a very considerable party, a dinner, just a pleasant social occasion. The Archbishop was a man of distinguished mien, charm, but we talked about nothing in particular. Then the men retired to his study where we had liqueur, and the men smoked. I should think that there could not have been less than twenty men at that dinner and in that room, but in ways still puzzling to me that I shouldn't have noticed, I suddenly became aware that I found myself alone in the room with the Archbishop. One by one they stealthily—that isn't the word, but almost secretly—at all events unobservedly, left the room. Of course this was by prior direction, and I found myself tete-a-tete with the Archbishop. It was a fascinating performance.

Then we began to talk. What stood out and what remains as vivid as when he made the communication that night was that he was a very forward-looking person. He was deeply committed to that famous encyclical of Leo XIII, Rerum Novarum. He had a strong sense of the lowly and the disadvantaged. He was a leader in housing reform, generally for the alleviation of the poor and the lifting of standards. He knew a great deal about industrial conditions which were very bad in California because employers were determined not to allow unionism to gain headway. He was very illuminating about the whole business. What I remember vividly was his saying, "I know Tom Mooney very well. He and his family were parishioners of mine. I know him very well. Tom is a bad man, but he didn't do this."

I saw Mooney in San Quentin, and I had to wait what seemed to me an unconscionable time before he was produced into the warden's office where I was waiting. He didn't know I was coming. The warden told me, "You might be interested to know the reason for the delay. When we told Mooney that you wanted to have a talk with him, he said that he would have to shave before he saw you."

That's a nice touch, isn't it.

I remember much later saying to a great friend of mine, a leading lawyer in California, "Why don't a dozen of you leading lawyers memorialize the governor"—one governor after another would do nothing about Mooney—"to the effect that he should commute a fellow whose conviction rests so demonstrably on perjured testimony. Show the strength of the state instead of the weakness, that the State of California and its judicial system can endure truth as easily as it can't endure the suppression of truth?"

My friend who is a whimsical Scot said, "I'll do it on one condition: if you will allow me to say to the governor that he can parole Mooney in your custody"—an amusing suggestion.

The Mooney case went on and on and on. It came on to the Supreme Court. It was there several times, as a matter of fact, and led to one of the most important decisions of the Court, *Mooney v. Holohan* 294 US 103 (1935) in which the Court held that if a conviction is had in a state through the knowing use by the prosecution of perjured testimony there's a deprivation of life and liberty by the state without due process of law. If there were such allegations, there was to be an opportunity for the state to give corrective process. The case went back to California on the issue: not whether Oxnam's testimony was perjured, but whether the district attorney knew when he put Oxnam on the stand that the testimony was perjured. The Supreme Court of California appointed a master, and there were long hearings. They found that the prosecutor was not privy to the perjury. Then it came back to this Court, and *certiorari* was denied.

It wasn't until January 7, 1939 that Governor Olsen pardoned Mooney. By that time everybody knew that he'd been convicted on perjured testimony.

When we concluded the other day, I indicated that we had overlooked the Bisbee Deportation, that round-up and removal of strikers from Bisbee, Arizona by a force under the county sheriff and their enforced shipment by train to New Mexico where they were left to shift for themselves without adequate supplies of food and water. You said that the story of the deportations was well documented, but you wanted me to remind you to tell the effect of the investigation on your assistant, Mr. Lowenthal. As for the TR letter, based as I suppose it was on his belief that "rough rider" Jack Greenway could do no wrong, you wanted me to remind you to tell a remark made to you when you returned to Washington.

I said the Bisbee affair is well documented; that is, the circumstances attending and details of the rounding up of I forget how many, eleven, twelve hundred people by a sort of local vigilante under the leadership of Jack Greenway who was in TR's "rough rider" regiment in Cuba, and dumping these people in New Mexico without food and water where they were rescued from the consequences of starvation and inordinate thirst by American troops, the intervention of the army—all that's set forth in a special *Report on the Bisbee Deportations.*

We spent I don't know how much time in taking depositions, or rather listening to the testimony of those who were left behind, the families of the people who were deported, the way in which they were rounded up, the way in which people came to their houses and picked the people they wanted to, and also the testimony, I think though I'm not dead sure about this, of some of the victims who made their way back.

Max Lowenthal is a very sensitive fellow, particularly responsive to cruelty and hardship, and a very fine disciplined brain. He really took to bed after this experience, after being with me and hearing and eliciting the story of the facts about this rather brutal affair. I remember saying to myself, "Doubtless this is the first time Max has encountered man's cruelty to man in the concrete, not merely by way of books, or in imaginative projection," but he saw, as it were, that kind of brutality and injustice in the raw. The realization that there may be injustice in this world, not on a small scale but on a large scale, had hit him with the result that he literally became ill. He was in bed I don't know how many days, the reaction of a nervous, sensitive temperament to the brute forces of life. This made a great impression on me because that was a just verdict on, a just response to, the cruelty, ruthlessness and callousness that were involved in what was done in Bisbee in routing out these people and just dumping them in the desert where they might have starved and come to their end through hunger and thirst.

This was done by otherwise perfectly nice, decent people. Jack Greenway was a very nice man. I knew his widow when I came down here in 1939. She was the representative-at-large for Arizona, I think, in the House of Representatives. She was a very nice woman, indeed, and incidentally a very handsome woman. He was doubtless a good man in all relations of life in which passion didn't supplant his fairness and reason, and it left a deep impression on me as to what cruelty means and how cruel conduct affects those who are immediately the victims of it.

There also ensued correspondence between Colonel Theodore Roosevelt and myself on the basis of his failure to read or adequately attend to the facts set forth in the *Report on the Bisbee Deportations*. He took as gospel the patriotic pretensions, or rather the explanation, that this was done as a matter of what we would now call "security."

The other item I wanted you to remind me of was an encounter I had with Mrs. Nicholas Longworth—Alice Roosevelt, the eldest child of TR by his first wife who was a Boston Lee. I had known Mrs. Longworth in my earlier Washington days, and we had been in a manner of speaking friends. I hadn't seen her for some time when this episode happened. It was some time in the course of the summer of 1918 after I got back from the western trip. I'd been shipped abroad on some job in March, particularly for Colonel House, or through Colonel House for the President. I didn't see Mrs. Longworth in the intervening period until one day in August—I think it was August 18. I had been to dinner at the house of a friend of mine. He was a bachelor, he entertained, and he was a friend of the Longworths.

Nick Longworth was at that time in the House. I don't think that he had as yet become Speaker, but he was a prominent Republican member of the House of Representatives and prominent, of course, as the husband of Alice, "Princess Alice." I remember that Porter asked me to this party, and I said that I could come, provided I could leave rather early. I had some work to do. I left his apartment near ten o'clock, and in the hall as I was going out, Mr. and Mrs. Longworth were coming in. They'd said that they would come in after dinner. I greeted the Longworths and received to me a rather surprising, perfectly courteous, but chilling greeting from Mrs. Longworth. She said in an icy voice, "I'm sorry you're going."

I said, "I'm sorry I'm going, too."

I forget the word she used, but she indicated that if I stayed, we might have a row, and whatever it was she said, it gave me an opening and I said to her, "Oh, I see. You share your father's biases and prejudices in the correspondence that we had, he and I."

She said with a kind of haughtiness—she is at all times a distinguished person, she's distinguished even when she's haughty, in her haughtiness—"And why shouldn't I?"

To which I replied, "I'll tell you why you shouldn't. Your father's a great man and is entitled to biases, but you're not."

"Oh," she said, "You can't go now."

I said, "Certainly not," and I walked back in with her to Porter's place, and we began to go at each other hammer and tongs. I remember very vividly I was trying to expound to her what the I. W. W. movement was and what it wasn't, and how it came into being and how unsatisfactory, remediable social conditions, if unattended, give rise to radical movements far transcending the original impulse and that these people, those deported from Bisbee, represented that disregard of fairness and decency in the treatment of people in the mines and in the mills. This discussion went on back and forth until about half-past one—it must have been around that time because it was two o'clock when they took me home. Nick was substantially silent throughout the discussion between her and me, and finally she turned from me to him and said, "Nick, I've always told you that this was a good man."

From that time on the debate was between her and her husband and I was out of it. She and I have been warm friends ever since and are to this day. We've always batted the ball of controversy and are free spirited in our talk with each other, but that made a great impression on me; the impression was great in the sense of indicating that if you have time enough to probe these problems and the mind you're dealing with isn't really imprisoned, has any sense of pursuing reason and a desire to know, is open to consideration of relevant facts, unless you yourself are unreasonable you can get somewhere. In short, as my wife says, I'm a romantic believer in reason.

In the report of the President's Mediation Commission you wrote that "the eight-hour day is an established policy of the country." This "policy" brings on the Judge Gary confrontation which, in the light of what transpires later in the steel strike of 1919, is worth a word.

That's worth more than a word.

Our offices, the offices of the War Labor Policies Board of which I was chairman, were in a charming old house, one of the houses where there now is the United States Chamber of Commerce. It had been a private house. Then it became a school. There were living facilities there, and so I told my executive secretary, George Bell, that in a week I wanted him to say, "We're all ready to have you come to lunch."

He said, "That's impossible."

I replied, "That's why I want you to do it," and the staff did eat there. There was a nice garden outside.

My office was a relatively small room, and that played a part in this story. It seemed to me that since steel was the leader industry, it was the bottleneck to progress on the eight-hour day. They were still on a ten-hour day. I decided to get some sense, if I could, into Judge Gary who was then chairman of the executive committee of United States Steel. I sent him a polite letter and asked him to come down for a consultation. No attention, complete disregard. I waited a more than decent interval, and then I wrote him a note saying, "I'm enclosing a copy of a letter which has doubtless gone astray in the mail."

No attention. I then sent a copy of the copy registered and got a return receipt. No attention, absolute flouting of this communication which, after all, was sent by a responsible official of the government. I used to laugh a little bit at these individuals, including myself, saying, "the government this" and "the government that," and here the government meant a little fellow like me, but nevertheless for this purpose I was clothed with the power of the government certainly to ask Judge Gary to come down. There was a surprising number of steps, but finally I indicated to him by telegram that if I didn't hear from him I would have to make the matter public. Whereupon I had a phone call from somebody —I don't know who, but on behalf of Judge Gary—saying that the Judge would be very glad indeed to see me, would be pleased to have me come to the room, whatever it was, 375 of the old Waldorf.

I said, "That's very sweet of him, but my office is in 1607 H Street."

I let it go at that. Finally, in due course, I had a phone call saying that he'd arrived with his associates in Washington, was staying at some hotel in Washington where he had retained a suite and that he had a parlor where we could have lots of room. I said, "That's nice, but I can accommodate the Judge's party."

My room was a small room, but I said, "I've got lots of room."

"Well, there will be about thirty or forty people."

"We can make room for them."

We cleared out the furniture. I remember ordering all men aboard to get in lots of chairs. The room was full of chairs. I was obdurate, very quietly, but I knew that I was not going to yield a thing to him. I told my old law school roommate who was then living with me at the House of Truth about Judge Gary, "He's coming tomorrow. I have to encounter him."

"Have you prepared your remarks? Have you put down on paper what you're going to say to him?"

"Why Sam, I wouldn't dream of doing that. My head is prepared on the subject. I'll let the words come. I know the substance."

I wasn't going to bind myself by preparing a soliloquy the way some lawyers do who come before the Supreme Court. You ask them a question, and it doesn't fit in with what they've planned, and then the whole thing goes to pot. They keep on telling you what is unconvincing instead of dealing with your difficulty. I said, "I have to adjust myself to the course of the discussion. I know the central things I want to get into his head."

Judge Gary finally turned up. Here we had all these chairs ready. He needed a big room. He talked as though Madison Square Garden was required, and he turned up with the then president of the United States Steel Corporation, Mr. Farrell. We had long hours of talk. Out of my window I could see the White House across Jackson Park. Throughout the talk the president of the Steel Corporation said not one word. Judge Gary did all the talking. He was a man much older than I, and I had with me Max Lowenthal and I think George Bell, also a Harvard Law School man. We talked about why the eight-hour day was right and inevitable. I pointed out that that was the official working day for the workers of the United States by statute. I remember at one point saying to him very blandly and apparently with great seriousness—the argument was serious, but the implied compliment wasn't—"Judge Gary, if you were sitting in that white building across the park there, as you well might be, would you recommend to Congress that they repeal the eight-hour law?"

At my remark, "if you were sitting in that white building across the park, as you well might be," I was conscious that his opinion of my brain, wisdom, and good sense appreciably rose, that I should think of the desirability of ever having him President of the United States. We went on and on, and the talk got nowhere. He wouldn't budge, and I wouldn't budge. It was an amiable enough talk, he yielding nothing and I yielding nothing, but as he started to go he said, "Professor Frankfurter, you work more than eight hours every day."

"That happens to be so."

"I work more than eight hours every day. You and I work more than eight hours every day. Why shouldn't these men in the factories?"

"Ah," I said, "Judge Gary, but think what interesting jobs you and I have."

With that he walked out in a huff. But, of course, that makes all the difference in the world, what you're working on and for. Well, that was quite an experience, a striking illustration of arrogance, the sense that they are really more important than government, and, of course, the importance of standing your ground. People don't understand these things sometimes. Nothing is involved in formal dignity. If it had been a little fellow with whom I had to deal, and he said, "It's awfully difficult for me to come there. I only have three people working for me. Couldn't you help me out and next time you are in New York, come talk to me?" that would be a different story, but this fellow thought that when the great Judge Gary makes a request, you ought to grant it. Well, he had to be put in his place.

Here's an interesting episode. It was carried on under my direction at the War Labor Policies Board, and it sheds light on ghost writing, proving that there are ghosts and ghosts. As things moved on in 1918, greater and greater demands had been made on labor through persuasion rather than coercion. All the talk in the last war of having a labor mobilizer, a labor controller, by people who said, "Well, you control goods, material supply, you must also control labor . . ."

They assumed that things and people are to be equated, and that you are to control them through the same coercive measures. Of course nothing could be farther from the truth than that. In short, one has to use the controls of persuasion much more with human beings than the physical controls with which you move things, the production of things, or the curtailment of the production of things. It's one thing to say, "You can't grow or produce more stuff." It's another to say what men should or shouldn't do. But it became necessary to use, or exercise, some controls. I was charged with working out such a policy, and it seemed to me clear that it would have to be made persuasive to labor, and also a generalized appeal to the country with labor as part of it, and that required the power of persuasive statement.

I thought hard as to who would be intelligent enough to do that and also gifted enough to phrase it so that it would carry great weight by the manner of statement and not merely the matter. The upshot of my reflection was a telegram asking a friend of mine, Alice Duer Miller, to come down. She wrote that wonderful poem, "The White Cliffs of Dover." She was a Duer, a famous, old New York, patrician family. She was a professor of mathematics at Barnard when she gave that up and married Harry Miller who was a shallowly attractive, rather handsome fellow, a broker. She was one of the leaders of the suffrage movement, a woman of great charm and distinction in every way, distinction in mind and distinction in presence, and we were friends. I thought that Alice Miller had clarity of mind to understand these things and gift of pen to make her understanding contagious. I asked her to come down and told her what I wanted her to do. She said, "I don't know anything about it. I'm not a student of economics."

I said, "No, you're not a student of economics, but you have the means of understanding the economic problems; namely, a good, clear brain. I will give you the general outlines, sketch the general factors of the problem, give you some literature which you will master in no time. At least there's ample time. When you get all through you must write this out for the understanding of people who know as little about it as you do now. The final task, and this is in a way the main task, is to write an appeal to the public of the United States to be issued by the President of the United States, and to that end, here is a mass of speeches and messages of President Woodrow Wilson. You soak yourself in his style so that that which we will eventually send over to him as a suggestion for his statement will be so good that he will be glad not to disown it, but own it as his own."

That was a rather interesting enterprise, and she was a venturesome person. The upshot was that she did a superb job. My immediate boss was this benign temperament, William B. Wilson, the Secretary of Labor. I wrote him a letter saying, "This is what needs to be done," and suggesting the kind of a letter he should write to the President of which I enclosed a draft for his consideration, and in his letter I made him say, and he signed the letter just as a matter of course, that the enclosed was the "outline of the kind of statement I venture to suggest would be appropriate for the President to issue to the people of the United States, and this is sort of a scratch pad which may save you time in drafting your own."

I suppose Wilson was about as efficient, in the narrow business sense of that term, a President as we ever had. I mean he was punctual, he was prompt, he cleared his desk, I suppose, every day. Really, he was his own assembly line. And so in no time back came a letter to Secretary Wilson, that he'd gone over the document, he thought the proposed draft entirely satisfactory, congratulated him on how good it was, and then it was issued, published, front page articles.

The reason I tell this story is that there was an editorial in the *New York Times* speaking of the "inimitable Wilson touch" in this "irradiating document," etcetera, etcetera. In England the *Manchester Guardian* said, "How proud a nation to have a President who can write this kind of a public document," and all this time not one word had been written by Woodrow Wilson, and every word had been written by the undisclosed Alice Duer Miller. It gave me a great kick and her a great kick for the sheer fun of it.

Well, of course, even a literate, literary President can only write a small fraction of the material he signs as his own. Wilson was a literate, literary President, and I don't mean to suggest that Wilson didn't write his major speeches. He did. He wasn't ghosted, but things like this—you know, they had to be. If this document hadn't been well written, he wouldn't have put his name to it. He could have either turned it over to somebody else, or typed it out on his Blickensdorf on the basis of the information it contained, but she was so good! It was the "inimitable touch" of Woodrow Wilson because she'd soaked herself in his style and just mimicked it, and on the whole, I think it rather showed the qualification of the distinction of his style. I don't think anybody could do that with Lincoln's writing. I really don't, but Wilson's itself was an artifact. Wilson's style was so largely patterned on Bagehot and Burke, synthetic Burke, that, since Wilson was synthetic, you could have a synthetic Wilson—rather fun wasn't it.

15. *Morgenthau Mission*

I suppose there never was a more fantastic mission on which I found myself sent, or included, than the so-called Morgenthau Mission in June and July, 1917. Henry Morgenthau was the treasurer of the Democratic Party in the Wilson campaign of 1912, and was deemed to have been one of the important leaders among those who guided the Wilson campaign and therefore, I suppose, he was one of the men who needed some reward, and the reward came in the form of the Embassy to Turkey. He came home in 1916, to further President Wilson's re-election. He was now out of a job after having tasted the pleasures and the sense of importance of high political office. To have everybody bow and scrape and call him "Mr. Ambassador" was a kind of scent that thereafter he couldn't live without. The problem was to "do something for him"—as the phrase runs—when he was out of a post. He created a job for himself by bothering everybody with a great thought that he had of detaching Turkey from Germany and Austria. To detach an important member of the coalition against you in a war was very appealing. Everybody agreed with the aim and the effort to get Turkey out of the war. There was only the little problem left of how.

Turkey is a far land, and Morgenthau glibly talked about Enver Pasha and Mustapha Kemal and about people who seemed awfully remote even to those in power. Finally, after some diplomatic negotiations, President Wilson got the agreement of Prime Minister Lloyd George and the French prime minister, a long-whiskered old gentleman named Ribot who didn't amount to much, to join in the American-Anglo-French commission to look into and bring about, if possible, the detachment of Turkey from the Central Powers.

I was then an assistant to the Secretary of War, and Baker broached the subject of my going along with Ambassador Morgenthau. I'd never seen Ambassador Morgenthau. I didn't know anything about him except in the way in which we're all influenced by what we hear and read. I assumed he was a considerable personage, but something in me resisted Baker's suggestion. I didn't want to go with Mr. Morgenthau. I finally met him and was puzzled by him. He wasn't my kind of person, in the sense that his talk was inconsequential and not coherent, but loose and big and rhetorical. You couldn't get hold of anything, but I assumed that was just the froth of the man. I didn't realize that the froth was the man. Anyhow, I resisted. I didn't want to go. I had other things I wanted to do in connection with the war. Then one fine day I had a letter from the President saying, "I learn with much satisfaction that you've agreed to go with Ambassador Morgenthau."

I hadn't agreed. This was just a polite way of saying, "It is my wish that you should," and I acknowledged the letter in a few lines saying, "I thank you for the confidence you repose in me. Sincerely yours." So I found myself drafted to go along on the theory that they needed an international lawyer. I wasn't an international lawyer, knew damn little about international law. I knew where Turkey was on the map and not much more, but, as is the way of lawyers, I began to study up this case. I got hold of the literature on Turkey, but, more important, a few days before I sailed I got hold of a brother of a friend of mine, Dr. Carl Alsberg who had been the chief and, for all I know, was then the chief of the Bureau of Chemistry which was in charge of the Pure Food and Drug Act. He succeeded Dr. Harvey Wiley, a very controversial figure in the Roosevelt Administration, because, believe it or not, there was terrific hostility to the enactment and enforcement of the Pure Food and Drug Act, something which we now take so for granted that we assume that it began with the Republic. Carl Alsberg had a younger brother, Henry, a Harvard man, who was a literary, cultural fellow, and he had been sort of a press attache of Morgenthau in Constantinople. I knew he had just got back from somewhere. I asked him to brief me about the personalities in the Turkish Government, who was who, and what was what, and I spent a whole day being pumped full of knowledge. Then I put to him a whole lot of questions and asked him if he could put his answers on paper, and he stayed up all night to give me a briefing on the whole Turkish situation in his own hand in twenty or thirty pages.

By the time we got aboard the *Espagne* I knew more about Turkey than Morgenthau had acquired in all his years there because my knowledge was critical and analytical, and his was just general, hot-air impressions. I got hold of a library on Turkey and persuaded my friend Max Lowenthal to join me as my assistant. In the party there were Mrs. Morgenthau, Ambassador Morgenthau, a stenographer-secretary he had along, Max and I on a Spanish boat. Spain was a neutral, and this boat was ablaze with light to let the warring vessels know that this was a neutral vessel. As is the way of a disciplined lawyer, I told Ambassador Morgenthau that we ought to have regular sessions every forenoon to map out the whole strategy of this enterprise. The first session convinced me that he was just a lot of hot air. He just had no sense—"When I see Enver Pasha, I will tell him."

I said, "Well, how will you get hold of Enver Pasha?"

That was another matter. He was incapable of continuity of thought, or effort, and I soon saw that his preoccupation was, "Who will be at the green table?"—the green table meaning the peace conference. "Now who will the President have at the peace table as peace commissioners?"

Here we were just beginning the war, and he was already talking about the peace conference. I soon realized that his ego was enormous, insatiable, and I was very mean. I'd say, "Well, I suppose he'd have to have," and I named Taft, Root and Brandeis. "Whom else would he need?"

It was as plain as day that he was just reeling out to catch this trout, and this trout would never bite. It was really outrageously mean of me. "Don't you think he'd have to have a Jew?"

"Well, he'll probably have Brandeis, Baruch, or Jacob Schiff."

After one or two sessions I couldn't bear it. We ate together. Lunch and dinner were plenty for me. I forget how many days we were on the water—ten, I think—and I became inaccessible thereafter. At lunch he'd say, "Where were you?"

"I was up on the upper deck waiting for you," or the lower deck, whatever it was. I really played the game of hide-and-seek so as to avoid talking with him because I soon saw that he hadn't a brain in his head. Well, what about this man? What gave this man what he had? What did he have? Money. He was a great dealer in New York real estate, and I concluded that simply because you can make money in New York real estate doesn't mean that you have an understanding of the relationship of people, or nations, or know the history of forces that made the past and therefore will influence the future. Oh, it was such a boring thing! It must have been a day or two after we left the New York harbor there were some letters to be answered. I remember his saying, "Let's send for the secretary and dictate an answer."

I said, "Before we do that let's agree on the theory of the reply."

He said, "What do you mean, the theory of the reply?"

That was something new to him; that you had to have an idea before you expressed it.

Mrs. Morgenthau whom I liked very much was a very nice lady, and I remember her telling me one day that when Henry first attended a political meeting in the 1912 campaign, as treasurer of the Democratic National Committee, he was asked to take a bow. "When he was asked to take a bow, he was so shy and timid about it. Gradually he'd take a bow, and one time they asked him to say something, and he'd say, 'You're very kind, and thank you very much,' and he got a hand. The next time he was asked to one of these meetings and said a few more words, and gradually," as she said, "his shyness left him."

The applause was very sweet, and it got to the point where he really wanted it, ached for it. The interesting thing to me was that after a while she made speeches, and the very seductiveness which victimized him got her. It was a great lesson of the insinuating influence of flattery and massaging the ego. After the ego

begins to be massaged and it feels good, then you're perfectly reconciled to having it massaged, and gradually you have to have it massaged.

My refuge, my release was Max with whom relations were very happy and congenial. We finally landed at Cadiz and took cars down to Algeciras, and then got over to Gibraltar. There was a French delegation and an English mission headed by Dr. Weizmann whom I met for the first time, and he made a profound impression on me. We put up at a hotel in Gibraltar, the Ambassador, Mrs. Morgenthau, Max and I—a dreadful hotel, very—well, not simple. I wouldn't mind that, but bad food, crude and unattractive. Across the water was the Reina Cristina, that admirable hotel with perfectly lovely vines, in Algeciras. I suggested to the Ambassador that we live over there, that that was more consonant with comfort and work. Our sessions were held inside of the fortress in Gibraltar with British soldiery walking up and down, guarding us while we sat inside and pursued this problem of exploring ways and means of detaching Turkey. He said, "No. Spain is a neutral country, and this hotel would be better."

I said, "If the British can live over there, I guess I can live over there," so I moved over and had a wonderful room looking out on the Mediterranean.

There was deference to the Ambassador, the "great" Ambassador to Turkey, America's representative and specialist on Turkey, and day after day after day we just beat the wind, and after weeks, we concluded that the aim that Turkey be detached was "very laudable, most desirable," but the "moment wasn't right." The Central Powers were then riding high. These were hard months for the Allies. The Central Powers were on the up and up, and people don't desert their allies when they are winning, which reminds me of a Churchill story. Israel was licking the pants off the Arabs, and somebody asked Churchill about some reason for criticism, and Churchill said, "I've been a Zionist all my life, and I'm certainly not going to desert them in their hour of victory."

Morgenthau had the bright idea that if he could only get hold of Enver Pasha—that was his idea. Enver Pasha was a great friend of his, and if he could sit down and talk with him, by the persuasiveness of his tongue he could get him to see how wrong they were to be with the Central Powers. They should be with the western powers. It fell to me to draft a cable giving the result of our deliberations. A fellow named William Yale who is, I believe, a professor of history or something at the University of New Hampshire, searched the documents on the Morgenthau Mission, and he refers to this report written by the then Professor Frankfurter as being sort of ambiguous, strange, elusive. It never occurred to him that it was purposely so. I couldn't say 1) This was a wild goose chase; 2) We spent six weeks proving it was; 3) Nothing doing. William Yale afterwards was attached to the famous Crane Commission to take a plebiscite of the Arab countries to find out whether they were for or against the Balfour Declaration and its implementation—well, you know, that was a crazy idea too, a plebiscite of people most of whom were living under the most degraded conditions, humans and animals huddled together, deeply illiterate: the idea of polling their political views!

We then left Gibraltar and went to Madrid to write the report. I remember that word was sent to the secretary of our legation and a fellow who afterwards became important, Leland Harrison, arrived in the morning after a long trip from Southern Spain. He was to meet the great Ambassador. Harrison arrived with all the formalities, top hat—everything. He said, "Where's Professor Frankfurter?"

I said, "That's my name"—and he looked at me. I was probably unshaven. I had a cap instead of a top hat, and I think I wore knickerbockers and a sweater, generally dressed not at all according to protocol. That was a very hard dose for him.

We moved into the Ritz in Madrid, and the hotel was just a center of German spies—dreadful. We were there I don't know how long. Then there were some cables. We had two code books along, and they were like two different shoes, deciphering books for two different codes. Oh, what a time we had! The problem was what to do from there on. The papers had it that there was to be a meeting of the Allied powers to discuss the Balkan situation. Morgenthau said, "I'm going there to attend, to represent Wilson," but Wilson hadn't asked him to represent him. Wilson had a policy not to sit in on Allied conferences. He wanted to keep his hands free. As I wrote afterwards, he was theoretically "going to keep his hands free while the Allies tied them behind him." I said to Morgenthau, "You can't do that."

After a while I realized that the real purpose in having me go with Morgenthau, the thought behind the insistence on sending me, was that they thought that I could control him. I had a nurse's function, to prevent the wilful, but imperious, child from being any more foolish than could possibly be avoided. I sent a cable to Frank Polk, the Undersecretary of State, whom I knew pretty well, that they should somehow call Morgenthau home, get him away from Europe. He was dealing with Europe the way he'd dealt with parcels of real estate in Brooklyn and the Bronx. There were strict instructions that he mustn't do this. We got to Paris, and he held a press conference. He was hell on press conferences. I said that he shouldn't talk to newspapermen, and he said, "You don't understand. I tell them something, and then in exchange they give me something for what I told them."

That was his notion of diplomacy: if he were just a little indiscreet, these newspapermen—you know, with the great secrets of the world—would let him in on some of them.

In Paris we called on Pershing. It was perfectly plain that having been balked by the fact that the Central Power cause was going too well for peacefully detaching Turkey, Morgenthau's next thought was to knock out Turkey militarily. If the Ambassador wanted to see Pershing, he could see him. Pershing had his temporary headquarters on the left bank near the Chamber of Deputies, and he was duly impressed by the fact that here was this great Ambassador to Turkey, obviously a great authority. Well, Morgenthau talked to him in general terms, and I thought that Pershing didn't quite follow how easy it was to knock out Turkey. Morgenthau asked me to go along, so I went along, but the stuff was so puerile! I remember sitting in Pershing's room and sliding way down in my chair with the thought that I could make myself even less conspicuous than my small size inevitably makes me so that Pershing might not remember that I was even there. I wanted to disassociate myself so completely from Morgenthau. But the high point of that conversation was when Pershing said, "Of course, Mr. Ambassador, we'll have to have some more talks and go into details. You have maps, of course?"

Morgenthau said, "Oh yes."

When we left Pershing, Morgenthau said, "Let's go to a bookshop. Where's a bookshop?"

I said, "There's a Brentano's in Paris."

He said, "Let's go there and get a map."

He bought for maybe a franc, but I think it was twenty-five centimes, a little pocket map. He had no idea what a military map was like, so he bought this little pocket map to show Pershing when he next had a conference. I don't know whether he saw Pershing, but I didn't see Pershing on that score again. I wouldn't go with Morgenthau and have him bring out that little map on which to plot a great military campaign.

That's unbelievable, isn't it.

That was the Honorable Henry Morgenthau, the Ambassador to Turkey, one of the important figures in the campaign that brought Wilson to the White House. Morgenthau just took it for granted that if you worked for a man and he became President, of course, you got a job out of it. I remember seeing him shortly after F.D.R. became President, after the inauguration, on a train going from New York to Boston. He had grandchildren living, I think, in Cambridge. He was going up to Boston, and there we were. We talked away in a desultory fashion, and he said to me, "What job do you want from Franklin?"

I said, "I don't want any job."

He said, "Well, what do you mean, you don't want any job?"

I said, "That's what I mean."

"But you could have anything you want. What do you mean telling me that you don't want anything?"

On this European mission he finally went to Aix-les-Baines, and I came home.

There's a very witty remark about Henry Morgenthau made by Colonel George Harvey who was the original prime mover in promoting Woodrow Wilson's candidacy for the Presidency. Then he broke with Wilson, became Wilson's bitterest enemy. Wilson found it inconvenient to have a fellow who partly represented Wall Street use Woodrow Wilson's name on the masthead of *Harper's Weekly,* which Harvey edited. One day there was a lunch at the Metropolitan Club here, and somebody said, "How do you account for Morgenthau's apparent important influence with Wilson?"

Somebody else said, "He was one of the important contributors to his campaign fund."

Harvey said, "Uncle Henry doesn't contribute. He collects."

16. *Paris Peace Conference*

The Balfour Declaration was an announcement of a policy by Great Britain, concurred in by the United States, that Palestine be established as a Jewish National Home. It was issued after detailed consultation, even changes in the phrasing, between the Lloyd George Government and President Wilson in person. It also had the benevolent accession of France, but everything turned on the Peace Conference. I need not tell you that the phrase, "that Palestine be established as a Jewish National Home" was a phrase of purposeful ambiguity and gave rise to a good deal of subsequent discussion. Did it mean that there should be a home for Jews in Palestine, or was Palestine to be the national home? Events have largely answered the question as events usually answer the lawyer's ambiguity—that is, in so far as ambiguities deal with really serious problems, experience and events pour meaning into the words and give them one vitality rather than another.

The implementation of the Balfour Declaration by the Peace Conference was one of the concerns of Zionist leaders, and it looked toward a mandate by the conference. Mandate was a new legal, political, diplomatic conception. The territory and people within a territory would be under the tutelage of the governmental authority of some power, a trustee, expected to be more or less short-lived, and carried on with responsibilities to some international organ to which report must be made as to how the mandate is being discharged, how the trusteeship is being carried out. A mandate is a constitution setting forth the powers of the mandated power and the rights or guarantees of the people in the mandated place. The constitution was a legal document and called for lawyers of experience and understanding, and our English Zionist friends and our leaders here, Justice Brandeis and Judge Mack, were very anxious that I should go, to be, as it were, the American responsible for working with the British, particularly the British, on the terms of the mandate in doing what one could do to get an appropriately worded, or appropriately formulated mandate issued out of the deliberations of the Paris Peace Conference. I therefore, having resigned from the government, for the war administration was being dismantled, went for that purpose, holding a "watching" brief for Zionists before the Peace Conference.

There were many people in the British War Office, educated military people who were interested in Palestine from the English strategic point of view. They looked ahead and saw that this western, as they were confident, Jewishly populated Palestine would be western oriented by the very dominance of the minds, the outlook, the intellectual orientation of the leaders. They might come from Poland and the Pale in Russia where Weizmann did, but they were scientists and the like and intellectually western bred. My friend Aaron Aaronsohn, the agronomist, was of great service to them as a brain of the first order, of imagination, intrepid in body and in spirit. They had collaborated a lot, and they realized that Palestine was a bridge between East and West and that the bridge masters better be people who would be good people in charge of a bridge, not letting it fall into disrepair.

One saw early that it would be important to knit a relationship of friendship with the Arabs. Prince Feisal was the spokesman for the Arab people, and Lawrence was not only his interpreter but his guide, so it was arranged that I should see him and tell him that we were American Jews with a tradition against colonialism, with strong affirmative traditions in favor of the dignity of man, and the last thing in the world we would go in for was restoring Jewish civilization at the expense of Arab peoples and Arab civilization, that one involved the other. I called on him—he lived in a villa in the *bois de Boulogne*—in the forenoon. Here was little me meeting this Arab prince, and I didn't know the wrinkles, how you meet Arab princes or what you do with them, but I thought you just acted on your instincts or your discipline of courtesy. My good sense taught me what I should have known, that when an Arab asks you about eleven o'clock or ten-thirty in the morning, "Would you like to have some coffee? May I serve some coffee?" the answer was, "Yes, you may serve." It would have been terrible if I had said, "No, thank you," and so we had excellent coffee in the forenoon.

We exchanged assurances, and it was agreed that each would put his remarks on paper. We went back to the Hotel Meurice where Lawrence was staying and I wrote my letter, and he wrote his, and then they were duly signed. Lawrence's eyes transfixed me. There was something very compelling about them. He was short and stocky, a quiet voice. It was an interesting little interlude. In those days I only knew him as Lawrence of Arabia. His *Seven Pillars* and his translations of Homer came later. Naturally I followed all that with interest, but we never had any further contact. We dropped out of one another's lives.

The condition of Jewry in Poland, their plight, was too awful abstractly to contemplate. Something had to be done about it. It was arranged that a commission would be sent out. It was headed by Morgenthau who was available for something important, something worthy of his great dignity. The Jewish leaders had no confidence in Morgenthau—not that they didn't have confidence in his general humane outlook, nor that he didn't have deep sympathy for the plight of Jews, but when you deal with a man of his ego, you don't know how that ego might be massaged for one purpose rather than another. Anyhow, it was felt that it was important for him to know that he was being watched, so it was arranged that I should go to Poland.

I attended a session of the Siem. Paderewski was President of Poland at the time. My friend Philip Kerr, later Lord Lothian, then private secretary to Lloyd George and one of the most influential members of the government, asked me to take a look into affairs there because Poland was nip-and-tuck rocky that the Bolshies would take it over. I was in Warsaw, then went to Lodz and other cities, nosed around and came back, got in touch with

Philip Kerr to tell him that I was back, and he invited me to lunch with Mr. Balfour who was then Foreign Secretary. I lunched with Mr. Balfour, that wonderful, charming creature, and Philip Kerr told him my story, what I'd observed, what needed to be done, and Mr. Balfour cross-examined me, asked me many questions, and at the end of it turned to Philip Kerr and said, "Philip, let me give you a note."

The upshot was that then and there Mr. Balfour took some action on the basis of what I reported, the burden of which was, "That's a very rickety structure. It needs to be buttressed."

I think it was on the same day after I lunched with Balfour who acted on my report after cross-examination, that I began to tell Herbert Hoover this story, and he was aggressively hostile, "Don't you want us to support Paderewski?"

He was really fierce, and I remember saying to him, "I'm suggesting to you that the very things we want to accomplish there require a reinforcement of the administration of President Paderewski. You don't have to believe these facts, but I didn't make them if they're true."

This was an illuminating experience. I'd known Hoover rather well, seen not a little of him because he used to come to the House of Truth when he was Food Administrator. He was a great friend of my housemate, Lord Eustace Percy, but this hostility against facts that he didn't like, that quality of not facing facts if they're disagreeable, is characteristic of the difference between Balfour, who used his sharp brain to ascertain whether I was a reliable reporter and whether the judgment on what I reported had validity, as against Hoover who didn't attack the facts, but didn't want me to discover them.

I had hardly landed in Paris when I was pulled into various other interests at the Peace Conference. When I got there in early March they were in the midst of working out what became the International Labor Organization Charter which was a separate part of the Treaty of Paris. There were various problems: what kind of provisions for the promotion of labor standards through international agreement would be constitutionally valid assumptions of obligation by this country. The fact of the matter is that one of the last things that I did before leaving Washington I was asked to do by the State Department. They asked me to be responsible for the preparatory materials for our delegation in regard to labor matters. There is a bound volume containing maybe a score of separate monographs that for months a staff of people under me had worked on with a view to ascertaining what the various labor movements of the western countries would be promoting. I was instrumental in getting appropriate people to prepare a study of labor policies and labor purposes of the British Labor movement, the French Labor movement, the Scandinavian countries and so on. Those studies were taken over by our delegation, so I had familiarity and was known to have concerned myself with these problems. Almost the day after I got there I was pulled into consultation on legal questions on the scope of our treaty-making power.

I had a lot of friends there. Many of the younger people on our peace delegation were friends, associates, Harvard people—all sorts of Harvard people as members of the House Inquiry. Oh Lord! That man of mystery! I saw Colonel House on Labor Day, 1918, at Magnolia where he was staying, and he took me in that secretive way of his—he didn't trust conditions in his own cottage—back into a little wood that he had, back where only nature was present, trees and grass, to tell me the great, great, great secret: namely, that the President had decided to attend the Peace Conference in person. I said, "I'm very sorry to hear it."

House said, "What do you mean? Why?"

I then expounded to him my conviction that by leaving the White House where he could thunder from Sinai from time to time, he was giving up a great advantage of being a *deus ex machina.* Not only that. He was throwing away the great advantage our commissioners would have of saying, "Oh, we have to refer that back to the President."

"If he's going to sit down at the table, he can't say, 'No, no, no' all the time. There's an inevitability due to the task of doing business every day with people that you can't always be in opposition. The mere camaraderie, however limited, of it compels certain compromises. Moreover, every well-trained lawyer knows the difference between an adverse decision and the terms in which the decision is cast in a Court of Equity. If you sue for money and a jury brings you in a verdict, why, that's that, but if a Chancellor in a Court of Equity decides against you, then a decree has to be drawn to formulate what it is that you're forbidden to do, what it is you're directed to do, and many a shrewd lawyer who lost the case won it because of the terms which he persuaded the court to formulate in carrying out the adverse judgment. That isn't the President's great faculty. He's not a fellow who would be very good at drawing an equity decree which plucks victory out of defeat. That's a lawyer's job. People like Root and Brandeis can do that. So he's not only surrendering the advantage of his aloofness and isolation, and the majestic status of the President remaining in the White House, but he in all ways enters upon a process of negotiation in which a person like Lloyd George can out-trump him every time because Wilson hasn't got that agility and flexibility that negotiation allows. He's a great fellow for laying down postulates and avowing principles, but not for translating them into the myriad variants into which general principles can be translated."

"Oh, you're all wrong," said Colonel House.

I remember writing a letter to Justice Brandeis giving an account of this conversation and saying, "Yesterday was blue Monday for me."

Early in the year, March of 1918, the Allied cause had a very precarious look, severe reverses, but I never had any worry. I had such reasoned confidence in Foch as a military leader that I just regarded these reverses as a setback, inevitable in the flow of the tide of war, but this "secret" from Colonel House was really for me the saddest day since the war began because I knew that Wilson was incapable of doing the kind of thing that a Peace Conference called for. Almost everybody else thought that it was wonderful. Very few people thought that what was "wonderful" might be a very different thing—you know. "Isn't it wonderful that Chamberlain will fly to Berchtesgaden!" I nearly wept. I knew he'd get trimmed. There are some things your experience tells you, but you have to have experience in that kind of thing and some insight.

House was a secretive character, a recondite character. I think he was absolutely devoted to the "Governor" as he always called

Wilson. Also he loved the role of being behind the scenes. I remember that my friend Percy came to Washington. He had a letter from his chief, the Foreign Secretary, Sir Edward Grey which he didn't want sent through the pouch, and he asked me how to get it to Colonel House. I said, "I have to go to New York tomorrow. If you don't mind, I'll take it in person and deliver it in person."

Percy was perfectly delighted with that. I went to see Colonel House in his apartment, 115 East Fifty-third Street, and said, "I have a communication for you from Sir Edward Grey," and House took it with the most indifferent, "I've been wondering where that letter was," and he put it down like a man who knoweth all things and wasn't going to be impressed by anything.

I was saying that there were many friends, associates, etcetera at the Peace Conference. Walter Lippmann was in Paris in uniform as Captain Lippmann. He'd been a member of the House Inquiry, drafted more or less the Fourteen Points, but with great instinctive wisdom, great knowledge of himself, had left the Inquiry very early. Walter knows that his job in life is to sit in a noise-proof room and draft things on paper. He's never been through the heartbreaks in making paper walk, of getting agreement out of people who also have views and getting agreement on sensible compromise and stopping short of where you shouldn't compromise. As you know, he does work in a sound-proof room, a corked room where none of the raucous voices of the world break the serenity in which his thinking is done, but there were lots of people in Paris—colleagues of mine from Harvard, Sam Morison, Allyn Young who felt as Keynes did about the economic terms of the treaty and wrote the kind of thing that Keynes published, but just didn't think he ought to "rock the boat," as the phrase runs. I'd been on the War Industries Board with Mr. Baruch, "Dr. Fact," as he called himself, and he was there. The headquarters of the American delegation was the Hotel Crillon. Then I knew some of the Britishers very well. Two of my closest friends were on the British Empire delegation, Eustace Percy and Loring Christie, the right-hand man of the Canadian Prime Minister, Sir Robert Borden. Another friend of mine, Lloyd George's Secretary, Philip Kerr, afterwards Lord Lothian, was there, so that it was a swirling crowd of familiars.

The best book I know on the Paris Peace Conference is Harold Nicholson's *Peace Making.* He was there, and the reason why I say it's the "best book" is that he gives you the sense of disorderliness, the hubbub, the hallabaloo, the tears, the melange of generous disinterested emotions, endeavors, the special interests, the axes that were ground and the axes that weren't ground, the interplay of forces—a very vivid account of the melange of hopes and fears, desires and passions and thoughts that constituted the conference.

I remember at one stage of the business a doctor who was there looking after the health of the British delegation said, "If they don't shut down pretty soon, or take a recess, there will be a goodly portion of them who will have breakdowns."

The conference started with such high hopes. They came in on the tide of Wilson's idealistic rhetoric—"war to end war," the "common council of the nations," the kind of thing he said when he was up in his grandfather's church in Scotland. With all these large, beautifully expressed, moralistic, exalting and exulting speeches of his, people really thought that heaven was coming on earth just because he was going to be there. In the course of some talks in Paris when he met delegations he said a number of things that left a deep mark on me and partly confirmed and partly helped to shape my feelings about my judgment on Wilson. He said, "If I didn't feel that I was the personal instrument of God, I couldn't carry on."

In no time it got to be a sordid pulling and hemming and hawing, and old hands at this kind of business, Clemenceau and Lloyd George, who knew that life is more complicated, that the tensions and tangles of Europe would be firmer and tougher than ever Wilson realized, just wore Wilson out and down. Ray Stannard Baker was the biographer of Wilson. I wrote a review of a little book he published when he came back, *The Americans in Paris.* Baker was a very nice man, an Amherst man by the way, and he got my dander up because he said that we failed because we were so pure and the Europeans were so wicked, so nefarious. He said, "They all had something that they wanted to get out of the peace conference, and we didn't want anything."

The book was so self-righteous! I wrote, "We wanted more

than anyone else. We wanted to further a decent world order, and we didn't do what they did. They were pushing their more or less limited objectives, and we just thought by announcing these noble principles they'd translate themselves into action."

The self-righteousness in that book—you know, "We were so noble, and the other people were so ignoble." The assumption was that ignobility should recognize nobility and kowtow to it, and that's that. As a matter of fact our people made compromises galore. Heavens! And then the ground on which Wilson stood where he wouldn't compromise, like Fiume. He gave Shantung to Japan—that didn't bother him—but to make any concession on Fiume, that seemed to be the end of the world. Of course one is struck, as I was struck in going over his books in connection with the little piece I wrote for the London *Times* on his centenary, that nothing about Europe was in his head until he was confronted with its problems and then he had solutions overnight. I suppose historians will discuss and debate, as well as they may forever, whether it was wise to break up the Austro-Hungarian monarchy rather than to secure a federal state, making Czechoslovakia a component. I think I know a little bit of the arguments pro and con, but Wilson just pronounced overnight that the Austro-Hungarian monarchy must be destroyed, and he was suggesting a surgical operation of a kind that called for a little more knowledge of the body he was going into before he began to cut.

Paris was like a session of Congress. You finally had to shut up shop. The effort at negotiation and settlement sort of became a rout, any old thing to close up shop. It was the most disheartening of experiences. One came to Paris when hope was riding high, and each day you could see these hopes just—well, you soon detected that it was a great enormous balloon and gradually all the air was coming out of it. It soon settled down to a kind of sordid play of selfish and ignorant and impatient forces. Then there was Russia, a vast black cloud that overhung the whole thing.

To me the most impressive figure at the Peace Conference was General Botha of South Africa. Smuts had a subtler, finer brain, but Botha was my fellow, my hero. I remember dining with my friends the night the German reply to the draft treaty had been circulated among the various delegations. Loring Christie and Eustace Percy were telling what went on. Botha made a speech in the course of which he said to his colleagues, Lloyd George, Balfour and everybody else, "I have an advantage over all of you in that none of you have had the experience of ever having been a defeated enemy. I know what it feels like to be a defeated enemy, and I can assure you that it made all the difference in the world that Great Britain gave us more generous terms after the defeat and did nothing to make defeat any more rankling than it inescapably has to be. This treaty is full of pin pricks against the Germans, and you ought to withdraw all those pin pricks."

Didn't Smuts make a statement at the signing?

After the signing, but he was intellectually as much responsible as anybody for probably the worst feature of the peace treaty; the reparation terms, because it was he who wrote a legal document that they could charge against Germany all the derivative costs. By the terms of the peace treaty Germany should pay for the "cost" of the war. The question was, "What is cost?" and Smuts worked out this lawyer's document that you could carry it on to the ultimate, indirect costs, and that persuaded Wilson.

Of course the leitmotiv of all of Wilson's utterances and expressed attitudes during the conduct of thc war was trying to separate the people from the Kaiser. The Kaiser meant the German General Staff. "We are conducting the war on the assumption that there is a distinction between the German government and the German people." After the tentative treaty was made public, there was great consternation as to the harshness of the terms. You can imagine the sadness that was stirred in me at Wilson's reply to a delegation of important leading citizens from neutral countries who came to Paris and I think through the intervention of Thomas W. Lamont had an audience with President Wilson. When they respectfully and soulfully pointed out how harsh and severe were the consequences to the German people of some of the terms, particularly the economic, Wilson said, "We mean them to be harsh because we want to etch forever on the minds of the German people that the people are responsible for the conduct of its rulers," which, of course, was the very opposite of what he'd been saying throughout the war.

I was at the Hall of Mirrors in the press section when they were all seated and then the door opened, and two little fellows in black came in and signed on the dotted line for Germany. Gosh! Just that sight!

17. *Return to Law School*

What moved me to make such an unexpected choice to join the Harvard Law School faculty—"unexpected choice" because the opportunity to make it was so unexpected—was the atmosphere, or what my friend Laski used to call the "ethos" of the time. This was a very fermenting period in American history. Things had been stirring. There was "a great awakening" of which TR, "Battling Bob" La Follette and Hughes were both expressions and promoters. 1912 was the Bull Moose Campaign. Wilson's "New Freedom" was abroad in the land, and the very contentiousness among the parties made each go beyond where they would have gone if they had had no real opposition. I should think another important factor in the general trend of events was the publication of Herbert Croly's *Promise of American Life* out of which grew the *New Republic* about which we've talked. I think one may call this period a minor renaissance in feeling, if not in thinking, of people who either by age, or by native woodenness of mind, weren't absolutely settled and impervious to the new currents that were floating about, the new needs that were asserting themselves, the new nostrums which were being peddled around and partly criticized and partly promoted. There was the realization that new forces were afoot, new interests were urging their claims, new responses were made to them through minority representation in the Congress, through absorption of some of them by political parties not excluding the "Old Guard" in the Republican Party.

The *Wisconsin Idea,* as Charlie McCarthy expressed the whole forward, progressive movement in the State of Wisconsin, had a lot to do with awakening interest in the universities and in the various professional schools as instruments of a better life in the United States, the university as a promoter of civilization, because Wisconsin beyond any other state in the United States utilized its university as a seed bed for its practical ideas. One of the great things about La Follette was that he turned to the specialists, the experts, the disinterested and preoccupied with ideas in different fields of human endeavor as his advisers when he was governor of Wisconsin, and the fact of the matter is that when he came to Washington as a Senator he continued to utilize, so far as he could, that kind of trained, disinterested intelligence in the promotion of his "progressive" ideas. All this naturally influenced me.

Another important factor was the tendency of Supreme Court decisions to block legislation in the states as falling within what Judge Hough called the "vague contours of the due process clause" by reading into that clause "liberty of contract" nowhere mentioned in the Constitution. This tendency led Holmes to say in his famous dissent in the *Lochner* case, "The Fourteenth Amendment does not enact Mr. Herbert Spencer's Social Statics" which was a kind of bible of the *laissez-faire,* Manchesterian view of economics. Holmes' powerful dissents—powerful despite their brevity; as he said on one occasion, "Judges can be weighty without being heavy"—naturally were congenial to my own mind and to the kind of direction I'd had at the Harvard Law School of the nature of the Constitution and the judicial function in relation to it, all flowing from that most important, single sentence in American Constitutional Law, Marshall's "It is a Constitution we are expounding," not an insurance clause in small type, but a scheme of government formulated in 1787, got under way in 1789, but intended for the undefined and unlimited future. Since we have a written Constitution to which appeal can be made, as de Tocqueville foresaw so clearly, almost every question can ultimately be put to the test of legality, or constitutionality. That being so, it was natural for me to think of the Harvard Law School as not being merely a guide to antiquity, but as a disciplined promoter of thought in the minds of the lawyers of the country.

I was asked to go up to the Harvard Law School precisely because of the kind of experience I had had in the law, both in the United States Attorney's Office and afterwards in Washington, with legal questions growing out of modern problems and to a considerable extent concerned with the enforcement of legislation that seemed productive of the ends toward which the legislation was directed, the kind of response the judgment of the legislature deemed reasonable to the situations with which legislatures were dealing. While the call was for a scholar at the Harvard Law School, meaning by that the full-time preoccupation with problems growing out of the legal materials relevant to our day, the particular things I was concerned with, namely, legislation and regulatory measures, what we now call administrative law, were materials of the law which the law had to absorb, just as more than a hundred-odd years before it had to absorb changes in commercial life through the vitality of the common law in adjusting itself to new conditions.

That's not only the general attitude and spirit in which I went to the Harvard Law School, but was, as I understood, the spirit which was expected of me and which led to my being called. It was first thought until circumstances changed that I was to have some concern with the criminal law with which, of course, I had a good deal to do in the United States Attorney's Office, and I did teach criminal law for a time and remained interested in it and am interested in it to this moment very, very greatly. I know that the then dean of the Harvard Law School, Ezra Thayer, who was the son of the great James B. Thayer, knew about me through Mr. Stimson who had been a classmate of his at the Harvard Law School, and thought I would bring the kind of experience, the kind of temper of mind, the kind of ardor that was precisely what, in his opinion, the school needed and which he was looking for. There was an additional specific reason, as he told me, for wanting me at the school.

There had come to the law school, partly on my suggestions to the people up there, Roscoe Pound, a native of Nebraska who was a great botanist before he became a great legal scholar. He had been professor and dean of the University of Nebraska Law

School. From there he moved to Northwestern University Law School then to the Chicago Law School, and finally he was brought on to the Harvard Law School. He was an American legal scholar who was widely read not only in German juristic literature, but also realized what Holmes had taught in his *Common Law,* but Pound spelled it out, applied it and amplified it, that law isn't something that exists as a closed system within itself, but draws its juices from life. Law being a response to life had to concern itself with life. Life was being studied, sought to be understood by scholars in other fields, sociology, economics, anthropology, and Pound was a great fellow for associating with students in other fields instead of treating law as a closed system with premises of its own in relation to its own ends. I remember Ezra Thayer telling me that one reason he asked me to come to the Harvard Law School was that he thought Pound needed a companion with a sympathetic outlook. He thought that I would serve as an intellectual companion to Pound, and, indeed, my relations to Pound became very quickly very close. This melange of reasons I've given you, this potpourri of factors that were in the air and that partly formed a congenial conclusion in my head explain the reasons why I was attracted to the kind of life the Harvard Law School offered and explains the spirit in which I went there.

Now everything was hunky-dory until the war broke out and I packed my bags for a weekend stay with Secretary of War Baker and didn't get back until the opening of the academic year of 1919. In the meantime I'd been doing various things in the War Department and at the Department of Labor and taking these trips to Europe, none of which would have impinged on the consciousness of influential people in Boston, or influential people in the affairs of Harvard outside of Boston. None of these activities would have mattered. What mattered were two things largely exploited by others, and especially by Theodore Roosevelt: namely, my *Report on the Bisbee Deportations* and my Mooney Report. This was directly referable to the Russian October Revolution which brought the Bolshies to power and quickly led not only to tremors, but terrors in the breasts of so many people. I was the spearhead in the *Report on the Bisbee Deportations,* and then the Mooney Report, and these were deemed to be manifestations that the Bolshevik Revolution was coming to America. Here was this professor of law at the Harvard Law School on behalf of the government of the United States lending himself to a sympathetic attitude towards these dangerous people! That's what stirred up the animals!

Of course, people don't read reports. Very few people ever read anything except the headlines and the commentators, those great miseducators of the American public in giving pepsinized knowledge and sometimes half-knowledge, so that all sorts of good people began to worry about this terribly dangerous man Frankfurter. The pack was led by none other than the ex-President of the United States and wide publicity was given to his letter to me, usually without people printing or even mentioning my reply. The idea of expecting people to read a thing like that!

By this time Dean Thayer was dead. Pound had become dean. Pound was essentially a timid creature. Looking back, it was on the whole tragic that he should ever become dean because a great scholar was largely spoiled in not making a good dean. His weakness was weakness, and these complaints were made to him. When I got back from Europe Justice Brandeis told me that Pound had come down to see him, said that he was greatly troubled about the criticism of and opposition to me, was worried about it. Pound himself was clear-headed about these matters; indeed, he had joined in the protest against the inexcusable performances of Mitchell Palmer as Attorney General. He himself was not critical or worried about my doings, all of which, looking back, were quite inoffensive; indeed, I was certainly in my naive way just doing a lawyer's job, investigating the Bisbee Deportations and bringing out the facts and their character. The mere fact that TR's great friend, Jack Greenway, was the leader of this performance didn't make it pure and good; indeed, didn't prevent it being reprehensible. How anybody could criticize the mildness in the Mooney case! It was a quietly persuasive document, but Pound was a scare cat. He was timid. Not only was he timid, but he wanted to be all things to all men. He was afraid to stand up to people. He wanted to be thought well of by everybody. He was a near genius. He once told us at a faculty meeting when he did something that ordinary people don't do, "Well, you have to pay a price for a genius."

That's what he said about himself, and so when these complaints came in, instead of brushing them off, or quietly disposing of them, he came down to Washington to put his troubles to Mr. Justice Brandeis who was, of course, a great friend of the school and a long, great influence in the direction the school had been taking, a supporter of the school. Brandeis said, "Well, what are you worried about? Hasn't Frankfurter got tenure?"

"Oh, yes, but they'll want to take away his courses in public law by which he might corrupt the young and their outlook on American public law."

Brandeis said, "Oh, don't worry about that. It doesn't matter what he teaches. If he were to teach Bills and Notes, he'd be teaching himself."

I always thought that was about as good a definition of a teacher as you can have. That indicates, in essence, why I've always been left cold by curricular discussions. Oh yes, I know they are important, but not very.

I wasn't back long, and one day I had a call from Judge George W. Anderson, United States Circuit Judge, who asked if he could see me. I went in, and he told me, "Important *habeas corpus* cases are before me"—a lot of aliens had applied for *habeas corpus* because of their detention by the Department of Justice. He said, "The lawyer who represents them is plainly inadequate for the issues at stake. He's doubtless a conscientious fellow, but not equal to the problems presented by these cases," and Judge Anderson very much wanted me to appear as an *amicus curiae,* as a friend of the court, without retainer. "Would you do that?"

I was then teaching administrative law which is concerned with these matters, and I said that I would be very happy indeed to serve as a friend of the court, but I hoped that he would associate with me and invite also my colleague, Professor Zechariah Chafee who had come to the school shortly after I did. He'd written articles on freedom of speech, made these questions his concern, and he and I were very congenial colleagues. Judge Anderson said that of course he would.

I talked to Zach Chafee, and he said that he would be glad to appear with me as *amicus curiae.* We were in court a good many days, and the upshot was the famous opinion—"famous" because it's had a great deal of influence—*Collyer v. Skeffington* 265 Federal 13. The chief legal point in that case, as a matter of fact, was the legal proposition on which the recent *Service* case turned. Judge Anderson says somewhere in the opinion, "I hear from the government no convincing answer to Mr. Frankfurter's proposition," and then he quotes my proposition which was, in essence, and this is the essence of the *Service* opinion, that if the executive head has formulated an administrative procedure for the determination of issues before him, he must follow his own procedure and not let it go hang in a particular case. That's the whole point in the *Service* case, that while undoubtedly the Secretary of State had authority to dismiss under the so-called McCarran rider on his own determination of whether a fellow should be fired or not from the State Department; in fact, he had issued a code of procedure whereby one charged in the State Department: i.e., Service, had to go through a certain procedure, and that was not followed. That was a disregard of the applicable law.

In the course of the war I became acquainted with Sidney Hillman because he was a very useful, important figure in seeing that equipment for the "Yanks" was forthcoming. I saw him in connection with the settlement of certain labor difficulties, and we became friends. A labor proceeding was brought in 1920, partly because of the hysteria influenced by the vast convulsion in Russia and partly because of the traditional hostility of American business to the trade union movement. The Amalgamated Clothing Workers tried to unionize Michaels Stern in Rochester, and there was picketing. An injunction was brought to bar this. This was very serious business because the bill of complaint charged the Amalgamated with being an "illegal organization" and the litigation sought not only to enjoin the picketing, but to disband the union as an "illegal conspiracy." This was very serious for the union, and Sidney Hillman came to me and asked me if I could take charge of their defense.

I regarded the nature of the proceeding and the legal claims that were made of great public importance, not merely to the Amalgamated Clothing Workers, and I said I would take charge of their defense subject to several conditions. The first was that I was not to accept any retainer, that "since I go into this matter not for the sake of the Amalgamated, but because public issues are involved," I didn't want to be paid by the Amalgamated. I regarded this as the kind of thing a scholar in the law should do provided he does it disinterestedly and has no stake, certainly no money stake, in the outcome.

The second condition was that I couldn't do it all, that one needed legal assistants, that I'd been out of the business of actually trying cases for some years and that I should want somebody more skilled in cross examination than I deemed myself to do that active part of the trial of a case, and therefore I wanted to be free to choose as my associates professional lawyers who ought to be paid. I picked Emory R. Buckner and Max Lowenthal who was then practicing law with Bob Szold, a very good lawyer who had been assistant to John W. Davis when he was Solicitor General.

Antecedent to all this I said, "I would not"—and throughout my years at the law school I never did—"subordinate the school work to anything outside no matter how important the public interest." I never cut a class, nor shifted hours because of some outside engagement or interest. I said that I would do this if the trial could be arranged for my Easter holiday. "Some of my colleagues go off and play golf, some do this, and some do that. I'll do this."

That was an antecedent condition, but the third professional condition was, and this was done for the first time and had important consequences, that these legal issues were not problems the answers to which are to be found in law books. "The law derives from facts, facts of industry and facts of life, and the relation of the law's response to the right of picketing, the nature or the kind of picketing, or under what circumstances, depends on the whole industrial context, and that's the business not of lawyers, though they can dig it out, but of economists and sociologists, and therefore I want to be free to select not only legal associates but an economic adviser."

Sidney Hillman being a far-sighted fellow said, "You name the ticket. It's all right with me," and I picked Leo Wolman. That is how Leo Wolman came to be known to the Amalgamated and became the economist for the Amalgamated for several years. I believe that was the beginning of unions' realizing that union efforts aren't merely parading with placards and such like, but unionism, both as a force and a quality, depended on intelligent direction.

Well, these conditions were fulfilled, and we all moved to Rochester in force into one of these good hotels that is hell to live in. This trial lasted I don't know how many weeks before an incredibly wooden judge to whom all these matters were foreign. Certainly the chief aim of the complaint failed; namely, to dissolve the Amalgamated as an illegal organization. That was the gravamen of the suit, and in a relatively short time Hillman organized the market.

While you were in Rochester the House of Representatives moved against Louis F. Post, Assistant Secretary of Labor, for "high crimes and misdemeanors against the United States," and you wired Secretary of Labor Wilson offering your services.

Louis Post was a reformer whom the Wilson Administration had brought on from Chicago. He was a single-taxer, a very kind and thoughtful man, and he had no truck with, indeed opposed, the raids of the Department of Justice, these wholesale raids for which Mitchell Palmer was responsible and which were lawless. Immigration matters were then within the jurisdiction of the Secretary of Labor, and they were more particularly delegated to his assistant secretary, Louis Post. Some resolution was introduced against him seeking his impeachment on the ground that he was blocking the deportation of alien enemies, more particularly alien enemies in the words of the resolution "who would undermine and overthrow the Government of the United States."

These illegal practices of the Department of Justice piled up, and there was submitted a *Report upon the Illegal Practices of the United States Department of Justice* signed by twelve lawyers of standing at the bar including Roscoe Pound, Tyrrell Williams, who afterwards became dean of the law school at Washington University, Francis Fisher Kane, who was United States Attorney and a leading lawyer in Philadelphia, Ernst Freund, one of the most distinguished of all legal scholars in the whole history of the legal professoriate, Zechariah and myself. We submitted this document addressed to the American People showing that the Department of Justice had been guilty of illegalities and, more particularly, arrests without warrants, illegal searches and seizures, use of provocative agents, etcetera, etcetera, fully documented, a report which Charles E. Hughes, then perhaps the country's leading lawyer, characterized in a public speech: "Very recently information has been laid by responsible citizens at the bar of public opinion of violations of personal rights that savor of the worst practices of tyranny."

I do not speak by the book, but my recollection is that that document, soberly worded and so responsibly sponsored, had a good press. Nevertheless there it was, another matter to worry the timid and conventional minded—Bisbee, Mooney, Hillman and the Amalgamated, and now worrying about being a little rough with people who were a menace to this country.

There is another item. Asquith and I think Lord Milner—in other words really solid, conservative, leading statesmen—had urged the recognition of Soviet Russia on the theory that recognition was merely the recognition of a fact, not the conferment of moral approval. Moreover, some very substantial people, indeed some who had been in Russia in connection with the Red Cross—William B. Thompson, a very rich man, Thomas D. Thacher, and Alan Wardwell, a partner in the J. P. Morgan law firm, said that the thing to do was to recognize Russia. A public meeting was arranged. I cannot now tell you who the conveners were, but they were certainly responsible people. They were going to hold a meeting in Faneuil Hall in Boston directed toward urging our government to recognize Russia, to legitimatize the thing and thereby to exert some influence of moderation, at all events, not to have Russia in the undesirable condition of a great power being treated as an outlaw. The speakers were to be some very conservative people. They asked me to preside. I told them I thought it was very undesirable for me to preside, that they ought to get a good respectable Beacon Hill Yankee to preside. I knew several such, particularly Thomas Nelson Perkins, a member of the Harvard Corporation and a partner in the old law firm of Ropes, Gray and Gorham, whom I'd seen on and off during the war and who had expressed himself very unequivocally on this question in

Washington. I told them they ought to get somebody like Perkins to preside, so I gave them a list of people. They said, "Well, we'll do our best. We'll see everybody we can possibly see, but if nobody else will do it, will you do it?"

I said, "You go and come and tell me when you've exhausted all the possibilities."

They did come and tell me that they had seen everyone on the list, and most of them agreed that it should be done, but they didn't want to preside. I said, "I'll be damned if I'm going to be as timid and cowardly as all the rest. If nobody else will do it, you'll simply have to take the loss of having me preside."

I wasn't born yesterday. I'd acquired a good deal of experience by this time, and I very carefully prepared my chairman's speech simply by stringing together quotations from Asquith, Smuts, Lord Milner, Bob Cecil—you know, people like that, three hundred percent kosher, and that was my speech.

In due course there was a rumpus that I should preside at a "Bolshevik meeting"—"Bolsheviks" meaning people like Sam Morison of Harvard and John F. Moors, a leading banker of Boston. I remember Thomas Nelson Perkins having me to lunch. He said he wanted to talk with me. So I lunched with him. He was a very charming person and friendly in his heart toward me. His refrain was, "Why do you rock the boat?"

I said, "You get General Wood to stop rocking the boat which he is doing by these violent speeches, and I will stop doing my best not having him capsize it. That's all I'm trying to do. Why don't you talk to him about not rocking the boat? Why do you talk to me? You talk with the fellow with whom you agree, and ask me not to rock the boat because what you yourself admit were perfectly reasonable utterances rile people whom you regard as unreasonable. Then you come to me instead of dealing with your unreasonable friends."

He said, "You're a very unreasonable man."

I said, "Yes, I suppose that's what it adds up to."

Chafee without my knowledge wrote a long, detailed study of the *Abrams* case (sustaining the Sedition Act) in which Holmes wrote his famous dissent. Some people said that Chafee was inaccurate and therefore guilty of conduct unbecoming a scholar, and several of us, Pound, Frank Sayre who was a professor then at the law school, Edward B. Adams who was the librarian, Zach Chafee and I signed a petition saying that the President of the United States should commute the sentences from heavy sentences to lower sentences. That was our great offense, that we thought these people shouldn't be getting these heavy sentences which Holmes in his dissenting opinion so strongly condemned, though he couldn't do anything about it.

On May 21, 1921, a meeting was held by a committee voted to be appointed by the Board of Overseers, which is the vetoing body of Harvard University. Harvard University is governed by two bodies, a self-perpetuating body called the Corporation. There are seven Fellows of the Corporation of Harvard University with life tenure who perpetuate themselves, and then there is the Board of Overseers who are elected by the alumni of the university. Harvard is run by the Corporation, by the President and Fellows, but the Board of Overseers must approve permanent appointments and honorary degrees. They have the veto power. Well, the Board of Overseers voted to appoint a committee to look into the nefarious conduct of Chafee for writing this article and us for signing a petition to the President of the United States recommending that he use his pardoning power. They appointed a committee consisting of all lawyers, several of whom were among the most eminent in the land, Judge Sheldon, a very distinguished member of the Supreme Court of Massachusetts, Cardozo, then on the New York Court of Appeals, Judge Julian W. Mack, then a circuit judge, Augustus N. Hand, then a federal district judge, Grant, a probate judge in Boston, Morton, a federal district judge, and Jerry Smith, Marvin, Thomas and Dunbar who were lawyers.

This meeting was held on a sizzling hot day. Lowell took charge. He was the champion of the accused on a ground of his own. He told the Overseers, "If any of these people are fired, or anything is done to them," they could have the resignation of their President too. He was vindicating an important principle of his: that matters of this sort were none of the business of the Overseers, that the Board of Overseers isn't a disciplinary body, and so that which was to have been an inquisition against Chafee & Co. soon turned into a battle between President Lowell and Mr. Austen G. Fox, the lawyer for the protestants against Chafee.

Chafee gave a calm, detailed, factual account of the *Abrams* case, stated the grounds why he thought the result was unfair and why it was unwise to deal with what Holmes called "these poor and puny anonymities" as threatening the destruction of the nation and to give these brutal sentences. When Chafee got through he said very quietly what I always thought was one of the most impressive sentences I ever heard in my life. He said, "I come of a family that have been in America from the beginning of time. My people have been business people for generations. My people have been people of substance. They have made money. My family is a family that has money. I believe in property and I believe in making money, but I want my crowd to fight fair."

Then he sat down, and I tell you that really was a wonderful avowal of faith. More is said in that sentence than the famous credo of David Lilienthal before the Senate Committee sitting on his nomination on what it means to be an American, because Lilienthal's was a carefully prepared rhetorical manifesto, but Chafee's was a concentrated expression of devotion without rhetoric.

A little later Harvard needed to raise some money, and people said that they were told that they wouldn't give any money as long as Frankfurter was on the faculty. Either Sam Morison or Grenville Clark who was a member of the Harvard Corporation, said, "People wouldn't give anyhow. They always like to have a good excuse for not giving, blame it on somebody." Well, the upshot was that Harvard really profited by these alleged defections of mine because somebody must have brought it to the attention of Julius Rosenwald, or he heard about it, and he gave a very sizable contribution out of regard for the kind of things he thought Harvard represented for having me there.

18. *Zionist Movement*

I hope you will surround the correspondence I've shown you relative to the proposed elimination of yourself and others of the Brandeis-Mack group from Zionist councils, made apparently at the Cleveland Convention in 1921, with more in the way of illuminating insight.

I do not know what interests will be served, or who would pursue the interest of the ins and outs of Zionist personalities, difficulties and policies from the time a divergence emerged between the rigorous, economically oriented outlook of Justice Brandeis and the entire consequence of the disciplined, even if inspired, mind that he was, and the kind of passionate, romantic, quasi-messianic temperament of Weizmann so far as the realization of Herzl's dream of a Jewish Palestine. That doesn't mean that Weizmann wasn't shrewd, that he wasn't hard-headed, that he wasn't even in some respects cunning and crafty, and it doesn't mean that he wasn't a disciplined scientist, as he was, but when it came to the promotion of Zionist interests he wasn't preeminently a scientist. He was preeminently a man filled with a great dream which because of its adventuresomeness, daring to his mind and anyone's mind, required something more and beyond the careful calculation of an enterprise influenced by economic considerations, or the kind of hard-headed regard for details that was so characteristic of Mr. Justice Brandeis. That doesn't mean that Brandeis wasn't a dreamer too, but the whole bent of, not his temperament, but certainly what experience had done to his temperament, made him not oratorical, not passion stirring, not sky-scaling in his speech and even in his thinking, but made him so much more—what shall I say, well, disciplined is the word, than Weizmann. Different pressures had molded the two men. Brandeis's pressures were intellectual and the pressures of imagination. They weren't the pressures of felt anti-Semitism, the pressures of the whole background of the Russian Pale, the pressures of actually being in communion with masses of Jews in Europe under the awful weight of squalid conditions, triumphing over them by a spiritual serenity. They were indeed—Jews in the mass are not now—people of the Book, and there was this sense of immediacy, or urgency, of not counting costs financially speaking but having a daring, micawberish outlook on life, that somehow or other God will provide, that the messianic grant given by Providence to the Jews will somehow or other answer the difficulties. Brandeis wanted it answered by a balance sheet.

In addition to that there was the inevitable clash of two powerful personalities and also, I suppose ever so much more in Weizmann's case than in Brandeis's case, the sense of rivalry. The notion of leadership in the Zionist Movement was a very potent factor in the movement. Theodore Herzl was the undisputed leader—magnificent, handsome creature that he must have been. Herzl was succeeded by other people, and then by Weizmann through the force of circumstances, his own genius, his relationship to the British Government in the First World War, the way in which he fired the imagination and, if not phlegmatic, certainly skeptical natures of people like Balfour whose imagination was not easily fired, or a hard-headed fellow like Smuts. These were great triumphs which vindicated to Weizmann the sense of power which he must have felt. Out of the West comes not young Lochinvar, but a judge with a composed temperament, a non-oratorical temperament, and almost inevitably challenges Weizmann's predominance, Weizmann's position of leadership.

I saw that very early. I became thick with Weizmann early and realized that through circumstances this jealousy would develop without any one wanting it to develop. The temperaments were different. I saw early that they would clash since each naturally felt that he was a master of his respective situation. Moreover, Jewry in eastern Europe, theretofore the mainstay of Zionism, more or less collapsed; at least it was weakened in its resources, its facilities, its strength and therefore in its total influence by virtue of the First World War. All that was transferred to America. The center of the Zionist Movement had been Berlin, and the war had made it impossible for the center of the movement to remain there. America was becoming increasingly the power that called the tune. There was the same strain between European leaders, Weizmann particularly, and Brandeis and the Americans that there was between the leaders of the English Government and the leaders of the American Government, just a natural friction. Almost in the nature of the situation there was involved a certain amount of subordination on the part of those who were previously on top.

Weizmann knew I was a Brandeis man, and he couldn't indulge in open warfare against Brandeis. Brandeis had too much authority with the other European leaders. Naturally you go after the subordinates, and he thought that I was probably as close to Brandeis as anybody. Our relations, Weizmann's and mine, were never strained. In the Cleveland Convention the Brandeis-Mack group were displaced by those who supported Weizmann in the contest between the Brandeis view and the Weizmann view so far as there was a difference in the plan for the development of Palestine. Brandeis wanted all the organs of the movement, the banks, the funds, everything to be as conservatively competent as the National City Bank, then the leading bank in New York. Weizmann's relations with me never had any strain, though since he was for ousting the Brandeis-Mack group naturally I was on the other side.

I remember vividly partly his shrewdness, partly his gregariousness—he was a very gregarious person, but he could also retire into a deep groove. He was a temperamental fellow. On the whole he was much more manic than depressive, but I remember that as we were about to go into the hall where the convention was held, and according to the order of events I was to make a speech that night attacking his crowd, defending the administration as it was called, the Brandeis-Mack group, he warmly shook hands with me, and I felt, "How shrewd that was. You can't attack a

man who warmly shook your hand two minutes before—at least I can't."

But I had a very good time because I was on my feet for four hours—four full fours!—and they tried to hoot me down and generally behaved the way the Irish contingent did in the House of Commons when Parnell was their leader, that is, make as much trouble as possible. I remember saying, "I have as much time at my disposal as you have. I can stick this out just as long as you will, so you'd better listen."

There I was—four hours! But I don't think that Weizmann ever harbored any ill feelings toward me. Quite the contrary. We became after a while even closer friends than ever before. He was very eager to try to persuade me to move to Palestine. There was a breach between him and Brandeis that was never healed because Brandeis thought he was guilty of a sharp practice in a certain negotiation. A man once asked Brandeis to "forgive and forget," and Brandeis said, "I can forgive, but if you ask me to forget, you ask me to give up experience."

De Haas is a different story. He was an Englishman, an early disciple of Herzl. I don't know how or when he came to this country, but he was the editor of a Jewish paper in Boston. Justice Brandeis was a man of great loyalty and personal devotion. He had a sense of indebtedness to de Haas because it was de Haas who really, effectively, got him interested in Zionism. De Haas was a man of very considerable ability, but also of very considerable irritabilities. Irritability implies that he was irritable. What I want to convey is that he irritated other people. He had very few friends. The only people who were really for him in the movement were Justice Brandeis, Judge Mack and I. I think I can fairly say that we were less perturbed than others by his egotism. With full awareness of the limitation of a man we go for his qualities. De Haas was a little crude. He lacked tact. He didn't realize that there are various ways of skinning a cat, and he would skin the cat the hard way, the insensitive way. Instead of saying, "Well, I hadn't thought of it that way," he'd say, "You're wrong!"

Instead of leaving the impression on his hearer that he was wrong, he took a meat axe with which to demonstrate that he was wrong. Also he was absolutely devoted to Brandeis and regarded Weizmann as an unworthy rival of his hero, just as Harry Hopkins had a feeling of a mistress toward President Roosevelt which had to be taken note of. In the first encounter between Hopkins and Churchill, Churchill was made to realize that he mustn't say anything that would make Harry Hopkins feel that he, Churchill, was as good as Roosevelt. De Haas had this feeling, that he was the servant of the great man, and Weizmann was a rival.

Also there was a period in the Zionist Movement when the British Government proposed a vast tract of Uganda as a homeland for the Jewish people. The British Government was going to work that out with the Jewish leaders. That begot a great schism in the movement between the Ugandists and the anti-Ugandists, those who thought that Palestine has a spiritual, inherent historic connection with the Jewish people, while Uganda was merely a piece of land. Palestine wasn't a piece of land. As a young man de Haas was against Uganda, and I think Weizmann came, as a very young man, to the note of the Jewish leaders through his opposition to Herzl on that score. The difficulties between de Haas and Weizmann dated back to some historic rivalry at the Jewish Congress. There was friction between those two people, and Weizmann was less than wise in dealing with de Haas, and de Haas was less than tactful in dealing with Weizmann, so the request for de Haas's elimination was not a surprising thing because he got on the nerves of most American leaders.

De Haas by virtue of his close relation to Brandeis would arrogate to himself the right to speak for him. Some people resented that. They would take it from Brandeis, but they wouldn't take it second hand, sometimes suspecting, not knowing whether he professed to speak with authority, or underwrote his authority by claiming that he spoke on behalf of Brandeis—oh, the kind of frictions among personalities, the kind of rivalries and difficulties that exist in every movement, every collectivity. These men were concerned with Palestine, the achievement of securing a declaration which became the Balfour Declaration, then getting it formalized, institutionalized, internationalized through the peace conference and finally, actually making the thing move in Palestine. Well, whether it's this or that, or whether it's the Republican Party or the Democratic Party, or the Labor movement, internal difficulties are the history of every movement.

Weizmann had a very charming wife. She was herself a minor scientist. They were studying science when they met at one of the Swiss universities where they married. She was a very handsome, distinguished looking creature—absolutely, wholesouledly absorbed by him, devoted to him, a person quite in her own right who absolutely fused her life with his. I've seldom seen so striking an illustration of a woman having an important and full life though not having a job of her own. Unlike so many American women of lesser quality, she thought she could be a person even though she fused her life with his. She didn't fuse her independence. She didn't think that she could only sustain her independence by licking stamps, envelopes, doing bell ringing for somebody else.

Weizmann was a man of great charm. He was linguistically very gifted. I don't know how many languages he mastered thoroughly so that he could make eloquent speeches in all of them. He was an excellent debater in German, French, Hebrew, Russian and I believe Italian too. He was very persuasive and very quick. He put his hooks into Balfour whom he met at Manchester when he was a reader in chemistry at the University of Manchester. I think that it was through C. P. Scott, the editor of the *Manchester Guardian,* that he met Balfour who got talking with this interesting youngish man and asked him, "Well why do you want to settle in Jerusalem? Why don't you want to settle in this large available land in Uganda?"

Weizmann turned to Balfour and said, "Why do you want London? Why don't you go somewhere else?"

"Oh, we have London," said Balfour.

"Well, the Jews once had Jerusalem."

That made Balfour sit up. He was this kind of a detached aristocrat and liked great self-confidence, daring and challenge, and they became great friends. Weizmann was a most persuasive person. He was of a very affectionate nature. He radiated authority. He was temperamental. He would move from gaiety to ferocity of speech. The gamut of his powers was very extensive. I suppose you have to count him among the great men of our time without any question; indeed, my friend, Isaiah Berlin, who became enamored of him, thinks that he was the greatest of all these people, was a greater personality than Churchill or Roosevelt. Berlin knew him intimately. That Weizmann should affect a person like Isaiah Berlin that way tells a lot. Weizmann seized the imagination and enlisted the will of people like Lloyd George, Balfour, Winston Churchill and Smuts. Winston Churchill was devoted to him. Weizmann had entre to all these people. His passion was contagious. He was a wonderful raconteur, and when he stood up to make a speech, he lifted himself in such a way that he was much taller than he was. He was a sizable man: he had that something that makes a difference, that makes the great man, that something which when Toscanini ascended the podium made him a different fellow from other distinguished conductors. There was something electric about him.

He was implacable in the pursuit of his object—implacable! And also, the other thing about him—and that I should have left it out! it's the most important thing—he himself said, "I have blinders on."

Nothing else interested him except the realization of a Jewish Palestine, but he had the kind of insight, understanding and imagination that made him realize that a lot of other things were relevant to that. He was interested in everything that was relevant, but he had blinders on. He didn't care what else happened. He wouldn't read the newspapers about anything else, except in so far as his instinct told him that this, somehow or other, was related to Palestine. The whole of life became for him a function of the realization of the reclamation, the rehabilitation, the investiture of Palestine by the Jewish people. And in that respect I've often thought—I knew Weizmann of course very, very intimately—how he reminds me of another friend of mine, Jean Monnet. He too has blinders on. For the things that he's interested in he doesn't dissipate his energies, or doesn't take time off, or doesn't listen to anything else. They are very much alike, powerful wills. In government affairs the realization of objects depends on the resolution of men—that's the difference between statesmen who matter and statesmen who don't—resolution, pertinacity, patience and persistence, and in Weizmann, as in Jean Monnet, the central quality that I call resolution, will, was manifested to an extreme intensity. Most people scatter their energies, or enfeeble them, or say, "Yes, but. . . ."—well, there were no buts in Weizmann's makeup.

People said a Jewish national home was a "dream." It was Herzl who said, "If you will it, it is no dream." Weizmann realized this dream. He was a volcano either in eruption or in training, and he couldn't go on to be as old as Gladstone, or, in a totally different way, Holmes, and so there came a time when it required some other energies, another messianic character: i.e., Ben Gurion, the present prime minister of Israel.

At the Peace Conference was Weizmann a good organizer of other talents?

He was no organizer. He was a soloist. Weizmann was no administrator at all. He had no sense of time. When he had an appointment with the prime minister at eleven o'clock, you may be sure that he was there at eleven o'clock, but if he had an appointment for eleven o'clock with you, you may be sure he wouldn't be there. Then too he always had a devoted crew that could attend to administration.

Take TR. Talk about a good administrator. He soon found that his then Attorney General wasn't a good sound limb to lean on, a good solid oak tree, or to change my figure, that he wasn't a wise adviser, and so he paid no attention to the Attorney General, but would consult a subordinate of the Attorney General, i.e., Henry L. Stimson at the time he was United States Attorney. Or TR would read an article—this happened while I was in law school—on rate regulation. Somebody called it to his attention, or he read it. Off went a wire asking this fellow to come down, and he turned out to be a student at the Harvard Law School. In short, these are men who represent the creative in that most difficult of arts, the art of government.

I remember during the war when I was in England in 1918, finding myself at Cliveden, residence of the Astors'. Lady Astor's sister and I were friends, and I got a message to come down. Balfour was there, the second most important member of the cabinet. Lord Milner was there. It was one of these English week-ends. I always thought that if I ever wrote a book on English government, I'd call it *Weekends.* Lady Astor got going on Winston Churchill, a vituperative speech against Churchill. I don't know what the source of the enmity was between them, but she got going lambasting Churchill. Churchill in the First World War was involved in the Gallipoli business in which, I think, all the best thought now is that he was right, that it was simply ineffectiveness of execution through no fault of his. She went on and on and on. Balfour was sitting next to her. I was drinking all this in and finally—all things come to an end, even Nancy Astor's powers of damning Churchill—Balfour very tenderly put his hand on hers and said, "Nancy, all you say about Winston may be true, but Winston has ideas, and to a statesman with ideas much shall be forgiven."

When you have ideas and the will to translate them into action and institutions, conduct, then you've got some powerful forces. One can't think of a character less like Weizmann or Churchill than Lincoln, but I'm prepared to defend the thesis that he had as much pertinacity and also the blinders on to everything except winning the war as those two men with reference to their objectives. Nothing swayed him, no nonsense from friends, no provocation, no fuming, no vituperative onslaughts by Horace Greeley would make a difference. No outcry about emancipating the slaves until he thought the time was right. He was swerved neither to the right nor to the left on what he clearly saw. He was a quiet man. He didn't blow up. He wasn't temperamental. He wasn't ferocious in speech as Weizmann could be, nor did he weep as Winston Churchill has been known to weep, but he had that iron will, that inflexible determination to pursue the road that leads to an end.

Those qualities seem to be very rare in combination—insight, seeing the goal and realizing the long, long trail that lies ahead before you can reach the end. I suspect that it operates in all manifestations of man. Anybody can construct wonderful policies on paper. If you don't have to persuade anybody, if you don't have to overcome opposition, if you don't have to keep a show going, you may be completely uninterested, or inimical to organization, but you've got to have secretaries and typists, and they have to be paid, so that success depended on organization even though Weizmann paid no attention to it.

Weizmann was a challenging figure of great intellectual and emotional, prophetic powers. He also had some interesting idiosyncrasies, or odd talents. He never forgot a telephone number of anybody. It was perfectly fantastic! Ten years after he'd keep it in his head, "I don't know whether it's still that number—Oliver 6735." He was perfectly uncanny about telephone numbers. I think on the whole as I visualize Weizmann in my mind's eye, as I talk here, and as he comes back cinematographically, I think he got more childish pleasure out of that quiddity of his than almost anything else, a kind of stunt—you know, like the fellow who could keep ten balls in the air. This was in London, and he'd remember the New York numbers of so-and-so. He'd never carry a book. It was all in his head.

Was there much humor to this man?

He was a very witty man—oh, yes. "Humor"—well, wit and sardonic, of the graver kind. During the Second World War I remember his coming from Portugal. He'd been in Lisbon where there was a concentration of people trying to get away from the Nazi countries, and he was describing this scene. He said, "They tell a story of an old Jew with a long beard, a very old, orthodox Jew. There was a long line and finally he gets into the presence of the American consul in Lisbon to get on the quota list. This competent official, hardened consul, 'Your name?'

"He was very meek, humble and deferential. This fellow represents the United States, is the United States in his eye. He determines his fate, his destiny, and he gives his name.

"Where do you come from?"

"Roumania."

"Where are you a citizen of?"

"Roumania."

"Very sorry. The quota is all filled for Roumania for the next eight years. If you come back here eight years from now, you can get on the quota."

"The old Jew said, 'Eight years?'

"Yes, eight years."

"He bows deferentially, takes off his hat, and leaves. He gets to the door and then comes back and says, 'Mr. Consul.'

"Yes, what is it?"

"You said that I should come back eight years from today?"

"Yes, yes."

"Shall I come in the morning, or in the afternoon?"

That's what the Germans call *Galgenhumor*—humor of the gallows. The poignancy of that story!

19. *The Election of 1924*

A colleague of mine at the Harvard Law School with whom I got into a tangle about some question of law once chided me, indeed, closed a contentious argument between us by saying, "You take law awfully seriously."

I said, "That's one accusation against which I plead guilty without reservation."

I am bound to say hardly another member of the Harvard Law faculty would have thought of making such an accusation. I do take law very seriously, deeply seriously, because fragile as reason is and limited as law is as the expression of the institutionalized medium of reason, that's all we have standing between us and the tyranny of mere will and the cruelty of unbridled, undisciplined feeling. And since the Department of Justice for me doesn't merely have the name of Justice, but really is concerned with the guardianship of Justice in our political national life, naturally nothing aroused me more than that the headship of that Department should be a sordid corruptionist like Harry Daugherty. Not only was Senator Wheeler not supported by good men in his effort to bring to the light of day the truth about the corrosive, corrupting developments, methods, preoccupations of the Department of Justice under Daugherty, but influences within the Government tried to unhorse Senator Wheeler by what I believed to be a continued case, what we call a "frame-up." This aroused the deepest feelings in me which I afterwards expressed in rather pertinacious, persistent correspondence with Harlan F. Stone when he became Attorney General who, it seemed to me, continued on lame grounds an indictment which I thought had been most outrageously brought to pass by his corrupt predecessor.

The spoliation of our inestimable, irreplacable natural resources with corruption of cabinet officers in getting them, which Senator Thomas J. Walsh of Montana disclosed in his investigations regarding the oil leases by Secretary Fall, and the investigation of his junior colleague, Senator Burton K. Wheeler, into the lack of guardianship of others in addition to his own corruption and the unsavory crowd about Harry Daugherty were projected into the campaign of 1924 since Senator La Follette was himself, I think, the original prime mover regarding the matters which Senator Walsh was investigating. The third-party movement was, I suppose, fundamentally a moralistic movement because the basic, rudimentary cleanliness in government had been projected as the immediately transcendent issue. Tragic that ordinary honesty should be a campaign issue, but that which so often was the proper slogan in American municipal campaigns—"Turn the rascals out!"—really became a relative issue in the 1924 campaign.

Relevant to all this was the general materialism of the country. "Prosperity" was in the saddle. People were more or less prosperous, and there was fantastic money-making on the exchange through gambling in securities. A professor at Harvard who is still alive in his ninetieth-odd year wrote a book to prove that this thing was a sort of self-perpetuating, "non-reversible trend" and a "new plateau of prices." Really it was the American South Sea Bubble Era. It wasn't 'til five years later that the bubble really burst, but it got bigger and bigger and bigger.

This was brought home to me in very concrete ways; namely, through the bright students, the best men intellectually speaking, the top men at the Harvard Law School. They were sons of ministers, farmers, mechanics and small storekeepers, and the whole drive, the whole propulsion, or compulsion almost, for their future were the attractions of New York. It was a perfect illustration that if leadership at the bar meant being a key figure in a New York law office, meaning by that a fellow who makes a vast amount of money, if the men who won the most esteemed gifts or prizes of the profession were deemed to be the great leaders of the bar, the law of imitation operated on the young. That's what they wanted to be. The man who goes in for the practice of the law not only wants to exert his powers and have the satisfaction of that kind of fulfillment, but how does he know that he has fully satisfied his powers, or is functioning to the full, except by seeing how the prizes are awarded. And so it was to me a saddening thing the extent to which fellows who came from smaller towns, or cities—and by "smaller" I mean Cleveland, Dayton, Seattle, let alone really small towns—looked to New York. The New York offices made monetarily attractive responses. They started them off with much more money than they could get in small towns. They didn't count the cost of living in New York, or its non-material costs, or they'd say that they would go there for a short time.

I'd say, "You don't go there for a short time. The possibilities are that you'll marry, have a family, and you don't just pick up stakes and go back to Youngstown, or Kalamazoo, or Lincoln, Nebraska. You live in New York, and you'd better find out what kind of life it is. You're a young fellow. You'll park your wife and your baby in some suburb and around 6:30 you'll phone your wife, 'Darling, I'm awfully sorry. I have to stay in tonight. Don't wait for me. I might or might not be able to make the eight o'clock, or the 9:27.' Then the competitive spirit sets in, and you become more and more geared to this materialistic pursuit. To concentrate the brains of the country in New York isn't good for the country; it isn't good for you."

The bar was indifferent. They were too busy themselves shoring up rickety structures, being in on cuts. Then the mere intellectual excitement of doing these things that seemed so big and so important—front-page news how one concern after another was consolidated, front-page news that stocks yesterday reached astronomical figures, etcetera, and the whole atmosphere of the profession was that of a feverish pursuit which expressed itself predominantly in not merely money returns, but the influence and the position of esteem, being president of the bar association, or this, that and the other thing, these so-called money-making leaders had achieved.

I remember an experience of a third-year man, a Boston man, a Yankee, the son of a rather important Boston lawyer whose intellectual endowments made it reasonably certain that if he went into one of the Boston offices as an apprentice, in no time he would gain recognition there and eventually obtain a partnership with a sufficiently lucrative practice, but there was the lure of New York. I remember talking with him and suggesting that he would be happy in Boston, staying in his habitat, but there was the lure of the *ignis fatuis*. He thought that he'd go to New York and canvass the offices, and I said, "All right. I'm sorry that you too fall for this lure."

He went down to New York, spent two or three days, came back, and he said that he had decided to accept the offer he'd had from a Boston firm, and I asked him, "What made you so clear, as you now say you are clear, that that's where you want to practice?"

He said, "I had an experience that sort of took all the savor and flavor of New York out of my mind and made me feel that that isn't the kind of a life I want to lead."

"What was it?"

He said that it was a leading lawyer in the big firm of Cravath and Henderson. He'd had a note to this lawyer whom I knew. He was a little after my time at the law school. "He spoke of the opportunities in New York, that they excelled the opportunities of any other place. 'A man with real guts, real fire, ought to go where the biggest opportunities are, and New York affords the biggest opportunity. I was the son of a poor minister, no money at all, brought up on a farm, came to the Harvard Law School with no money at all. I then came to New York and this firm, and now I have an apartment which has eight bathrooms.' That finished me," said my young friend, "that he should talk of life's success in terms of eight bathrooms! That finished me!"

Of course one can say that's an unfair example—I don't offer it as a statistical sample—but it sheds its own light, and it might come within the doctrine of the sociological quantum theory. If you're once able to live on Park Avenue, that's supposed to show something. It does. It shows that your standards are all wrong. To me one of the striking things was the difference in appeal when the great South Sea Bubble burst in 1929, and when the New Deal came in. Then the best men wanted to come to Washington because they were excited by the nature of the problems.

Of course fashion has a lot to do with it. The old set the standards, and the young, until there's a rebellion or something happens—happily there is that discontinuity—and the young respond to it, but New York was the attraction, New York was the drive, New York was the fashion, New York was the lure until after the depression, not that New York had ceased to be the lure to some extent, but other things were competing with it, other opportunities. But there isn't any doubt about that era, what I call the Byzantine period of American history, that William A. White has well characterized in his life of Coolidge, *A Puritan in Babylon.* Coolidge was a kind of Puritan, but he thought the Babylonians were the thing. He made a speech once about George Washington as a businessman. Coolidge was a great hero. A crowd of us in Cambridge sat around one night after dinner—you know, the way people play acrostics—and the game was what single word most comprehensively conveyed the quality of Coolidge. I think the prize was awarded to my wife. She said, "Arid." But it pleased the Babylonians that their priest should be such a Puritan. It pleased them to think that while they were country club and all the rest of it—you know, that was the life for the people—in the White House there was a "representative of virtue." They knew that the flesh pots aren't all there is to civilization; in fact, not the most desirable part of civilization, but while they were pursuing the flesh pots there was the priest tending the eternal flame.

I remember that I made some speeches. The 1924 campaign was a three-cornered affair. I remember debating Eliot Wadsworth, a prominent Republican, a prominent Harvard man, with whom I had the pleasantest and friendliest relations, and we debated in the Harvard Union on the campaign. Eliot Wadsworth recalls the debate, and it's nice of him to be so generous as he is to this day in telling the story of what I did to him in the debate, but he was so helpless there. He said that he came there to discuss the issues in the campaign, namely, should we elect Coolidge or Davis or La Follette, and "Professor Frankfurter is talking about economic matters."

The idea was that that wasn't fair. I took the position, I took in every statement I made, that the question for me was what direction are you giving the country, what are you building? The campaign was for me an educational opportunity and not giving reasons why Coolidge was a better man than John Davis or vice-versa, so that I hardly mentioned the candidates except to say what was in their heads in talking about what kind of direction they would give to the country if they got into the White House.

There was, as there always is, talk connected with the third-party campaign, "You throw your vote away. You throw your vote away."

Well, it all depends on what you conceive the vote to be for, and if you think of an election not merely as a discrete, isolated episode, but as part of a process of the unfolding of American life, then you don't throw your vote away. If enough people vote for La Follette so that the other parties say, "Hello. Here are people who can determine the election. Why did they vote for this fellow? What is there about this?" In other words, third parties whether they survive as the Republican Party survived after the Fremont election, or whether they do not survive as the Bull Moose Party did not survive after 1912, and as the La Follette Progressive Party did not survive after 1924, may serve as a ferment, and through their death new things are born. It's like the chrysalis that dies and something else comes out of it so that merely getting the patronage for the next four years isn't all there is to politics, though that's what the politicians think.

Wasn't there any difference in your mind between Coolidge and Davis?

I didn't have to vote for either, happily. Of course John Davis was an extremely attractive figure. He was a man of great charm, one of the most charming men I encountered in my life. I'd seen something of him when he was Solicitor General and I was in the Wilson Administration. We had some professional work together. He was an admirable type of lawyer—in the sense that he was one of the few successful lawyers who cared strongly about the standards of the profession. When he was in the House, he made one of the best speeches in favor of the provision of the Clayton Act restricting the use of injunctions in labor cases. He was an engaging, a most engaging personality, a great success as Ambassador to the Court of St. James's. He was a widely cultivated man, read and retained what he read, spoke with elegance and distinction, had great humor and grace. I think he got into debt as Ambassador. He had an offer to go to that important New York law firm, Stetson, Jennings and Russell. Frank Polk who had been the Undersecretary of State in Wilson's Administration was a great friend of his, and Polk in turn was a very attractive fellow—very.

Frank Polk was a fellow who had played a part, and it might have been a decisive part, in my life. You know, if Cleopatra's nose had been one millimeter shorter, Antony might not have fallen for her as he did, and a lot of other things would not have happened. That doesn't mean that everything is chance in the world. Bury defines "chance" as "the valuable collision of two or more independent chains of causes"—valuable meaning that it is attended with more or less important consequences. Now the fact that Cleopatra's nose was what it was and the fact that Antony was there when he was are two independent causes colliding. I'm more and more struck with chance in that sense, contingency. When Frank Polk was Corporation Counsel under John Purroy Mitchel, a great reform Mayor in New York, he asked me to come and head the appellate division of the Corporation Counsel's Office. That is one of the biggest law offices in the world. That was an attractive offer in itself. I was at that time getting forty-five hundred dollars as law officer with Secretary of War Stimson, and Polk offered me ten thousand dollars. Had I had a strong money sense which I never had and haven't—a great friend of mine said that I have a bias against money, and I said, "The world isn't suffering from that"—but had I had that sense I would have been tempted to do that. Well, if I had, a lot of things would have been different. Frank Polk was a charming person, a delightful person, and he was the instrument of persuasion in getting John Davis to practice law with Stetson, Jennings and Russell. Davis was a much more attractive figure than Coolidge. In the White House he undoubtedly wouldn't have been as complacent, as passive as Coolidge was.

I forget now what the source of my knowledge was, but I do remember that the source was dependable. It concerns George Harvey, that strange, cynical figure in American politics who was in a way the begetter of Wilson as a presidential candidate. Wilson jettisoned him because he was tied up with Wall Street, and Harvey became an implacable hater of Wilson. Harvey was one of the people around Harding, one of the king-makers of the Republican Party, and he became Ambassador to Great Britain. On his way home he saw President Coolidge, and the President consulted Colonel Harvey. President Coolidge at that time was grappling with two major national issues. One was whether we should join the World Court. For a number of years that was a bothersome carbuncle on the neck of the Republican Administration. The other problem was a strike in the coal mines which was getting more and more ominous.

The President consulted Colonel Harvey about the World Court. The virus of isolation strongly infested the body of the Republican Party. Root was the begetter of the World Court, and there was constant pressure on the part of the goody goodies in the United States to join it, as though the World Court had much relation to peace maintenance. The issues that are justiciable between nations are very limited, and Coolidge asked Ambassador Harvey, "Should we join?"

Harvey is reported to have said, "I don't think there's any hurry about our joining."

Coolidge said in effect, "I'm so glad to hear that because that's what I think."

The other question was what about the coal strike. "I've just arrived from London and don't know anything about it. I don't know what the issue is, but I think that on the whole generally it's undesirable to have the federal government interfere in a local strike."

"That's what I think," said President Coolidge.

That's the way great issues were decided! Any advice that expressed the principle of negation seemed to manifest the fount of statesmanship.

If you're going to get many parties representing the various economic and social interests in the country having such diversified interests, you're bound to get government badly balanced where the result is a bargaining coalition. Two parties give a kind of assurance of stability, strength, but you can't have two parties unless each party is within itself a loose federation of these diverse interests. So the reasons for our federal system are reflected in the federal aspect of our parties. The Democratic Party has in it people of varying and conflicting views. This is brought out sharply in the recent debate on civil rights, but it's true also of the Republican Party. The hope then was that you could introduce loosening influences so that the community that there was and is between liberal-minded Republicans and liberal-minded Democrats as against conservative Democrats and conservative Republicans would give you a real division.

Everybody recognizes that society can't remain stagnant, and change is the law of life. There are of course temperamental differences, reinforced by reflection, regarding the pace at which change should be introduced in the conduct of affairs, the response of institutions and laws and action to changes, if life itself is not to become dead, and the rate of change. I suppose that's the most interesting aspect of the times in which we live, the rapidity in the rate of change brought about not by law but brought about by events and circumstances to which law must conform more or less. I used to ask my classes, "Who was the most important law reformer of the Eighteenth and Nineteenth Centuries?"

They'd guess, "Blackstone, or Mansfield, or Jeremy Bentham," and after I'd get all their guesses I'd say, "Watt, the inventor of the steam engine."

That's an illustration of the transforming events outside of law, the central problem of how organized government is to adjust itself to events outside it. I've sworn to live whatever years are allotted to me without ever using the phrase, "This atomic age," but the changes that have taken place within the last ten years in nuclear physics and the effect of those changes are of course enormous, and profoundly influence politics. The thought in 1924 was that somehow or other you can bring like and like together and then have a real difference.

I wrote a piece about La Follette and said of his program that I probably disagreed with nineteen out of twenty planks. It was something like that. The specifics I didn't care about. I knew they wouldn't matter. On the whole I'm a great disbeliever in specific promises by candidates during election because they haven't any idea what they will face. This was illustrated in Canada recently. In Mr. Diefenbaker's cabinet, including himself, there isn't a single member who had ever been in a cabinet, not one. They'd been in opposition using slogans for twenty years, and they got elected and found what William James called "hard and intractable facts." The slogans don't have much bearing, and yet somehow or other most people aren't as jauntily irresponsible, or gay, or candid—call him what you will—as Wendell Willkie who said, "That's just campaign oratory." Responsible men who have been mouthing these slogans just can't say, "Well, it's all the bunk." Contrariwise, St. Laurent's cabinet who are now in opposition have never been in opposition. They don't know what it is to criticize the government. George Humphrey, the most self-confident of the lot in Eisenhower's first administration, said after he'd been in office, "I think I've learned a good deal since I've been Secretary of the Treasury." I wonder, though, how much he learned.

That's why the opinions of most public men on important issues are relatively worthless because they don't know the details, and it's the details that determine judgment. Generalities don't amount to a hill of beans. Everybody agrees with them. Everybody's for Justice, Right and Decency, and everybody wants to have lower taxes, fine school houses on the basis of lower taxes. Everybody wants security, but security which does not in the slightest affect the finances of the country, and so on and so forth. Everybody wants to preserve the natural resources, but there's all the difference in the world in how you preserve them, or how you exploit them. People who are out of office don't know the hard, inescapable facts that you have to encounter, or disregard, and if the latter, they bust in your face.

The law is full of that. Most lawyers hand out these generalities which nobody disputes. Holmes said, "But the point that matters is whether the boy got his finger pinched."

I remember seeing Theodore Roosevelt after he was out of office and leaving him and having the feeling that expressed itself in a remark I made to a friend, "I just saw the most tragic case of unemployment." Roosevelt could only function when he had to deal with a problem. Al Smith also is a striking and tragic illustration of that. If his pragmatic mind had to deal with a problem whether penology or unemployment, his hardheadedness and sense of justice came into play, but sitting up on the eighty-seventh floor of the Empire State Building and discoursing abstractedly on things he was no good at all. Holmes, the philosopher, could do that because he got his directions out of thought, but a man like Al Smith particularly, but even TR and most people, haven't got the capacity of imagination and insight that justifiably led Holmes to say, "I don't know facts. I merely know their significance."

The specific program of La Follette meant nothing to me, but the general direction in which he was going meant everything to me.

I wish you'd tell the story Mrs. Frankfurter likes to tell, the comment made in her hearing at the Forum in Boston the evening Laski spoke and you chaired the meeting.

Harold Laski would come to this country every other year, and he'd stay with us at Cambridge. He used to come up to Boston to talk at the Ford Hall Forum which was one of the earliest forums in the United States. I think the first one was the People's Institute down at Cooper Union, from attendance at which I got most of my education. Ford Hall was one of these things, and it was the center of a polyglot neighborhood, most of the attendants, the listeners, were radically minded. David Niles was a director of it, a most disinterested creature, absolutely disinterested, that rare thing. We dined at our house and then went to the hall in a taxi. Within a few minutes of reaching Ford Hall, located back of the State House in Boston, I said to Laski, "Harold, what are you going to talk about?"

"Oh," he said, "you know, a critique of our economic system."

"Harold, you know you give your audience a foundation, a philosophy, evidence for their discontent, but you don't have to stimulate that insight, that feeling, or that outlook in them. What you do need to stimulate is how hard it is to achieve a better society."

You know, most radicals think that all they have to do is just kick the other fellow out and everything will be lovely. He said, "Well, what should I talk about?"

"You've just been through the round-table conference"—this was the round-table conference with Gandhi, Nehru and Company with the British on Indian affairs, presided over by the then Lord Chancellor Sankey. Laski had been there as assistant to Sankey—"why don't you deal with that in making them realize how difficult it is to translate into actuality the dreams of your head, mind and heart. You know it isn't merely the Left in this country. All you have to do is canvass the professors at Harvard, and they think that all you have to do is to get the Raj to take his boot off the neck of India, and then India will be the Garden of Eden, or Heaven. That's all that needs to be done. Get the British out, and everything will be lovely. You know that is far from being true. Why don't you talk to them about India, tell them the nature of the problems, their complexities, their intractabilities, what will confront India when it does get home rule"—nobody thought then in terms of full, complete independence. "Interstitially you can get in all your grips, your Marxism, and all the rest of it, but make them feel that government is the toughest thing in the world, and make them see that rhetoric is something very different from governing and administration."

"All right."

By that time we had arrived at Ashburton Place where Ford Hall was. I was to be chairman that night. That's all the preliminary talk there was to that extraordinary performance of his. I don't know who else could have achieved it on either side of the Atlantic. It was then nearly eight o'clock, and in no time I had to be on my feet and introduce Professor Laski. There he stood, each hand on the lapel of his coat—no gesture—and for one hour he delivered an address on India which could have been taken down and published in book form without correcting anything—all these long sentences and all these qualifying phrases in apple-pie order. To be sure he was loaded. He had lived with this subject for several months or years, if you will, but that kind of quick mobilization of your knowledge and the capacity to put it out with such architectural completeness and finished beauty of speech was a feat of the highest order.

Then came the question period of an hour, and I, this poor professor who thinks relevance is important, said, "Well, now we've just had this wonderful address from Professor Laski, and your questions should relate to what he was talking about. We'll begin on this side with the balcony and then we'll move down, moving from left to right."

So I started to take questions, and the second question was, "What does Professor Laski think of Calvin Coolidge?"

That was not very closely related to India, and so I said, "That's a very interesting question, but some other time Professor Laski will answer it."

There was grumbling. Other questions came along, such as "Don't you think we should have a minimum wage higher than thirty cents an hour?" whatever it was. I began to rule out these questions and say, "Do please ask questions pertaining to India. That's a vast enough territory."

This went on, and there was a rumbling, a premonition of a revolution. My wife, sitting in the back of the floor, overheard a woman behind her say in a tone of exasperation with this presiding pedant, "Vat a chairman! Vat a chairman!"

My wife afterwards told me about it with great delight. Wasn't she pleased! Well, at last I gave up and let them ask anything, "Don't you think we ought to have proportional representation in Oregon?" or "What do you think of a unicameral instead of a bicameral legislature?"—though they didn't use those words, but they'd ask about Iceland, not about India, or "Don't you think we ought to have the people elect the judges?" And so on and so on. I learned a deep lesson, namely, the limited appeal that relevance has for a discussion.

20. *Sacco and Vanzetti*

Perhaps the "rapier" way to put what is essential to what you call the "drama of Sacco-Vanzetti" was expressed in a remark made to me by John F. Moors about "two wops." Moors was a Yankee of Yankees, a Bostonian of Bostonians, an intimate, close personal friend; indeed, a Harvard classmate of President Lowell and a member of the Harvard Corporation. His friendship with Lowell survived without strain despite Moors's nonconformist attitude, and indeed he fought hard for the cause of Sacco-Vanzetti. But he said to me after it was all over—this at once shows his breadth and his parochialism, his worthy parochialism—"It was characteristic of Harvard and in a way to the glory of Harvard that two Harvard men were the leaders of the opposing forces in the Sacco-Vanzetti affair. Here was A. Lawrence Lowell, the president of the school, and here was Professor Frankfurter of the Harvard Law School, who were the spearheads of those who expressed conflicting views."

That he should have derived satisfaction from the characteristic broadmindedness of Harvard's non-regimentation of thought illustrates his deep devotion to the law school, but in the course of that talk he said about his friend, Lawrence Lowell, this: "Lawrence Lowell was incapable of seeing that two wops could be right and the Yankee judiciary could be wrong."

That posed a dilemma for Lowell which his mind couldn't overreach, clear and hurdle with ease. His crowd, the Yankees, were right, and the alien immigrants were what they were—pacifists and draft dodgers. He was incapable of doing what men have done, namely, say their crowd was wrong. You have to transcend the warm feeling of familiarity and reject that warm feeling in a spontaneous loyalty that transcends to greater loyalties, abstract virtues, truth and justice. That remark of Moors for me goes to the root of the difficulty. Just as it was true of Lowell, it was true of many, many people, of lawyers who would suppress their beliefs that maybe something went awry, who would suppress their realization that no matter how disciplined or sterilized, as it were, their biases are through the habit of discipline, nevertheless, judges and courts may go wrong. I wrote in my book on the Sacco-Vanzetti case that, "Perfection may not be demanded of law, but the capacity to correct errors of inevitable frailty is the mark of a civilized legal mechanism."

Now there were any number of lawyers for whom the issue was not should justice be done, but should we weaken the whole structure, namely, respect for our courts. It was the realization that Lowell, a more civilized partisan than Judge Webster Thayer, couldn't transcend his belief in his crowd and entertain the belief that two Italian immigrants might be right, the realization that it was those forces and not merely individuals which saved me from ever seeing the affair in terms of devils.

A very important factor, and one that gnaws at my curiosity all the time, is the fact that men who know do not speak out. Any number of people privately were convinced all was not well, lawyers particularly. A dozen lawyers I can think of who had doubts would have added to the strength of those who did take action. There were a good many people who did take action. Moors was one of the fellows who went up to the governor and got the governor to appoint the Lowell Committee. Then, of course, the simple-minded, ingenuous people who don't understand thought that everything was going to be hunky-dory because the president of Harvard University was appointed. When the Lowell Report came out—it was so vulnerable in so many respects—they didn't say it was a report by Lawrence Lowell. Although it was well known that it was written by him, they did say that it was a report by the highly esteemed president of Harvard University. I remember saying to a dear friend of mine, "Don't talk to me about this report as the report of the president of Harvard University! You must go from the report to Mr. Lowell, not from Mr. Lowell to the report. You must deal with this report as though it was an anonymous report written on parchment, on papyrus, which was discovered way back in some catacomb, and some archæologist who was able to decipher it said, 'This is a report on the conviction of two men. I can't figure out their names—something like Sacco and Vanzetti. This is two thousand-odd years ago, and I'm happy to report that buried with it is the six thousand pages of minutes, so that we can check what was said in this report about these two men against the permanent and controlling facts—the stenographic minutes.'

"You are not thus led to the plausibility of this report by the author of the report, and, if the report is revealed as defective by the minutes of the proceeding, then you don't say that the report must be right because the president of Harvard University wrote it, but what kind of a man was the president of Harvard University to write such a report?"

It is very difficult for people to question authority and very difficult to get people to read documents. I remember being furious, really furious, with a friend of mine, a really intelligent woman, a strong supporter, deeply devoted to the cause of Sacco-Vanzetti. I was furious when I heard that at a private party—of course, the Sacco-Vanzetti case rent families, friendships and associations—people were discussing the case at dinner, and instead of debating with those who asked her questions she answered their questions by saying, "I don't know anything about it. It's enough for me that Felix Frankfurter has taken the position he has."

She hadn't taken the trouble to spend two hours with the little book I'd written in order to qualify herself to talk about the case and to answer the questions of doubters, the skeptics, who also hadn't read the book, who also hadn't familiarized themselves with the facts, but went on generalities about the reliability of Lowell's report. This was true enough in the overwhelming number of cases so that this was a combat in the dark by people who on either side eschewed the responsibility to find out what they were talking about. John Morley says somewhere—I think it's in his important little book *On Compromise*—that the most important thing in a man's life is to say I believe this, or I believe that, on the assumption that when he says that, he has put behind that affirmation the necessary thought and inquiry. Here this woman—I was perfectly outraged—shot off her mouth all over the place, but she couldn't take one evening off to read my little book to find out what the facts were so that she could at least meet people who were honest and groping, if not the ignorant, the set, and the hopeless.

The Sacco-Vanzetti affair has almost every important, really sizable issue that cuts deeply into the feelings and judgments and conduct of the community, implicates factors that transcend the immediate individuals who, in the main, are instruments of forces that affect many, many beyond the immediate actors in the affair. It involves problems that still gnaw at my curiosity. Few questions bother me more from time to time than what is it that makes people cowardly, makes people timid and afraid to say publicly what they say privately. By "people" I mean not those who are economically dependent and who can't call their souls their own because they have to feed their wives and their children, but those who are economically independent, those who have position, those who by speaking out publicly would turn on the currents of reason and check the currents of unreason. What is it that makes so many men timid creatures?

I can give myself some answers. People want to avoid unpleasantness. Life is hard enough even if you've got a bank account. Life is hard enough as it is, Why take on something extra? "Why go out on a limb?" as the phrase runs. "Why stick your neck out?" that other lovable invitation to do nothing! Even people who are economically independent are not socially independent. They may have money in the bank, but that isn't all they want. They want to be asked to dinners at certain houses. They want to run for office. They want to become Grand Masters of the Masonic Order. They want to get a degree from some college or university. They don't want to make trouble for their wives. They have silly wives with social interests or ambitions. Or if they get into public controversies their boy in prep school will be a marked character,

"Oh, it's your Dad who says this." There are a thousand and one considerations beyond the immediate enslavement of economic dependence which I know make people hesitant, timid, cowardly, with the result however that those who have no scruples, who are ruthless, who don't give a damn, influence gradually wider and wider circles, and you get Hitler movements in Germany, Huey Long ascendency in Louisiana, McCarthyism cowing most of the Senators of the United States at least to the extent that they didn't speak out, etcetera, etcetera.

So the affair like Sacco-Vanzetti for me was a manifestation of what one might call the human situation. The upshot is that I didn't think that it should be minimized to the trivialities of a few individuals. Oh, sure. If another judge had presided, or if the governor of Massachusetts at that time had been a less crude, illiterate, self-confident, purse-proud creature than was Alvan Fuller, other things might have happened. There might have been Bury's "valuable collision" we referred to in one of our earlier talks. But these individual effects derived from the fact that there are causes at work on which they can operate.

As I understand your little book, your aim was a dispassionate examination of the record. In the Boston context in which the book was received, it was largely overlooked—that is, while it aimed at reason, irrationality won the day.

Without being Pollyannish about it, it isn't quite fair to say—and you haven't said it in those words—that this effort of mine was a dud in the sense that it didn't affect opinion. It jolted, particularly outside of Boston, minds and said, "Stop, Look, and Listen," and it gave discomfort and disquietude within Boston. You haven't asked me what I was trying to do. I think I can answer that question—what I was trying to do. Of course anybody who publishes as against a man who doesn't publish publishes not because he is an anchorite. An anchorite doesn't publish. A man doesn't publish because he doesn't want to touch men's minds, because he doesn't want an audience, because he doesn't want to influence conduct, because he doesn't want to persuade men to his way of thinking, or to his way of appreciation, or to his way of seeing things. A man who publishes publishes for the opposite reasons, because he does want to reach a public, and so it's no use saying, "Oh, I published this thing not because I wanted to persuade people to this way of thinking."

Anybody who says that is either a fool or a hypocrite or just self-deceiving. But I was once asked, "How did you come to write this book?" The Swedish Socialist Party, like the socialist parties all over Europe and all the other people who hadn't read the evidence and didn't know, was infected by a feeling that some harm was done. In some places in Europe they were glad to get something on the United States, and a generous emotion is contagious which is to the credit of mankind's heart, though not always of its head, so that there were widespread protests all over Europe in this case. So it was with the Socialist Party of Sweden. They wanted to pass a resolution saying, "We condemn" etcetera. The son of either the then or previous prime minister of Sweden, Branting, a very notable Swedish statesman, was a lawyer and was the lawyer of the Swedish Socialist Party, and he urged on them that before they resolute against the injustness or unfairness of a conviction in the United States they'd better know what they were talking about. He suggested that they'd better send somebody to the United States to study the case and then resolute on the basis of knowledge, instead of on the basis of infected feeling. The upshot was that Branting himself was dispatched as a lawyer to the United States, and one day there turned up at the Harvard Law School a rather serious-minded, solemn-spoken blond fellow, and he introduced himself as Mr. Branting and told me that he was sent to the United States to make inquiry on the spot into the Sacco-Vanzetti case with a view to guiding the action of the Swedish Socialist Party.

He studied the case like a good lawyer and when he got back to Sweden he wrote a book on the Sacco-Vanzetti case. He examined everybody, all the dramatis personnae, and he turned up at Langdell Hall in Cambridge and said that he would like to ask me a series of questions that he had carefully considered and would I be good enough to answer them. I said that I would be glad to do so to the best of my ability. He had a long series of questions. The first one was, "How did you come to write your piece for the

Atlantic, which is now the little book? How did you come to write that book?"

I reflected a minute and then answered what I now would answer, if asked that question: "It wrote itself. I will explain what I mean. I didn't decide to write a book. I didn't say, 'Here's an interesting case; I'll write a book about Sacco-Vanzetti.' That isn't the way it happened at all."

The Braintree crime was committed in the summer of 1920 while I was abroad. Needless to say it wasn't reported in the English papers, or the French papers. Most of the time I was in England. When I arrived here in time for the opening of the law school, I didn't know that there was such a crime as the Braintree holdup-murder. So far as I know I'd never heard the names Sacco and Vanzetti. I knew nothing about it—just nothing. Soon, however, it got into the papers, and I didn't read anything about it because it was my habit, is my habit, engendered from my experience in the United States Attorney's Office, not to read accounts of trials as reported in the press unless the press purports to report the trial verbatim. My experience during those years about trials in which I took part as I saw them reported even in the best papers was distortion, mutilation and at best an opaque account of what took place in the court room. If I was sufficiently interested in a trial, if I really wanted to know, I would try to get stenographic minutes.

To illustrate this pedantic attitude of mine I can give you an episode in my life that is almost ludicrous, not only ludicrous, but incredible. You remember the Hall-Mills trial—the pig woman and all that marvelous wallowing in sensationalism for the American people for weeks? What is more exciting, what is more sensational than a secret liaison between a rector and a choir singer! You know—it's the classic case resulting in the classic crime of passion, getting the husband out of the way. One fine day in Cambridge, as here, I would read my *New York Times* at breakfast. One day I said to my wife, "Marion, what in hell is this Hall-Mills business that I see?"

She said, "What do you mean, this Hall-Mills?"

I said, "It's some kind of a trial evidently. I see Hall-Mills, and it blocks my reading of the *Times*. For weeks now I've had to turn pages to get rid of Hall-Mills. What is it all about?"

"Don't you know what it is?"

"I haven't the remotest idea."

"You don't know anything about it? You don't know about the 'pig woman'?"

"I don't know what you're talking about."

The fact is that I didn't know until she then told me, and this after the trial had been under way for God knows how long and all the sensationalism preceding the trial had been under way for weeks. I had physically not read one line and so didn't know what it was all about, and to this day crimes can take place that have a front page in the Washington *Post,* and I couldn't tell you to save my life five minutes after I've seen something, just enough to turn the pages, what the criminal trial is about. So I haven't any idea what I saw, or what my eyes skipped, in Sacco-Vanzetti. All my life I've read newspapers avidly. I've told you about Cooper Union. One of the good things that I got out of those years of wastefulness is that I can read a paper very rapidly and with extremely profitable discrimination. I don't know what I saw or didn't see in the papers about Sacco-Vanzetti, but I don't recall having read anything. However, the case impinged on me because our dear friend, Mrs. Glendower Evans, became deeply involved, and I knew it involved some murder in which two Italians were charged. "Auntie Bee" as we called her was greatly exercised over it, and as the years went on my wife from time to time said, "Auntie Bee wants to know what you think about the Sacco-Vanzetti case."

We cared a lot about her. She was a woman of great benevolence. She lived in the household of Mr. Justice Brandeis. She was a Boston Gardiner. She was a very beautiful young thing when she married Glendower Evans, a most promising young lawyer, a great friend and classmate at the Harvard Law School of Louis Brandeis. Evans was a Quaker who came up from Philadelphia and remained in Boston. He had a very acute mind, extremely acute mind. Holmes told me that Glen Evans's criticisms of the *Common Law* published in 1881 were the only instructive criticisms that he had about the book. Evans married this charming

Boston lady, and he died a few years after their marriage. The Brandeises and the Evanses lived near each other, and it was a habit of Brandeis to pick up his friend Glen Sunday mornings for a walk. They took long walks and talked together. The Sunday following the death of Glen Evans, Brandeis turned up at the house of the Evanses and asked the young widow to take a walk, and he continued to do that, saw her through that awful period of devastation when everything went to smash for her and gradually directed her into ways in which she occupied her time, became, as it were, interested in social causes. She took some courses with William James. She had a very good brain, an awfully good brain. Brandeis didn't care much for abstract philosophy, but thought that it wouldn't do her any harm. She became the close friend of the Brandeis family and spent summers with the Brandeises. We occasionally saw the Brandeises during the summer, spent some time in Chatham down on Cape Cod. Incidentally because all this was going on while she lived in the Brandeis household, he disqualified himself when the case came before him and didn't sit in the case.

But Mrs. Evans—"Auntie Bee" she was called by the Brandeis children, and we picked this up—from time to time would ask my wife what I thought about the Sacco-Vanzetti case, and Marion would ask me. I would say to my wife, "Marion, you know very well that I have no opinion about a trial or a conviction unless I've read the record. I haven't read the record, and I don't know anything about it."

This went on over the years, into 1925, and I remember my wife once saying to me, "Why are you so sticky? Can't you give me some general opinion that I can tell Auntie Bee. She worries me so about it."

I said, "No, I can't," and I continued being what was called "sticky." There it was. I paid no attention to it, but one day I saw that William G. Thompson had became counsel for Sacco-Vanzetti, and that interested me. William G. Thompson was one of the most conspicuous lawyers in Boston and particularly conspicuous as a trial lawyer and an appellate lawyer. So far as we have any he was a barrister, not a corporate adviser, but a court man. I knew him, greatly respected him, admired him. I knew him somewhat because he was a great friend of Mr. Stimson. They were contemporaries at the Harvard Law School, and he was a great friend of Ezra Thayer, who, as Dean, brought me to the law school. That's how I had a kind of feeling of association with him. When I saw this notice I said, "Hello!" Up to that time Sacco-Vanzetti had some class conscious lawyers and a blatherskite from the west called Fred Moore, but William Thompson was something else. He was as good a lawyer and as esteemed a lawyer as there was at the Boston bar.

By this time, of course, the men had been convicted, and there was a succession of endeavors for a new trial, new proceedings following the conviction and pending the appeal. One day I saw in the papers, THOMPSON MAKES MOTION CHARGES FRAME-UP—whatever the scare headline was and a short story, and I read that. I found that Thompson made a motion for a new trial based on an affidavit of one of the ballistic experts of the Commonwealth, Captain Proctor.

The specific thing Captain Proctor swore to in his affidavit was: [Reading from his book, *The Sacco-Vanzetti Case*] "During the preparation for the trial my attention was repeatedly called by the District Attorney and his assistants to the question whether I could find any evidence which would justify the opinion that the particular bullet taken from the body of Berardelli, which came from a Colt automatic pistol, came from the particular Colt automatic pistol taken from Sacco. I used every means available to me for forming an opinion on this subject. . . . At no time was I able to find any evidence whatever which tended to convince me that the particular model bullet found in Berardelli's body which came from a Colt automatic pistol, which I think was numbered 3 . . . came from Sacco's pistol, and I so informed the District Attorney and his assistant before the trial. . . . At the trial the District Attorney did not ask me whether I had found any evidence that the so-called mortal bullet which I have referred to as number 3 passed through Sacco's pistol, nor was I asked that question on cross-examination. The District Attorney desired to ask me that question, but I had *repeatedly* told him that if he did I should be obliged to answer in the negative; consequently, he put to me this question: 'Have you an opinion as to whether bullet number 3 was fired from the Colt automatic which is in evidence?' To this I answered, 'I have.' He then proceeded. 'And what is your opinion?' A.: 'My opinion is that it is consistent with being fired from that pistol.' "

When I read that in the paper, something happened.

This is what I told Branting and what I tell you now and what is so. When I read that motion filed by Thompson based on this affidavit of Captain Proctor that the district attorney had "repeatedly" asked him, and he had repeatedly said that he could not do this, but finally the district attorney formulated this question, I said, "Hello! I don't have to read six thousand pages. Thompson is making a specific charge. I understand this, and I will now wait to see what the district attorney will reply."

When I read about that motion something happened to my insides. What reading it triggered was the experience I'd acquired under Mr. Stimson's guidance and rules, the standards he represented which had become habits of my mind as to how a district attorney should conduct himself. If what Proctor said was true, it was reprehensible beyond words, and it undermined any confidence in the conduct of the case, that a district attorney should try to get an expert to swear to something that he repeatedly said that he couldn't swear to. It took some time before the district attorney replied, and I don't see why I didn't give the date in my little book, but finally the district attorney stated that prior to his testifying Captain Proctor told him that he was prepared to testify that the mortal bullet was consistent with having been fired from the Sacco pistol, that "I did not *repeatedly* ask him whether he had found any evidence that the mortal bullet had passed through the Sacco pistol, nor did he *repeatedly* tell me that if I did ask him that question that he would be obliged to reply in the negative."

When I read that, that settled the matter because I didn't care whether it was "repeatedly" or only once that he asked Proctor whether the mortal bullet found in Berardelli's body was the bullet that came from Sacco's pistol. If he asked him once, and Proctor said, "I couldn't tell you," and then he got from Proctor his opinion that "it is consistent with having been fired by that pistol"—that is so misleading a matter to be allowed to put to a jury, because the jury didn't make that nice, subtle distinction. If they had, they might have said, "Why the hell didn't he say, 'It did, or it didn't?' " To them it meant, "Yes, it went through," and that's all it meant. That's all you can expect from twelve jurors whose minds aren't sharpened to taking the kind of sophistical and subtle and fastidiously accurate meaning out of words, careful that you allow no implication to slip in that isn't intended, or is intended. When I read the district attorney's reply I said, "That settles me. I'm going to read the record."

That's what I meant to Branting when I said, "The book wrote itself." I got hold of the stenographic minutes and said, "I'm going to study this case and find out what it's all about." I was propelled and compelled by the something in me that revolted against this conduct of a district attorney resulting in the potential death of two people accused of murder. If I hadn't been the kind of fellow I am, if I hadn't had my experience with Mr. Stimson in the United States Attorney's Office, if I didn't care passionately about the clean administration of justice in the United States, if I didn't feel as strongly as I do about law, it wouldn't have had that effect on me, but taking the total of me for granted, what moved me into action was not a nice, quiet determination, but the triggering of my convictions, my impulses to action, the triggering of my total being by the kind of disclosure that was made by the Proctor affidavit and the reply made by the district attorney. If in his reply the district attorney had said, "The fellow is a liar. He is mistaken. He must have misconstrued"—there would have been an issue joined, a claim on one side and a contradiction on the other, but instead there was for me a far-reaching indictment of the disinterestedness that should guide the district attorney by one of the state's two expert witnesses on a decisive aspect of the case, and a district attorney not denying it, but practically in essence admitting it by a pettifogging evasion of the crux of the matter, that Proctor couldn't connect the bullet with Sacco, but a question could be framed so that he would give the jury the feeling that he did connect the bullet with Sacco. That outraged my sensibilities, outraged my whole conviction of what the administration of justice calls for, and my whole antecedents propelled me into action. I began to study the five or six thousand pages of the record. The result was the article which eventually appeared in the *Atlantic*

Monthly, and then the little book which had footnotes that Ellery Sedgwick didn't have room to print in the *Atlantic.*

The story of how the article came to be published in the *Atlantic Monthly* always amused me. I had known Ellery Sedgwick for a great many years partly because he was a great friend of a great friend of mine, Winfred Denison, another Harvard man, and Sedgwick from time to time would come to Washington and stay at the House of Truth. When I came up to teach I saw something of him. He was an extremely able editor, had a gift of pen, was a shrewd, calculating, money-making man. He was also one of these compounded creatures like the rest of us. He wanted to be on the side of the angels. He wanted to be for decency. He wanted to be for "liberalism"—provided it didn't cost too much, particularly if it didn't cost him too much with what he regarded as the "right people." His first wife was a Cabot, and he once told me, "It's very interesting to be married to a Cabot." He had all that side of him. He was very careful. One day he called me up. He said that he'd heard that I was writing something on Sacco-Vanzetti, would I let him see it with a view to having it published in the *Atlantic Monthly?* He would be brave up to a point. I said, "Yes, it is true, but I'm very sorry. I'm already committed to letting Croly have it for the *New Republic.*"

Sedgwick was a very competitive creature. I thought I'd play with him. I was eager to have it published in the *Atlantic Monthly,* but I knew that I should appear to be indifferent. He was a great fellow to be wooed by, instead of sought after. He said, "What do you mean, you're committed to the *New Republic?*"

"What do you mean, 'What do I mean'? Haven't you got people who promise to write something for the *Atlantic?*"

"Yes, but you don't want to publish anything on this case in the *New Republic.*"

"I don't know. Why not? What's the matter with the *New Republic?* Anyhow I'm committed to them."

Well, I appeared more and more indifferent. Finally I said, "Ellery"—I may have mentioned some author he particularly cared about—"if so-and-so had promised to let you publish in the *Atlantic* an article he had written and then said, 'I'm very sorry, but I prefer to put it elsewhere,' what would you think of him?

How would you feel about it? I said that I'm committed to Croly. He's going to make a supplement of this."

Oh, Lord! He was hot on the trail. No jealous lover ever pursued a beloved object more than he did me. In the meantime I got hold of Croly and said, "Of course, if Sedgwick will really stand for what I've written, I'm sure you'll release me because it's much more important to have this in the *Atlantic* than in the *New Republic*."

Croly was a wonderful fellow, a devoted friend, generous, and had a real sense of the public good. He said, "I'm very sorry, but of course if you can get Ellery Sedgwick to publish this."

Well, I played cat and mouse with Sedgwick, made some conditions—publish it as it's written in full without editing. He was ready to give any old terms. The *Atlantic* paid nothing to speak of, certainly in those days. He was going to give me five dollars extra. I finally succumbed to what he then regarded as a great triumph, and that's how the article came to be published in the *Atlantic Monthly*.

As for the Wigmore business, somebody phoned me about three o'clock in the afternoon, "The *Transcript* is out with a front-page story, a full front page, an attack by Wigmore on you for the Sacco-Vanzetti article."

I told my secretary to pack up her things, "Let's go home. We'll buy a *Transcript* in the Square so I can answer it."

My wife loves to tell this story. We came home—took a typewriter because I didn't have one at home—and I was at work when I suddenly heard the house door and up rushed my wife. She said, "You're here!" She said that she was in a streetcar shopping in town when she saw this headline, WIGMORE ATTACKS FRANKFURTER, and she got off the streetcar and took a taxi to rush home to tell me about it, and "There," she says, "he was already in the middle of the answer."

I got hold of a great friend of mine, Frank Buxton, editor of the Boston *Herald*, a man of honor and justice, and said, "I've just read this, am preparing an answer, will give you a scoop provided you hold the presses so that it can get in tomorrow morning's edition," and they said they would. Here was newspaper rivalry, all these motives that come into play. While I was at my reply Ellery Sedgwick called up and said, "Have you seen what Wigmore has written?"

"Yes."

"I suppose you're going to reply."

"Yes."

"Now be temperate, be temperate, be cool," and he went on. Bill Thompson who was a good friend of Sedgwick's told me, "Sedgwick took to bed when he saw this attack by Wigmore."

Sedgwick was scared stiff, and he talked to me about how I should answer it, and I finally said, "Ellery, if you'll get off that phone, I'll be obliged to you, and maybe you'll be obliged to me when you see what I've written. Goodbye."

"Be calm, be temperate!" He was as jittery as he could be when telling me to be calm. I worked at it, corrected it, went over it, and took it into the *Herald*. They held the presses. There it was, a front-page story, and it really atomized Wigmore. I have no doubt that the attack was written by, or concocted by, or based on Judge Thayer, because it was the same kind of thing that Judge Thayer talked about. Wigmore just rehashed. He put things in there that just weren't in the record, and I asked him, "Would you please produce this. Where is this found?"

My senior colleague, my erstwhile teacher, Professor Williston said to me—this was after the two articles; two weeks later there came another Wigmore attack, and I replied, and it was in the *Morning Herald*—"Felix, I haven't read anything on the Sacco-Vanzetti case"—John Wigmore was a classmate of his—"but I must say you pulverized him."

When I wrote my little book I read, re-read, and re-examined the five or six thousand pages of testimony over and over again. I went over and over my little book again and again testing it against the record and so on. My wife and my secretary dropped out. They wouldn't read proof any more with me. My wife said, "Why do you go over this? You've done it twenty times."

I said, "It's humanly impossible to avoid some errors, but if I have a comma instead of a semi-colon, or a semi-colon instead of a comma, that will be blown up to some heinous, venal offense in an effort to discredit the whole, and so far as it lies within my power I don't want to have a mistake in punctuation."

The proof of that pudding was that when Wigmore tried to attack me he was just pulverized. Mr. Lowell said to Norman Hapgood who promptly came over to tell it to me, "Wigmore is a fool! Wigmore is a fool! He should have known that Frankfurter would be shrewd enough to be accurate."

Not that you would be accurate.

Yes, not that I would be accurate, but that I "would be shrewd enough to be accurate." As though you choose whether you're accurate or not. Maybe that was true of him, but a habit of mine is to be accurate.

That is the story of how I got into the Sacco-Vanzetti affair, how for years I was indifferent to it, what stirred my conscience, what led me to study the record, what led me then to write the book and then to deal with Mr. Wigmore's two articles. As I look back, I don't see why my wife and I were so calm about it all. At the time it was just a job I took on, the kind of thing that seems to me to be the most natural thing to do, and all the passion, the venom, the hatred of the community passed over our heads almost without awareness.

21. *Joseph P. Cotton*

My relations to public affairs in the Hoover Administration were largely related to the State Department because of my intimate friendship with Secretary Stimson. It is fair to say that I was responsible for the selection of Joseph P. Cotton as Undersecretary of State. Joe Cotton was a very distinguished New York lawyer, Harvard College, Harvard Law School, and as capacious-minded, as effective a man of law as anyone I know of in my time. Shortly after he got out of law school—a tall handsome son of a minister —he went to Cravath, Henderson, one of the biggest law firms in New York. He soon became a partner, eventually left them to form a partnership with John C. Spooner, a former Senator from Wisconsin who was a man of great influence in the Senate. After Spooner's death the firm became McAdoo, Cotton and Franklin. Cotton was a powerful person, wise as well as shrewd, shrewd as well as wise, a man who had great influence with other very able men. If you talk to John Lord O'Brian, he'll say, "Joe Cotton is probably the ablest man I've ever known." Cotton was a gifted fellow, an attractive fellow, and he made a great deal of money in what he called the "green goods business" meaning that he was legal adviser to big financial interests in affairs that ran into the millions, and therefore, the lawyers' fees were correspondingly large in the days before income tax amounted to anything. He also had scholarly interests and had a hankering for public affairs. He was very critical of the work he was doing and, on the whole, despised his rich clients. He squared his conscience by charging them very heavily, and since he was very good anyhow, that made them respect him more and more.

To my knowledge he was tempted to several public offices. Mr. Stimson wanted to make him his senior assistant when he became United States Attorney, and Cotton said, "No." A short time later he asked him to be Attorney General of Puerto Rico, and he said, "No." He was asked to become a professor of the Harvard Law School, and he wanted to, but didn't. He was asked later on to become dean of the Harvard Law School, and he wanted to, but didn't. He wanted to make money for his two children. One was a girl, and the other was a boy to whom he was deeply devoted. Cotton was a man of outward cynicism and inward devotions. When this boy of his became ill and for weeks his life was in the balance, Joe Cotton was unremittingly at his son's bedside. He told his office that he didn't care who called, or who wanted him, he was not to be reached. For weeks he just sat in his son's sick room, absolutely incommunicado, and he didn't give a damn what happened to his law firm. That was the kind of a fellow he was.

When Mr. Stimson was named Secretary of State, he was in the Philippine Islands as Governor General. Manuel Quezon said that Mr. Stimson was "the best Governor General" they had. Stimson, a rather withdrawn, noneffusive Puritan, also had a strong sense of justice and was intrinsically democratic. Mr. and Mrs. Stimson were the first pair who opened the residence of the Governor General of the Philippines to what were oddly enough called "the natives," and Mr. and Mrs. Stimson danced the native Filipino dance with the Filipinos. Quezon and all the others were absolutely devoted to Mr. Stimson. Since he was out there when he was named Secretary of State, he came back to his post belatedly. I forget when it was, but it was after the fourth of March.

Stimson was not Hoover's first choice for Secretary of State, and I think Hoover was never happy with him. Hoover writes in his book, "He wasn't really a diplomat. He wasn't a statesman. He was a soldierly kind of a fellow," or words to that effect.

Herbert Hoover has a lot of brass to say that about Stimson! What it really meant was that Stimson constantly tried to prevent

Hoover from doing things that shouldn't have been done and to make him do things that should be done. Hoover himself had a lack of sensitiveness toward public affairs. Really, he had no touch at all for politics in the best sense of the term. Some of the factors that certainly contributed toward the deterioration in European affairs and gradually brought Hitler to his apogee, to his power—Germany was then and is now the center of gravity in international affairs—were largely Hoover's doing. At the bar of history I think Hoover will bear a considerable share for promoting the disintegrating forces as against the health-bringing forces. More particularly there was the Smoot-Hawley tariff. Mr. Stimson, old Republican that he was, saw clearly that if we were going to build tariff walls, other nations would build tariff walls, and feverish nationalistic forces would be encouraged. At the very outset Mr. Stimson tried to make the President see that he ought to tell the leaders of the Congress that he would not stand for the raising of the tariff on commodities. McKinley—the last speech he made way back in 1901—indicated that we had to change our tariff policy, that we can't always be sellers and not buyers, that these empirical, *ad hoc* economic remedies aren't absolutist principles. Mr. Stimson begged Hoover to assert his power as the President, and Hoover, not unlike Eisenhower in the early years, said that his job wasn't to tell Congress what to do. It was this old struggle between the Presidency as leader and the Presidency as a coordinate branch of the government. Months went by, and the tariff proposals became worse and worse, and when the bill was enacted it was so bad that it was bound to stir reaction in other countries. Mr. Stimson tried to persuade Mr. Hoover to veto it, and he said, "I can't after all these months." Having said that he couldn't intervene in the beginning, when the months passed and they put a tariff on his desk, he said, "Well, now I must sign it."

The evil of that action or inaction I saw that summer, 1930, when my wife and I were up in Canada. They had a general election. I remember being struck by the transparencies in the election, "If America for the Americans, Canada for the Canadians." That led to the Ottawa Agreement, imperial preference, and so on.

The other disturbing matter was the whole question of reparations. The country was still in an isolationist mood; at least, the President feared that it was. Moreover, Hoover himself had strong isolationist impulses, or directions. He was strongly anti-British. I don't know what that was due to. Apparently he had a bad experience with the British in a law suit concerning some engineering matters when he was in the Far East. The fact of the matter also is that events have shown that he could fairly be deemed to be a believer in "Fortress America." He was probably much more in sympathy with General MacArthur than he would be, let's say, with Senator Vandenberg in his converted days. Mr. Stimson wanted to deal with the reparation problem and lift that load of fear. Anybody who knew anything knew that we could never get anything. You can't make a conquered nation pay for the cost of the war. The cost of war is due to the ineptitudes of man all around. Suppose we'd saddled the South with the cost of the Civil War!

Finally Mr. Stimson persuaded the President to allow him to give a moratorium in 1931 when things were bad. Then Stimson indicated that it was no use giving a respite for one year. You should do it for two years to enable Germany to catch its breath. Also Hoover was rather hesitant in regard to our response to Japan's attempted absorption of portions of China. He was constantly afraid, always worrying about what "The Hill" and "public opinion" would stand for. The people who are most ignorant about that elusive thing called public opinion deem themselves the greatest experts on it, and Hoover is a striking example. When you go to his book, you'll see that he clearly indicated that he didn't think Stimson was much of a statesman.

Stimson was not Hoover's first choice. He tried to persuade Harlan F. Stone to be his Secretary of State, so Stone told me himself. Stone said that he spent a week looking into the State Department and that he concluded that he would have to institute "such far-reaching and radical reforms" that he didn't suppose the President would consent to them. Of course Stone was a very considerable self-deceiver. I think that you can almost lay down as a postulate that a man of great vanity is a great self-deceiver, and Stone was that. The fact is, according to Stone, that Hoover wanted him to be Secretary of State, and Stone finally declined.

He didn't say, "I said no because no man should leave the Supreme Court to do a political job." He beefed about that a lot in reference to Robert H. Jackson's going to Nuremberg, and generally talked high-minded, "You know a man on the Supreme Court should never do anything else." But it never occurred to him to say that when he told me about Hoover's asking him to be Secretary of State.

I don't know whom else Hoover had under consideration, but I think Root strongly urged Stimson on Hoover, and so he was named Secretary of State. When he came home he needed an Undersecretary, a man who would run the department, and he did, I think, a surprisingly shrewd thing. He put the suggestion for his selection of his Undersecretary under commission, as it were: he asked George Roberts and me to select his Undersecretary. George Roberts was one of his partners and a great friend of mine. He was a year or two behind me at the law school, a hardboiled Republican, a very conservative Republican, really conservative, but a terribly nice, high-minded fellow. We were great friends personally, really warm friends. He disapproved of me politically very much. I didn't disapprove of him. I just thought that politically he was an old fogey, but, as I said, our relations were very happy. Stimson I thought very shrewdly said, "You two fellows have to agree. I will select as Undersecretary whomever you two fellows agree on."

That was very smart of Stimson. For some time Roberts would bat a ball to me, and I'd volley it back. I'd bat a ball to him, and he'd volley it back. "What do you think of so-and-so?" I'd say, "I don't think anything of so-and-so intellectually speaking," or "He's too stodgy," or "He isn't even as open-minded as you are, George," or George would say, "Gosh, he's even more radical than you are" to me—he in New York; I in Cambridge. It was sort of taken for granted by us and by Mr. Stimson that he wanted a lawyer, quite rightly I think. As I've said on more than one occasion, "The worst public servants are narrow-minded lawyers, and the best are broad-minded lawyers," for reasons that I don't have to go into. I once made a speech on that subject from which you can profit if you haven't already seen it.

This went on and on until some weeks elapsed. Mr. Stimson was fretful that he had no Undersecretary, and one day I came back to my office at the Harvard Law School after having been out overtime for lunch. My secretary said, "Mr. Roberts called from New York and is very anxious to talk to you."

Well, in due course Mr. Roberts was on the phone, and he said, "Felix, what do you think of so-and-so?"

I said, "I don't think anything of so-and-so. He's much too narrow-minded. His vision is extremely limited."

He said, "All right. We'll try again."

I said, "Now wait a minute, George. Don't ring off. What do you think of Joe Cotton?"

He laughed—just a warm-hearted laugh. Roberts is a very nice, warm-hearted fellow. He said, "Why don't you suggest Jesus Christ?"

"I'll tell you why, George, because you cannot get Jesus Christ, but you can get Joe."

"What do you mean?"

"Take my word for it. If you agree, if you say that's fine, as I'm sure you will, if I tell you this is someone we can get, you telephone down to HLS and say if he wants Joe Cotton, he can have him."

He could hardly believe it, and I said, "Take my word for it, and I'll tell you the story some other time."

The story was this. The day, in 1929, of this telephone call that I've just narrated there was an event at the Harvard Law School. We had a lunch for the guests in the corridors in the L of the building of Langdell Hall. I found myself sitting next to Joe Cotton. He was already a big figure when I came to New York in 1906 as a kid, but through a senior associate of mine in Mr. Stimson's office, Winfred Denison, I became friends with him. He had been president of the *Harvard Law Review* when he was a student at the law school, and there are these ties between law school men—not school ties, but ties. We became very warm friends, and later in Washington I became a house mate of one of his closest friends, Robert G. Valentine. I found myself sitting next to him that day. As I sat down I said to myself, "By jove, that's the fellow who ought to be Undersecretary." As we were eating lunch I said, "Joe, how would you like to be Undersecretary of State?"

He was a man of quick decision and just like that he said, "I think I'd like it."

Right across from us was Mark Sullivan who was a lawyer to begin with, a product of the Harvard Law School. He finally was seduced by Norman Hapgood to become an editor of *Collier's Weekly*. That's how he got into journalism. Mark Sullivan was a great friend of Hoover's. He was one of the medicine ball party with whom President Hoover played at breakfast time in the White House. He was sitting right across from us, and I didn't want Mark Sullivan to overhear this, that I was engaged in matters affecting the Hoover Administration, so Cotton and I talked sort of *sotto voce* after he said, "I think I would like it." I said to him, "You're a friend of Hoover's aren't you?"

I knew that he had been the legal adviser—what we now call general counsel—of Hoover's Food Administration in the First World War, and I knew they had relations. He said, "He thinks I am."

He then said, "Let me ask you something. Do I have to give up drinking if I take that job?"

"Not so far as I'm concerned," and then I said, "Joe, where are you going when we get through with this lunch?"

"I've got to go into town."

"I'm going in with you."

"All right."

We said not another word. In due course the lunch was over. We took a taxi, and I said, "Joe, this isn't just a game. This is very serious business. Are you prepared to have me tell Mr. Stimson that you're prepared to be his Undersecretary of State?"

"Certainly."

"Stop this cab. Goodbye Joe," and I took another cab and went back to Cambridge. I've already told you what happened. When I came in my secretary said, "Mr. Roberts wants you."

Stimson was simply in seventh heaven. Here was Joe Cotton. I'm sure Stimson thought that Cotton was as well qualified as he was to be Secretary of State. He was of that caliber. In due course in went his nomination. Presidential nominations then were considered by the Senate in executive session. In those days when "I call for executive session" was heard, the galleries were cleared, the reporters were kicked out, and it was a closed secret session. At the time of Cotton's nomination, McAdoo, a former Secretary of the Treasury, was a partner of his. Weeks passed, and one day my secretary said, "Mr. Stimson wants to talk to you from Washington," and soon there was this vigorous—Stimson had a vigorous —do I mean contralto voice? Well, stop that machine a minute, and I'll go consult my expert on these matters.

When I asked my wife what kind of voice Stimson had, she said, "He didn't sing."

That's very good, isn't it.

Wonderful.

Well, soon there was this vigorous, deep, rich voice. Without any palaver—I can hear him now; when he was mad he was always a joy to me—he wasn't mad, but it was the intense expression of a vigorous, determined man, "Felix, will you get those damn progressive friends of yours to report out Joe's nomination! They're holding it up."

I remember saying to him, "And what are your damn Republican friends doing?"

"Never mind that."

"Now, tell me what's the trouble."

He calmed down, and he said, "Here they're holding up this nomination, and they ought to thank God that they can get a man like Joe Cotton to take this job."

"Who is making trouble? What is the difficulty?"

"It's his association with McAdoo."

I think McAdoo had been counsel for Sinclair, the oil man. McAdoo went in for money-making, and he was not reputed to be the most fastidious operator. This came after Teapot Dome and all that business. Mr. Stimson went on to say, "They think that Joe is involved because of the smell of oil, because of his partnership with McAdoo. I wish you'd do something about it," as though I could tell those "wild jackasses of the west"—remember that phrase?—that progressive group of Senators, Borah, Norris, Cummins, people like that, powerful fellows. I said, "I'll do what I can."

He said, "I wish you'd tell them the kind of a fellow Joe Cotton is."

I sat down and wrote a letter to Senator Borah, who was then chairman of the Foreign Relations Committee before whom Cotton's nomination was pending. I had pleasant, friendly but not at all close relations with him. My correspondence will show that he may have turned to me from time to time on questions about which I supposedly knew something, or I may have written to him saying, "I'm all for this measure," or "Do you realize what a bad measure this is," and so on. It's that kind of a completely public relation. These silly columnists! These penny-a-liners! These "scribblers," as Lincoln called them. They don't understand. They project their own notion that there must be some private interest, some personal interest, some conspiratorial interest! We say our democracy is dependent upon citizenship, but if a fellow exercises his citizenship as a serious office, that they don't understand. Whatever relation I had with Borah was that kind of a relation. My files will show the letter I wrote telling him about Joe Cotton, the kind of a man he was, that he doubtless sold his great ability to his clients, but not his soul, or his character, or his convictions, and that the government would be damn fortunate to have the whole-souled service which he would render as Undersecretary of State.

I had a very nice letter from Borah, saying, in effect, that he was glad to have this expression from me. He read it in executive session, and in relatively no time Cotton was reported out.

To illustrate the kind of a man Joe Cotton was, he used to smoke a corncob pipe, wore woollen socks rolled down, with his feet up on a drawer or on the desk and dressed in flannels. One day in came one of these striped-trousered creatures of the State Department—these were the days of great formality—and reported that at the western European desk they just had had a cable. After Lindbergh had flown the Atlantic he had imitators. Someone had concealed himself on one of those transatlantic flights and arrived at the airport near Paris as a stowaway. There he was, no passport, no nothing, and that presented a great problem to our Embassy in Paris. The American Ambassador in Paris, whoever he was, cabled over that they had an American on their hands, that he came over as a stowaway, and that the French were raising some question. What should they do? This fellow with the striped trousers stood there respectfully. Joe took his corncob pipe out of his mouth and said, "Send this cable to our Embassy in Paris: LAUGH IT OFF!"

"Yes, sir."

Out he went. That was a perfect way to deal with the situation. Hours afterwards he came back. Joe Cotton looked up and said, "Well?"

"Sir, that cable about that stowaway."

"Yes, what about it? I thought we were all through with that damn thing."

"The cable has not been transmitted."

"Why not?"

"There's no code word for 'laugh'."

"Make one up!"

Out he went. That shows Cotton's quality. Here's another. There were lying in the North River in New York following the First World War a goodly number of obsolete crafts, and the government—the Shipping Board as it then was—tried to sell them for junk for years and years with no takers. There they were. One day the chairman of the Shipping Board came in to see the Undersecretary and said that the Shipping Board had had an "unexpectedly profitable offer from Amtorg," the Soviet purchasing agency. They had received this unexpectedly opulent offer from Amtorg for the purchase of those obsolete ships, and they came to talk about that offer.

Cotton said, "What about it? You tell me it's a good offer."

"Oh, my yes, we never expected to get so much for them."

"What's the trouble?"

"On the Shipping Board we're troubled whether we could enter into such an arrangement in view of the fact that we're not recognizing Russia." Russia didn't exist on the map, you see. We hadn't recognized her. "We want to know whether it's all right, whether you approve, or have objections."

Cotton said, "For Christ sake! Put the deal through, but don't ask me."

He was something! Those are two typical stories about him. Cotton was a tower of strength. He died within two years. I don't know the details. It was too awful. I went up to his funeral in

Bedford Village, New York. Mr. Stimson was there, and he asked me to ride back with him to the station. I remember that that strong man, Mr. Stimson, was really in tears about Joe Cotton's death. I remember sitting there, and he clasped my thigh, and he said, "Felix, you know a great deal about the goings on of this administration, but even you don't know what Joe's loss means to the country." And then he made this statement, "He's the only man who can do anything with the President."

Well, that's the story about Joseph P. Cotton who became Undersecretary of State in the Hoover Administration and exerted important influences, prevented, I suspect—what Mr. Stimson was referring to—a great deal of mischief which without his presence would otherwise have taken place. Mr. Stimson used to say, "He stopped rat holes." And that's how I—this arch fiend of the New Deal—was really responsible for selecting the Undersecretary of State in the Hoover Administration.

22. *Supreme Judicial Court of Massachusetts*

I was at lunch in the Faculty Club in Cambridge just before the Democratic Convention met in Chicago in 1932, when one of the waiters came up and said that I was wanted on the phone. I was sitting at a table where members of the law school faculty used to lunch together. I went to the phone, and there was my wife. She's a person of equanimity, poise, and she said with some evident eagerness—a touch of impatience characteristic of a particular form of eagerness—"I wish you'd come home as soon as possible and take the reporters off my hands."

"What?"

"Don't waste any time. Just come home as fast as you can, and take these reporters off my hands. The place is crowded with them."

"What are you talking about, Marion?"

"Don't you know? You know what I'm talking about."

"I haven't the remotest idea," and I remember vividly thinking, "I wonder whether anything's happened."

"Don't you know?"

"I haven't the slightest idea what you're talking about."

"Well, the reporters and photographers are swarming all over the place. Don't you know that Governor Ely has named you to the Supreme Judicial Court?"

"I'll just gobble down my luncheon and come straight home as fast as I can."

I went back to the table, and one of my colleagues, Professor Barton Leach, said in a very sympathetically anxious way, "What's happened, Felix?"

"Why? Why do you ask what's happened?"

"You're white as chalk."

"All that's happened is that Governor Ely has named me to the Supreme Judicial Court, and I just want to gobble my food and run home," which I did. I couldn't get a taxi, and I walked home in a rush. As I came near our house, 192 Brattle Street, I encountered Mr. Charles C. Burlingham. It was a day or two before the Harvard Commencement, the day of the Yale-Harvard baseball game, and I bumped into him. He said, "I was coming down to see you. You're going to accept of course. You're going on the Supreme Judicial Court. Isn't that wonderful!"

I said, "I don't know whether it is or it isn't. I don't know whether I shall or shan't accept."

This was all out of the clear sky. He said, "You know the way to decide a question like that?"

Mr. Burlingham was a man of great decision, extremely confident in decisions other men should make. I said, "No, how do you decide a thing like that?"

"Do it Ben Franklin's way."

By this time we had reached 192 Brattle Street, and the place was swarming with reporters and photographers. They clicked their cameras. I finally got rid of them. "No comment." Those aren't the words I used, but that was the thought I conveyed. That phrase hadn't yet originated. "Wonderful phrase it is," said Mr. Churchill, "wonderful phrase," when he first heard it. "I'll have to use that. That's a great out." Finally the reporters and photographers were all cleared out, and Mr. Burlingham said, "Now let's sit down, and we'll decide what you should do about this. Give me a piece of paper."

He just took charge. He said, "You know, whenever Franklin had a problem, the thing to do was to take a piece of paper, draw a line right down the center of the paper and on one side put the arguments for a particular proposition, and on the other side the arguments against. Now 'the arguments for' and then 'the arguments against' "—he was writing the headings. All this time he was taking charge. He was putting down the arguments for and against, and it all added up, of course, that I should take it. That was that. Finally he said, "Come on. You don't want to bother Marion here. Take it off your mind. I've got two tickets. Let me take you to the baseball game."

I thought that was a good idea, so we went down to the stadium to the baseball game, and Mr. Burlingham, that wonderful, delightful, impish creature! He knew what was what. Instead of entering at the appropriate place where we could just slip up where he had seats, he entered at an entrance farthest from the place where the seats were, and I had to walk the full length of the field. People were yelling. By that time the newspapers were full of it. This was news, exciting news—on the one hand, to some people this was awful, and to some it was wonderful. Well, it was a Roman Holiday, and Mr. Burlingham had the time of his life—you know, sort of taking the Christian into the arena for the lions. Finally—we got to our seats, and we saw I don't know how many innings, only a few—and he said, "Well, we've had enough of this," and he yanked me out, and that was that.

I went back home, finally was all alone with my wife and looked at this thing, faced it, and I could not forbear wondering why Governor Ely should have done this, why he should have sent my name into the Executive Council without ever giving me the slightest hint, or asking me whether I wanted to go on the Supreme Judicial Court. Not only that. The papers said that the Governor had left for the Chicago Convention. I thought about it for twenty-four hours and then wrote a letter declining and had it delivered to the then secretary of Governor Ely, Robert Bradford. Later on Bradford became district attorney and then governor of Massachusetts. He was an old student of mine. I sent my letter of declination in to him.

In the meantime there poured in letters from all over creation, certainly "creation" to the extent of the United States. The next day Bob Bradford came out and said that he'd communicated with the governor and the governor begged me not to make public my declination until he had had a chance on his return from the convention to talk to me. For the next week or ten days—I don't know how long; certainly it seemed an eternity, certainly a week—my wife and I were prisoners because to the world we had to appear that it was a settled matter that I was going on the Supreme Judicial Court when as a matter of fact I'd already declined. We left the house as little as possible. I made no acknowledgement of any letter and to people who called on the phone, or whom I had to meet on the street, or at the law school I avoided any intimation of what was what.

I received hundreds and hundreds and hundreds of letters. What a mass of letters! There were very few that gave me very great pleasure. Among these was a letter from Joe Eastman of the Interstate Commerce Commission who said, "Well, this is fine, important and great, but I'm sorry because I think at the Harvard Law School you're doing more important work than to go on the Supreme Judicial Court of Massachusetts, important as that tribunal is and great as the honor," etcetera, etcetera.

Very few manifested any sense of understanding what a teacher is, or what he is capable of being or doing. I remember Mr. Justice Brandeis whom I saw saying, "People think it's wonderful to be a judge. I don't know why they think it's so wonderful to be a judge. They have this strange notion that a judge is something very special," and he, indeed, was glad that I decided not to go on the court and to stay at the law school. He said, "If ever the time comes when you should be asked to go on the Supreme Court, why then talk to me about it, and if you're then old enough, there might be some reason to leave the law school."

I didn't pay any attention to that. Then I told some of my colleagues at the Harvard Law School that I wasn't taking it. They were worried about it. Bart Leach went out to Holmes at Beverley Farms and told him that I was thinking of turning it down. I had a letter from Holmes who said that I mustn't do that. How could I do that after the governor had named me? I went out to see the old gentleman and asked him if he knew that the governor named me without ever asking me about it. He didn't know that, and he said that relieved me of all responsibility, that I certainly could do as I pleased if I was not consulted and there wasn't what we lawyers called an estoppel.

Well, the governor came back after this awful, terrible time during which the papers, particularly the *Transcript,* opened up columns "For Frankfurter," "Against Frankfurter"—oh, hundreds and hundreds of letters. When Governor Ely came back I went up to see him in the State House, that lovely Bulfinch building, and I said, "Why did you do this—much as I appreciate the high honor? Why didn't you ask me?"

He said, "I did it because there was a much better chance of your accepting it if I didn't ask you than if I had asked you in advance."

He was very anxious to have me accept. He said, "This present chief justice is a tyrannical kind of fellow. There ought to be somebody on the court who stands up to him." It was a well-known fact that nobody ever was allowed to file a dissenting opinion, and Governor Ely thought that court needed rejuvenation. When I was adamant, he said, "Why don't you go on there for a few years?"

I said, "No. I wouldn't dream of doing that. If I go on the court, I go on the court."

There were only two temptations that I had not to turn the nomination down. There were only two things that seemed to appeal to that part of my nature which is whimsical, why I should like to have accepted. In those days the seven members of the Supreme Judicial Court of Massachusetts went in lock step every day from where the court was sitting on Ashburton Place, right near the State House, to lunch at the Union Club in formal dress and top hat. I thought that would be an interesting thing—to go in lock step in top hat to the Union Club for lunch.

The other consideration that appealed to me was the desire to satisfy the curiosity of the means that Chief Justice Rugg used whereby if a fellow dissented from an opinion, his opinion wouldn't be filed. How did he work it that grown men of independent position—life tenure—would suppress their views when presumably they felt them with sufficient strength to dissent. I was confident that he couldn't suppress any dissent of mine, and I just wondered how that would operate, but these two considerations didn't outweigh my sober convictions that the opportunities the Harvard Law School afforded me were more significant than even membership on the Supreme Judicial Court of Massachusetts.

When finally my letter was made public, that I declined definitively, my wife and I were liberated. The cage was open, and the birds could fly out. We gave a dinner to our most intimate friends, and my friend and colleague Tom Powell said in a kind of snarling way at our own table, "Why would you ever think of going on the Supreme Judicial Court of Massachusetts?"

I said—I think very quietly—"Tom, I didn't think that a place that had been occupied by Lemuel Shaw and Oliver Wendell Holmes Jr. was beneath me, or too meager for my powers."

I had a telephone call from FDR in the midst of that dramatic flight to Chicago to make his acceptance speech for his nomination for the Presidency. He said that either Sam Rosenman, or Raymond Moley—and I forget which—had just told him that I was going on the Supreme Court of Massachusetts. He said, "I congratulate you, but I'm rather surprised that you would take such a lower court position."

I said, "You evidently are confusing the Supreme Court of Massachusetts with the Supreme Court of New York. The Supreme Court of Massachusetts is like the Court of Appeals in New York. It's the highest court in the state, not an inferior court."

He said, "Well, anyhow, you ought to be on the highest court in the land."

I said, "Thank you very much. That's very sweet of you. Good luck!"

That explains the episode of the Supreme Judicial Court.

23. FDR and the New Deal

What was your relationship to FDR and the New Deal?

We were contemporaries at Cambridge. I did not know him there at all, and I'm sure I never met him. Shortly after I came to New York in 1906, I found myself frequently in the library of the Association of the Bar of the City of New York which is a very good library. I was then unmarried and would go across to the Harvard Club for lunch, or stay over and have dinner at the Harvard Club because while the office of United States Attorney was in the old Post Office Building on Park Row facing that beautiful city hall, I did a great deal of work in the library of the Bar Association. There I gradually came to meet this attractive young fellow, Franklin Roosevelt. Probably I came to know him through Grenny Clark—I'm not sure—because they were in the same law office, Carter, Ledyard and Milburn. We became acquaintances, not intimate friends at all, but we knew each other pleasantly.

I went to Washington in the Taft Administration and stayed over after Wilson became President. Soon my old acquaintance, Franklin Roosevelt, turned up on the same floor of the then State, Army and Navy Building, that old, ugly monument to the Grant era of architecture which is now occupied wholly by agencies and officials of the White House. I had an office next to the Judge Advocate General and soon—the most natural thing—Franklin

Roosevelt and I extended our New York-originating acquaintanceship. I left in 1914 and went up to Harvard. I wrote one or two critical pieces, leaders on finance imperialism in the *New Republic* against action by him because it was the Navy that had a kind of receivership of San Domingo. I don't believe that we saw each other, after I left in 1914, until 1917. He was still Assistant Secretary of the Navy when I returned to Washington to the War Department, and naturally I saw something of, and saw increasingly, the Assistant Secretary of the Navy. He had a good deal to do with personnel problems with work in the Navy Yard, and I had to deal with those problems in the War Department, and we saw a good deal of each other in that connection. Finally through the competitive attitude of the different agencies of the government—the different agencies of the one, single, overriding authority and need, that of the United States of America, were dealing with each other as though they were rival grocery stores—there came into existence the War Labor Policies Board. It was a small permanent organization, and I was its permanent, full-time chairman. Each personnel-concerned branch of the government designated an important official to constitute the board, and FDR was the Navy member, and from the time that that agency came into being we saw a great deal of each other—not less than once a week for several hours with telephone conversations and talks in between.

Herbert Ehrmann, who figured as associate counsel to Mr. William G. Thompson in the Sacco-Vanzetti case, was then on the Shipping Board, and he very often sat in for, or with Bob Bass, the former governor of New Hampshire who was the permanent representative of the Shipping Board. In 1932, though he was rather a Republican and was against FDR for President, I remember his saying to me, "I'm bound to say that the chairman apart" —mine was a permanent full-time job; it was my job to have ideas —"of all those rather eminent people on that board, Franklin Roosevelt had the most resourceful mind and made the most important and fertile contributions at our meetings."

Franklin Roosevelt was very active and full of ideas, full of interest, and we became friends, close friends, the way men with genial common factors become friends when engaged in a common enterprise, and those active years of comradeship in important work of an official kind rather transformed a casual, pleasant relationship into what might be called a warm friendship.

After the war was over I went back to Cambridge, and I lost sight of him. He stayed on through the Administration, and then in 1920 he ran for Vice President. I was not active in the campaign, and I'm sure that I had no communication with him then, but we did exchange letters when he was stricken. I wrote him, and some small correspondence passed between us, a trickle. I did not actually see him again until after he became governor. During his governorship I saw him, I think, twice in Albany and I saw him in Boston. On a visit of his to one of his sons at Groton he came to Boston where he sought me out on two matters regarding which presumably I had some knowledge and competence. One was crime, and the other was regulation of a public utility.

He became governor during the depression period and manifested great vigor, initiative, eagerness, a questing mind in dealing with problems in strong contrast to the torpid, lethargic, somehow-or-other-God-will-provide attitude, that prosperity is around the corner, the crisis is over with a constantly shifting date, from the occupant in the White House. Roosevelt then showed, as he showed later, that he got about him people with ideas, that he listened to all sorts of ideas, sifted them and absorbed what was congenial to him and rejected that to which he was allergic, but temperamentally he wasn't allergic to new ideas. A good deal of correspondence passed between us. He had to deal with utility problems, tax problems, water-power problems, who would pay the bill for governmental expenditures and how it was to be paid. How anybody who watched affairs at Albany during the three odd years that he had been governor could make the fatuous statement that Walter Lippmann did in that famous sentence of his, Franklin Roosevelt is "a pleasant man who, without any important qualifications for the office, would very much like to be President" —you remember that classic statement? How anybody could make that! Well, he could only make it if he paid no attention to the powers of initiative, resourcefulness, and aggressive statesmanship which Roosevelt subsequently showed in the White House and theretofore had shown at Albany. Now to be sure he was careful as he was in the White House. To be sure he had the problem on his hands of how to get rid of Jimmy Walker and not alienate Tammany Hall, how to square the circle—that's the perennial problem of public men. How to do the right thing and not alienate the people who don't recognize the right reasons for wanting the right thing to be done, how to be ahead of the procession, "but not too much ahead" as TR said. If you're too far ahead, you've got no followers. If you're not ahead at all, then there's no leader for those who follow.

The fact of the matter is—I'd forgotten about this—I saw him twice at Albany and once in Boston apart from a rather active correspondence when he was governor. I forgot for the moment until I mentioned Jimmy Walker and Tammany Hall that I also saw him at Hyde Park. He asked me to come to Hyde Park and talk with him about the legal problems raised by the Jimmy Walker business. I worked out with him the legal theory on which Jimmy Walker had to go; the theory being that when a public official has acquired money during the time that he was in public office, the presumption of wrong doing lies there unless he can explain why he suddenly came into money that he couldn't have got merely through his salary. Anyone who reads, as I have read, the minutes of the hearings on Jimmy Walker in Albany and the skill with which FDR conducted them is not likely to say that he wasn't a man of great skill. I daresay he failed in some course at the Columbia Law School, and he didn't make much of a fist at the bar, but that performance showed an extremely skillful lawyer. Just as later on I was present in the White House merely as an onlooker when he dealt with the avoidance of a coal strike with Lewis and his cohorts on one side and the operators on the other. To be able to deal with tough babies like that is not child's play.

I remember that Walter Lippmann came to me as Farley was making more and more progress, as Franklin Roosevelt was emerging more and more as the challenging candidate for the presidential nomination. Walter Lippmann's favorite was Newton Baker. He wrote and said that he'd like to see me when he came up to the Harvard-Yale football game which must have been November. When he talked with me in order to make me realize that the man who really should be nominated was Newton Baker, whom

I knew well, probably at least as well as he did and about whose qualities I had as good a basis for knowledge as Walter Lippmann, I remember his saying, "Franklin is a dangerous man."

I was greatly disposed toward Newton Baker, but not for the Presidency, and I said, "Walter, a fellow who has your command of adjectives I should think could use a more felicitous one to describe Franklin than 'dangerous.' I can understand anything that might be said about him, but to say that he's a 'dangerous man' is straining the word 'dangerous.' "

Walter thought he was a rather meager, frivolous, not very responsible person—well, I leave it to you to decide how wise that judgment was. He had in him this so-called frivolity. There was a lot of that on the surface, a lot of shallowness on the surface, but Mr. Stimson came to a more perceptive realization of the depths of Roosevelt when he served under him. I remember Mr. Stimson once saying to me, "People who say that Roosevelt is impulsive don't know the man. There's a deep streak of the Dutch in him. When he digs in, you can't dig him out."

We formed rather easy, I might say intellectually intimate, ties in the course of his governorship. After his nomination I was for him, and I became enlisted. As you well know I was not of the so-called brain trust, a Columbia enterprise organized by Raymond Moley, but from time to time I would write suggestions.

There is a very funny episode connected with this. We used to spend weekends during the summer, and more particularly during the early fall, at Lyme, Connecticut with a great friend of ours, Katharine Ludington. She was a great suffrage leader. She was treasurer of the League of Women Voters, a New England lady, and somewhere in the middle of October her maid came in while we were at dinner and said, "There's a long distance call"—I forget from where. It was way out, Omaha, St. Louis—out West somewhere. This was a large weekend party Katharine Ludington had at her house. She was a very gracious hostess, charming surroundings and all that. I left the table. After I came back I said, "Guess with whom I talked?"

Somebody who thought that he'd say something irresponsible said, "Governor Roosevelt."

Well, sure enough, it was Governor Roosevelt. He was way out in the sticks somewhere—way out. He traced me down, found out I was there somehow or other and what do you suppose he was asking me, calling me up for? He said, "I plan to be in Washington two days or three days before inauguration," and he'd be staying at the Mayflower. He was very anxious to see Mr. Justice Brandeis, and he wondered whether I could arrange it. I said, "I rejoice at the presupposition of your suggestion."

He said, "What do you mean presupposition?"

I said, "The implication of your remark is that you'll be elected."

He said, "Don't bother about that. That's all right."

It was just like that. I told him that I thought I could arrange a meeting with Justice Brandeis. That was the purpose of his call. He was already thinking ahead about talking with a man with ideas, probably a man who had as many ideas, as much wisdom on social and economic matters as any man in the United States, if not more. He was thinking ahead, two weeks before the campaign was over, making plans for such a meeting.

During the campaign he came up to Groton visiting one of his boys there, and he was to receive a delegation of independents for Roosevelt. I never was a party man. My record of voting is that of a mugwump, a typical mugwump. That's why these silly newspaper people whenever they have to give tags to the members of the Court, think I'm a hide-bound Democrat simply because Roosevelt named me. Well, I'm a hide-bound nothing, let alone a hide-bound Democrat. I led this delegation of independents for Roosevelt, an interesting motley crowd, interesting as independents usually are. They are not regulars, and therefore they're interesting. I made a speech of presentation and then introduced them, each of the people who turned up, and one of them was Mrs. Glendower Evans who was, to a large extent, the angel of the Sacco-Vanzetti defense, not "Moscow gold," but this Mayflower product, this Yankee of Yankees, and I introduced Mrs. Evans. She startled all of us by saying, "I'm not going to vote for you. I'm going to vote for Norman Thomas, but I'm contributing sizably to your campaign fund."

Well Roosevelt laughed, and I remember his saying—imagine this happening to almost any candidate you can think of; imagine how Taft would have received this, or Hoover, or Wilson—"Norman Thomas is a fine man. I have only one thing against him."

She said, "What's that?"—quite challengingly.

He said, "I asked him to go on my unemployment commission shortly after I became governor to deal with the unemployment problem in New York when the depression really hit us, and he refused. I thought he should have gone on, but he is a fine man."

That was all done so simply, in such a civilized manner. He was elected and was President-elect. He asked my wife and me to come to Hyde Park two days before Christmas. He wanted to talk about things. I remember that Marion turned in around midnight, and we were up 'til nearly two o'clock. We talked about many things. He showed, having been out of Washington for a good long while, his limited knowledge of people in different branches of the government concerned with different problems that I'd had more alert interest in than he had had. Down with his disease, and then to come back, to be governor, his preoccupations were very different from mine. We talked about measures and men. I remember, for instance, that he didn't know about Joe Eastman. We talked about various problems that would come up. I said, "Well, if I had your problem, I'd talk to Joe Eastman. He knows more about that."

I remember Latin-American problems. We were still in the tail end of dollar diplomacy, Mexican relations—you know. I said, "The fellow who I think is more wisely informed on that subject, who has written a book on that subject and whom you ought to see is Ernest Gruening."

"Ernest who?"

He'd never heard of Gruening, and that's how they got together. Well, we talked of a number of things, and there were these suggestions of men. The next day I remember Marion saying to me, "You reminded me a little bit as though you were holding what I assume to be a seminar of yours. After all he is the President-elect."

I said, "I used to say to my students that in the realm of ideas there is no hierarchy, and I was friendly and respectful."

"Oh, yes," she said, "but he was taking down notes almost as though he were in a seminar of yours."

That very night I said, "Would you like to give great pleasure to a very old gentleman whom you admire?"

He said, "Certainly."

"Justice Holmes will have his ninety-second birthday shortly after your inauguration, on March 8, 1933. He will be ninety-two years old. I think it would be very exciting if you called on him by way of a surprise, and if you can work it out I will arrange with a wonderful maid who is in charge of him"—a marvelous Irish maid whom that very wise woman Mrs. Holmes installed to take care of him should she go and indeed she did before him—"Mary Donnellen, so that everything will go off according to Hoyle."

He said, "That's grand! Sure I'll do it. Will you be down there for this?"

"Yes, I'll be there for his birthday. Indeed, we're going to have a birthday lunch."

"That's fine. I'll turn up at four o'clock."

This was all arranged with Mary Donnellen. I was there. We had a wonderful lunch. In due course the wife of his nephew, Ed Holmes, produced out of a baize bag a bottle of champagne. Prohibition was still on, and he shrank back. She said, "Don't worry, Uncle Wendell, this is all right. This comes from the French Embassy"—I'm sure it didn't; she just made this up—"It's legal."

He said, "I never ask the source of champagne. I have no truck with bootleggers, but I do not reject their product. I assume it's legal. I assume people obey the law, but I have no truck with bootleggers."

While I was at lunch there were several phone calls, people who knew I was in town, and I was outraged. I told his secretary, "No matter who calls don't interrupt the lunch. Tell me after lunch is over if anybody calls."

When the lunch was over the secretary said, "The White House has been ringing."

I rang back Steve Early, the President's press secretary. He said, "Where have you been? Don't you know that the President has been waiting for you for lunch?"

"How should I know the President is waiting for me for lunch if nobody ever invited me."

He said, "What?" Then he said, "This will show that we've got to be more efficient around here. You come over here as soon as you can. The President wants to see you."

I went back in and told Holmes that the President was expecting me for lunch, that I didn't know about it, but that I wouldn't have gone anyhow for lunch. He turned, "You wouldn't. What do you mean? It's a command from the White House."

I said, "I told them I had a prior engagement, probably a better lunch anyhow."

He said, "It's rather fun to have the President's nose tweaked."

Eventually I went over to the White House, and as I waited to be ushered in, out came an old law school friend of mine, Arthur A. Ballantine. He had been Undersecretary of the Treasury under Ogden Mills and had stayed over. As he came out, all aglow, he said, "The President will doubtless offer you some post or other, and you must come into the administration."

I said, "I hope you're staying in it. Thank you very much for the advice."

I went in and there I saw him for the first time as President. I'd known him well, called him Franklin for what—fifteen, twenty years—and there I saw him, the American flag in that lovely oval room in the White House, and I paused. I was awed, not by him, but by the Presidency. That was the first time I had been in that room—this was 1933—since 1907, I think, when Mr. Stimson took me down to the White House and I then saw the President, Theodore Roosevelt. No, that's wrong. It was in that room that President Wilson met the Mediation Commission and instructed me on the *Mooney* case. Well, I saw Cleveland at the dedication of Grant's Tomb on the sidewalk as a little shaver with the crowd hissing him. Nevertheless, there was the President of the United States. I saw Taft, Wilson, and the Presidency is the Presidency. I feel about it the way I'm sure Winston Churchill did when he called Roosevelt, "My *august* friend." The "august" was a characteristically felicitous adjective to describe the majesty of the office. I saw FDR sitting there with the presidential flag in back of him, and I said, "Before I say another word, Frank—forgive me, but it will take me some time to say 'Mr. President'—forgive me, Mr. President."

He said, "You can say that when there are others around, but not when we're alone. Don't you dare say that when we're alone! Arthur Ballantine whom you may have seen—we were together on the *Crimson* and every other word is Mr. President this, and Mr. President that, and I don't particularly care for it. When there are other people around, that's different."

I said, "Before I sit down, Franklin, all I can say to you is that my hopes are as much engaged, perhaps more engaged, in the success of your administration than that of any President in my life time."

He said, "I know that and I want you to be part of it. I want you to be Solicitor General"—quickly like that. I have a memorandom about this meeting, and rather than give a rehash of it now, I'd prefer to rest on that contemporaneous account, dictated March 15, 1933, which reads, in part, as follows:

> This took me completely off my feet. It was the first reference directly or obliquely that Roosevelt had ever made to me about my holding any office, although at Albany and over the phone he had discussed with me and very intimately questions of personnel for the Cabinet and other places in the Government. I started to speak, but he stopped me with "I want to talk before you say anything." He then said, "I have wanted you to be Solicitor General ever since November." He said he had talked with "poor Tom Walsh" about it, and that Walsh was very eager to have me, and that it "just awaited the formalities." "When Walsh died I had to act quickly, and I put Homer Cummings in. Homer was scheduled to go to the Philippines, and he wants to go there still. I think he's a shrewd, level-headed fellow, and he's all right. I have talked to him about you; he said he thinks he met you only once, but knows all about you and admires you greatly and is most enthusiastic about having you as Solicitor General. Now, I want you down here, because I need you for all sorts of things, and in all sorts of ways. As you know, we are going in heavily for utility regulation, reorganization of the various Commissions, amendment to the Sherman Law and a lot of other things. I need your help on all those matters, and I want you to come very much." This accurately conveys the substance of the President's remarks in stating his desire in wanting me to be Solicitor General.

I said to him, in substance, that he would understand if I didn't put in words how I felt about what was implied in his desire to have me as Solicitor General. I said, "To a lawyer it is professionally the most interesting job. But confronted as I am with the situation, I have to decide whether I ought to come down and give myself up completely to being a technical lawyer, exciting as it would be to have charge of the Government's cases before the Supreme Court." The President interrupted to say that I could free myself for other work, there would be adequate help in the Department, etc., etc., to which I replied, "If you don't mind my saying so, I think I know the demands of that office perhaps more completely than there is any reason for your knowing them. I have known about the work of that office almost from the time that I left the Law School. It is exciting and profoundly important professional work. But if a man is to be Solicitor General, he must make up his mind that it will absorb sixteen hours of the day." I briefly tried to indicate the nature of the duties of the Solicitor General's office and why it would preclude participation in working out his Presidential policies. I then proceeded, "It is my genuine conviction—I am sure it is so—that I can do much more to be of use to you by staying in Cambridge than by becoming Solicitor General. The fact of the matter is that I could not have anything to do on any of the matters on which you would want my help and do my job as Solicitor General—it just can't be done. I am due to go to Oxford next fall. I won't urge that as an excuse, for while of course I am obligated, and it would disarrange matters if I didn't go, considering the exigencies of the time, I have no doubt I could be released if there were a compelling public duty. But I do want to say that no matter who will be your ambassadors abroad, I think I can be of use to you even while I am abroad, and of more use to you than as Solicitor General."

Having listened eagerly and with sympathy, the President made the following reply: "I think there is a great deal in what you say. I'm not at all sure it isn't true that you can be of more use to my Administration outside the office than you could as Solicitor General. But there is another consideration, and I am going to talk Dutch to you. I am going to talk to you frankly, as a friend. You ought to be on the Supreme Court, and I want you to be there. One can't tell when it will come—it may come in my time or not—but that's the place where you ought to be. Now you have, of course, a national reputation, a national recognition. But you know—and I said I was going to talk Dutch to you—that there are also objections to you. For a good many years now you have been a professor (smiling); you haven't actively practiced law, you've never held judicial office (again smiling); you've been the man who has refused to be a judge; then there is the Sacco-Vanzetti case (again smiling) and (this time with a grave countenance) your race. I can't put you on the Supreme Court from the Harvard Law School. But once you are Solicitor General, these various objections will be forgotten or disappear. I talk to you this way because I think for once you have a right to think selfishly, to think about yourself and not exclusively of the public interest."

My reply was: "Of course I very deeply appreciate not only what you say but the friendship that makes you say it. You know what any American lawyer thinks about the Supreme Court and a place on it, but so far as that goes, that matter will have to take care of itself, if ever the time may come. It's clear to me that from the point of view of such usefulness as I may have, I ought not to abandon what I am doing and can do to become Solicitor General, and I do not think it is a wise way of life to take a job I don't want because it may lead to another, which also I'm not at all sure I'd want. All that must be left to the future. I really don't think I ought to take a post at which I know I cannot be of the use I can be in remaining where I am, simply because it may promote my going elsewhere."

After a pause, the President said, "Well, there's no hurry about this. I tell you what I want you to do. I sometimes find it useful, and you might find it useful—I wish you would talk to your Mrs. about it. And I repeat that for once you have a right to think a little bit selfishly."

I eventually wrote him from Cambridge, saying no, that my answer was definitive and gave him the reasons. That same afternoon, on March 8, after our talk, I went back to Holmes and eventually FDR turned up. Tom Powell happened to be at the Brookings School which was on that block, or near there, and he saw the President's arrival. It took the President about half an hour to negotiate the stairs of that old brownstone house. There was no ramp. The crowd gathered. It was a wonderful thing. It was quite an experience. Suddenly the door opened and as he stumped in on the arm of Jimmy and Justice Holmes became aware that somebody was coming in, he looked sharp, leaned forward in his chair and said, "Isn't that young fellow the President of the United States?"

He stood up, and he could hardly—well, you know, he was a very old gentleman. He used to say, "The jack-knife won't open." It was a wonderful scene. Then it got into the papers. He was with him for about an hour, and I said to myself, "I'll bet they're all speculating what did the President of the United States and this most revered figure in the land, this wise, old, wisest of judges, what did they talk about? What great things passed between them?" Well, somehow or other the talk got on prize fights—John L. Sullivan and Jim Corbett. Holmes was telling of the first prize fight he saw, and they got talking about prize fights. As soon as President Roosevelt put him at his ease he quickly said, "What do you suppose I was doing just before I came here, Mr. Justice?"

"I haven't the slightest idea."

"I was signing an executive order calling in all the gold."

Holmes looked a little disturbed and said, "Does that mean I must turn over my gold medal from Congress?"

"Oh, I've made a special exception for that. That's taken care of," quickly improvised the President.

After an hour FDR stumped out on those stairs. It was hard for him to manage. I tell all this because you can't understand my relations to FDR and the New Deal without it. All this silly business! The "happy hot dogs"—you know, with whom I filled the Departments. It was the most natural thing for him to ask suggestions from me as he did from other people, and it was the most natural thing for me to have a wider acquaintance of people who were qualified for government service than probably anybody else. Why? Because I'd been at the Harvard Law School from 1914, and this was 1933, and because of the kind of people the Harvard Law School was turning out, because of their peculiar competence for dealing with governmental problems in a society and government that rests on law, I was doing for the administration what I had been doing for big offices from the time I was at the Harvard Law School, year after year after year. I used to say, "I've probably recommended more lawyers for Cravath and Henderson than I have for any department of the government."

This transcended economic views, social views. I was a professor at the Harvard Law School. I'm bred in the law. I'm a common-law lawyer. I've cared passionately about law and the institutions of law. I happen to have a penchant for relations, good relations, warm relations with young men who were students there and am probably endowed with a gift of spotting talent. I will admit to that faculty probably beyond the average. I was the recruiting officer. Most of the men who went into the United States Attorney's Office I brought in and not for any ideological reasons. They were Republicans and prohibitionists, people with humor and people without, but they had certain faculties and certain training, and so it was natural for the President to say to the Secretary of Labor, Frances Perkins, "If you need a very good lawyer, why don't you talk to Felix about it?"

That didn't mean anything ideologically. It meant no more than that Emory Buckner would ask me every few years to recommend him six men for Root, Clark, Buckner and Howland, or Winthrop and Stimson, or any number of New York law firms. Until I came down here each year God knows how many letters I had from lawyers "What do you think of this fellow?" and, "Can you recommend me that fellow?" and not only has it no significant other than professional meaning, but it has no sinister meaning other than the significance that turns you to a fellow who has some knowledge, some experience, some skill in regard to the needs you have. That is all there is to this newspaper hullabaloo—what Chief Justice Hughes was fond of saying, "The calumnists. I beg your pardon. I mean the columnists."

All this silly stuff that newspapers indulge in! Of course they have to dramatize. They have to personify. "This is a great plot!"

There's a very funny story, an amusing episode, bearing on this at the Hiss trial. One of the reputation witnesses for the defense was Mr. Justice Reed. Alger Hiss had been his immediate assistant, certainly one of his assistants, a very important assistant, when Mr. Justice Reed was Solicitor General. The prosecutor, Thomas Murphy, asked Justice Reed, "How did you come to hire Alger Hiss?"

The sedate, quiet-voiced Mr. Justice Reed said, "He was recommended to me by Judge Frank."

Murphy said, "You mean Judge Frankfurter?"

"No," he said, "I mean Judge Frank."

He referred to Jerome Frank, but what a lot that assumption of Murphy tells—you know.

The depression brought a change in the thinking of young men; the holy grail was no longer deemed to be exclusively in New York. When their thinking changed, their opportunities seemed different. Certainly in the case of the best of them, a good many of the best, the appeal of working for the country, the government, the people of the United States, in a time of dire need and distress became a sought opportunity. There was a great expansion of governmental activity and need for lawyers, and there was nothing more natural than that they should turn to the institution that turned out the best lawyers in largest number and to the man who probably was in closest contact with most of them or more voluminously in contact with the best men in the graduating class. It was the most natural thing in the world. If you want to get good groceries in Washington, you go to Magruder's, or in New York to Park and Tilford, or in Boston to S. S. Pierce. If you wanted to get a lot of first-class lawyers, you went to the Harvard Law School. There were contemporaries of mine, men I'd known who had been my friends, or men who were out and had been formerly students, and now themselves were heads of agencies and what not. It was the most natural thing in the world, and it so happened that there came to be a considerable percentage of Harvard Law School men on the legal staffs, among government lawyers.

This is so commonplace that I forget that I had been sending year after year—from the time I went to the Harvard Law School—law clerks to Mr. Justice Holmes and after Mr. Justice Brandeis went on the Court to him. I supplied Learned Hand with law clerks, Judge Julian Mack with law clerks, and so on. What's the great conspiracy? What's the subtle, below-the-surface reason?

This reminds me of a remark I heard William A. White, the editor of the *Emporia Gazette,* that wise fellow, make. A newspaperman was sent to Washington to be the Washington correspondent for his paper. He was very young, a hopeful one. He'd made good in his home town, but Washington—my heavens! He saw Mr. White and asked his counsel, suggestions, and advice. Mr. White said to him, "Every newspaperman wants to make scoops. You do too. It's a perfectly natural thing. Would you like to know how to have scoops as a Washington reporter, particularly of what goes on in Congress?"

He said, "Oh, certainly."

"I advise you to do this. You sit in the Senate gallery and listen hard to the debate. Most of the time very few other newspapermen will be there. They'll be looking for stuff underneath the asphalt. If you very often will report what is going on to which nobody else will pay any attention and assume that what you hear and see is the truth, you have no idea how often you'll make a scoop."

There is something in human nature that will not take the surface, if you please, the ingenuous, on-the-face view. They must look for some cunning, conspiratorial, sinister, extremely sophisticated, out of the way, exotic explanation, and so it is with all this business of how Felix Frankfurter filled the government with his cohorts, his disciples, whatnot. In the first place, they have no understanding of my relations with these young men. They have no understanding of the kind of independence—that we're just all in the same boat in being, as it were, part of the ministry of justice, part of the great company of lawyers who serve law, and that the bond was just the bond of fellowship of ideas and purposes and nothing more complicated than that. So often of course these efforts to seek for some ulterior motives and purposes are what the psychologists call "projections"—there must be some ulterior reason, either money, or wanting to join the club, or get a job, or marry off your daughter, or something. Well, I don't mean to say that there aren't ulterior motives in this world in people. It is true that very often there's more than meets the eye, but whoever said it for the first time said a profound thing when he said about Washington, "In Washington there's often less than meets the eye."

24. *Oxford*

The whole of Oxford—English life generally, Oxford life in particular—was so different from the atmosphere we were breathing and our accustomed ways in Cambridge, Massachusetts. The chair at Oxford to which I was appointed was the George Eastman visiting professorship, founded by George Eastman not in reference to any particular subject, a professorship-at-large as it were, an annual professorship not in any one field, but each year in successive fields of inquiry and filled by somebody presumably of standing within that field. All professorships at Oxford are attached to some college. This professorship was attached to Balliol. It was an exceptionally wise endowment, for a house was attached to the chair.

One day my wife and I arrived at the Oxford station where we were met by the Home Bursar of Balliol College, Colonel Basil G. Duke. He had charge of all the domestic arrangements for the college, the servants of the college, the kitchen, etcetera. Colonel Duke was a Scot and a veteran of the Boer War, a delightful fellow who added not a little to the pleasure of our stay at Oxford. He took us to Eastman House, 18 Norham Gardens, a house sort of off the general grounds of Oxford University, on the same street right across from the house that Sir William Osler had lived in during his years as Regius Professor of Medicine at Oxford. We got there just in time for my wife to preside over tea because not only did a house go with the chair, but a staff went with the house

—Mr. and Mrs. Golder. Mrs. Golder was the cook, and each morning my wife had a conference with her. Everything is very particular, very precise in England. Orders are definite. Things are done punctually, reliably and meticulously. Every day my wife sat like Queen Victoria receiving some privy councillor and gave the orders for the day, what to have for lunch, what to have for tea, what to have for dinner and who was coming, if anybody. Golder was a veteran of the First World War, and it took me some time to get over the fact that here was a fellow with God knows how many medals who was now merely attending to my animal, or more or less civilized wants. My shoes stood outside the door carefully polished each morning. He pressed my trousers, and everything was put away. Golder took care of me, and Mrs. Golder took care of my wife. There we were at four-thirty, my wife already pouring tea in her own going establishment. Every benefactor of educational institutions who founds a visiting professorship should always have a house go with it. For the professor's wife, especially, is it a great comfort.

While tea was going on there turned up the Master of Balliol, A. E. Lindsay, later the Lord Lindsay who was a Kantian scholar. On his retirement he became the vice chancellor of a new university up in one of the provinces. He was a charming fellow, a delightful creature, always addressed as the Master. The head of each college has a different title: president, provost, rector, dean. Balliol's head is Master. We put him at ease. He was a relaxed kind of a person, knew America.

When they invited me in their very courteous way, they told me next to nothing of what they expected of me. What my duties would be, my responsibilities, were all very loose, very vague, very indefinite, so I asked the Master when, where and to whom I was to lecture and about what—you know, what I could do within a limited scope. "Sandy"—Lindsay was a Scot, so it was "Sandy" —took out his little book. Everybody had their little blue appointment books, and "Sandy" wrote down in his that he'd have to find out and let me know. I soon found that I was to give in the three terms several public lectures and for the rest I could do what I pleased. They've got the tutorial system, but I would have no pupils, and I could do what I pleased.

I had practically no acquaintance at Oxford when we arrived. Strangely enough I did have at Cambridge, more particularly Keynes, which reminds me that when I told Professor Whitehead I was to be professor at Oxford, he was perfectly delighted, but added in his charming way, "I'm sorry it's at the inferior place."

Whitehead was a Cambridge man. Arthur Goodhart was the only fellow I knew at Oxford. He was an old American friend. He was professor of Jurisprudence, at University College, and he soon gave us a lunch. In order to lecture you have to wear a cap and gown, and I was made a supernumerary fellow of Balliol College which means that I could attend college meetings, like our faculty meetings, but not vote. Very promptly after we came there, we had a formal invitation to dine at the vice chancellor's—Lys was his name. He was then the provost of Worcester College, and he was vice chancellor of the university. That was a very memorable experience in my Oxford adventure. I went there in white tie. It was a formal dinner. Oh what a lovely green the college lawn was! My wife was ushered up to put her wraps down. I was waiting downstairs for her, and when she came down I said to her, "Marion, I'm sunk. I've disgraced myself and my country, Harvard—everything."

"What's happened?"

"It's terrible. Evidently I should have worn a gown."

A lot of guests came in, all of them gowned, even some of the ladies gowned. My wife said, "You'll have to make the best of it."

It was a beautiful dinner. Those were still the days when there were four lovely glasses at each place, four courses of wine. It was a big party. This invitation was addressed to us as I was addressed the rest of the year, "The Eastman Professor." I had no name. I wasn't a person—"The Eastman Professor and Mrs. Frankfurter." You were known by your title. I did the best I could. Mrs. Lys was a very charming woman; indeed, a delightful, forth-putting hostess. The dinner was excellent, and I care about good food and wine. I'm something of a gourmet. But there they all were in gowns, and I was not dressed as I should have been, and that gnawed at me throughout the dinner. All things come to an end. We went home. That was that.

The next morning I walked out. I forget where I was going, but

I bumped into an acquaintance of mine, somebody I knew. We stopped, and he said, "Aren't you clever!" He was somebody who was at this dinner, and he said, "Aren't you clever to get on to our ways so quickly!"

I said, "Why that remark?"

"It was so clever of you to know how you should have dressed last night."

"Oh, well," I said, "You know—we know these things in America."

It was very strange, but I found myself being rather chauvinistic. I wanted to do everything better, or at least as well as my English friends there. His comment was puzzling. Evidently what I did in my ignorance was right. I then found out the little twister. A formal dinner at the vice chancellor's calls for academic gowns. The formal head of the university is the chancellor, some eminent personage. When I was there Sir Edward Grey, the chancellor, had just died. I don't think Lord Halifax had as yet been appointed. He was the chancellor until recently. That's an honorific, life office. The actual executive headship of the university is in the hands of the vice chancellor who is one of the heads of colleges according to some system of seniority. He's head of the council that really runs the show. The chancellor is the titular head. The vice chancellor is the *defacto,* executive head, and when you dine at the vice chancellor's you dine in an academic gown. That's an academic occasion. But when you dine at the vice chancellor's and you wear an academic gown, it must be the academic gown of Oxford. In order to lecture as I was going to lecture—this was very early, before I got under way—you had to have an Oxford degree, so in due course I was given an honorary M.A., so that I could wear an Oxford gown, but I had not yet been made an M.A. I therefore had no Oxford degree, was not entitled to wear an Oxford gown, couldn't have worn an Oxford gown. It would have been improper to have worn a Harvard gown. Therefore, you wear what I wore, formal dinner tails. And so I started out propitiously, by good luck having complied with the mysteries of the custom of the country which you cannot find in any book at all.

For instance, when you dine in Hall, you dine in successive rooms. Take All Souls College. You have your dinner in Hall.

Then you go to another place for your dessert, then another place for your coffee, and the port, and you have to watch closely where you take your napkin along and where you don't, or when you take off your gown and when you don't. All this was very perplexing, and nobody tells you anything. You know that you're not supposed to ask, and your pride prevents you from doing so. It's like being out in the country asking directions, and the fellow tells you, "When you get to Jamison's Drug Store, you turn to the left," but you don't know where the hell Jamison's Drug Store is. I was told that you lecture in "schools." Well, I didn't know where "schools" was. That's a building, but where it is "Don't ask!" as in Potash and Perlmutter. You just have to smell it. This was all very trying, and my wife recalls—and it couldn't have been a fortnight, maybe a week or so after we got there—when I came home and said, "Marion, to hell with it! I'm going to stop trying to please them. I'm going to just try to be what I am, and they'll have to put up with it."

From that time on everything went smoothly. They didn't want an imitation Englishman. Such crudities and ignorances as I manifested! But if I'm not to be—not coy about it, not prissy, not self-conscious and not manifest the egotism that suppresses the ego—the fact of the matter is that what they liked was my spontaneity. I wasn't boorish, and I had more or less good manners, but they liked the spontaneity, the vitality. My explanation of why so many English like America so much is that they like our vitality. It's a sort of shot in the arm for tired people. The English use a word frequently when we use a very different word. They don't say, "He's a fool," or "He's a crook," or "He's a phony." They have one word that covers all sorts of uncongenialities, unsatisfactorinesses, "Oh, he's so tiresome." The word "tiresome" covers a lot of their incompatibilities, "Oh, he's so tiresome!" They're not all tiresome, but they all are a little tired, and to have a fellow who is as spontaneous, as enthusiastic as I am without being sappy, a fellow who is as spontaneous as I am and who is as critical—you know, who is a little sophisticated—was a refreshing thing. I suspect another ingredient that made the dish palatable was revealed to me one night as I walked home with a fellow who is now the Master of Balliol, Keir, a Scotsman, and he said—

well, I suppose it was the darkness, the anonymity of the night, that led him to be as candid as was his remark in saying, "You rather strike me as un-American."

I wanted to punch him only he was twice as tall as I was, so I abstained and asked, "Why?" thinking that I was a very fine specimen of an American. He said, "You have a strong vein of irony, and Americans are not a people of irony."

That's very true. My form of humor isn't a slapstick—you know, exaggeration and all that, so anyhow, I nailed my thesis of independence at the door of my house and said, "If you don't like it, to hell with you," and from that time on everything was hunkydory.

I soon asked whether it would be agreeable to them if I could have what amounted to a seminar in federalism. For a long time in the whole place I couldn't get a copy of the American Constitution. This was 1934. Things have changed a great deal since then. I got together a number of people including Arthur Goodhart, this fellow Keir who was a political scientist, a number of people, and we had a very good time at the Codrington Library, met once a week for two or three hours, on federalism. I tried another thing which was a complete bust. I found that the economists and the law teachers had no communication. Economics was Economics, and Law was Law and never the twain shall meet. So I was the convener of a discussion as to why there should not be an interchange, what you damn jargonists call "interdisciplinary study." The economists thought the lawyers were mud, and the lawyers thought the economists were—you know, "the dreary exponents of a dismal science." No progress was made in the interfusion of the two, but this seminar on federalism was great fun.

Then one day they asked me if I would take a pupil, a very, very brilliant fellow of whom they had great expectations that he was to be a law don. He was Jack Latham, the son of the then Chief Justice of Australia. I said I would, and he came. He afterwards became a law don, became a flier and was killed very early in the war, a very, very able, promising fellow. I think it must have been at our first tutorial, certainly not later than the second when he suddenly said, "I see you're a sociological jurist."

I said, "I'm very glad to be ticketed, but suppose we leave tickets behind and just find out what the problem is."

With that "I see" he sort of had me pigeonholed. He was an "analytical jurist," and I was a "sociological jurist." The end of man is categorization. The end of man is labels, not contents, but labels. Well, he and I became great friends.

I did odds and ends. I was asked to read doctoral theses for the University of Manchester and the University of Edinburgh. I visited the University of Manchester where I delivered a lecture I forget on what, but I went up primarily to see the then greatest living English philosopher, Samuel Alexander. He was a prophetic, long-bearded, wonderful bachelor. He'd written a book on God and a book on Beauty. He lived in a very modest little house and was one of the most benign, one of the purest creatures I ever laid eyes on. Just to be in his presence you were—I was going to say washed clean, but you had no consciousness of being dirty in his presence. He was benignity itself. No wonder when he walked out with me to get me a taxi the children just flocked around him. I was later reminded of it when the same thing happened to Einstein. Children loved him, had a natural affinity, and he would tell wonderful stories to children. It was cold as could be up in Manchester. It was biting cold, and he had a little bit of an open fireplace in which charcoal was being burned, and he held his hands in front of this thing to warm himself. I remember saying to myself, "While he warms himself by this fire, I warm my soul by his presence."

That was an interesting experience, just to feel him. I remember when Professor Whitehead got the Order of Merit, the greatest of honors, of course it made him happy, but there was a fly in the ointment, a big fly, because as he said to me, "It's Alexander who should have been given that honor and not I."

Marion and I went to dinners again and again up to London—you know the kind of life you lead at Oxford which is within less than an hour of London. You go up to opera, the wonderful ballet, etcetera, etcetera. Then Keynes was an old friend of mine from Paris days, and he had the good sense to ask me up to Grand Night at King's College. That was a wonderful experience—Grand Night. Colleges usually have a Grand Night in celebrating the founder of the college, eight hundred years ago, seven hundred years ago—whatever it was. I made friends with Lord Rutherford.

He was, I suppose, responsible for the "atomic age" beyond any one human being. He is the father of all these fellows: Niels Bohr, Kapitza who probably did the intercontinental missile for Russia—all these fellows studied at the Cavendish under Rutherford at Cambridge. He asked me twice to be his guest at the High Table at Trinity College. That's the famous Cambridge college. I remember the first time he said, "You might be interested to know that at that table there sit five Nobel Prize winners."

One man interested me most. I couldn't take my eyes off him—A. E. Housman, the *Shropshire Lad* man, because he sat there rigid, talking neither to the right nor to the left, just ate his food, and that was that. I never had a word with him.

Soon—I don't know how soon—we came to know a group of people two of whom since have become our dearest and most enjoyable friends. The origin of this relationship was a great friend we had in London, Sylvester Gates, who was a pupil of mine. He was a Wykehamist and as one of the first lot of Commonwealth Fund Fellows he was at the Harvard Law School from 1925 to 1927. I needed somebody to work with me on the record in the Sacco-Vanzetti case, and he's the fellow. If you want to know his quality, read his biography of Sacco-Vanzetti in the *Dictionary of American Biography*. He was then at the bar. A great friend of his was Maurice Bowra, an outstanding Greek scholar. Bowra was a don at Wadham College, and he had a broad, rather powerful, vigorous voice, was an emphatic, intense man and a great friend of Sylvester Gates. Sylvester arranged this meeting, and Bowra and I found each other very quickly. He's now the warden of Wadham College, and has written many important books. He was offered the professorship of Greek at Columbia, Harvard, and wherenot in this country, but he prefers life there. Through him we came to know several of the younger people who since have attained distinction. The kind of a fellow that Bowra is, is illustrated by a story that my wife and I like about him. He was a kid—sixteen or so—when he was in the First World War. His whole trench fell in, and he found himself way below the cave-in. The telephone rang. He picked up the telephone and said, "Bowra speaking." Well "Bowra speaking" describes him. He's witty, powerful, generous, uncompromising. He's abundant, an abundant source of life. His protege—I think I can call him that—is the now famous Sir Isaiah Berlin who had then been elected to All Souls. I don't have to tell about him because the world knows about him, a man of very great intellectual distinction who recently was elected to the professorship of G. D. H. Cole. Then there was Freddie Ayer, A. J. Ayer, the philosopher, the leader of the logical positivists. There was Roy Harrod, the economist at Christ Church and I suppose the most distinguished economist at Oxford who wrote that admirable life of Keynes. There was Lord David Cecil, a distinguished professor of English, Stuart Hampshire, a philosopher, and Sir John Maud now one of the leading civil servants, the Undersecretary, I think, in the Power Ministry, a very distinguished civil servant. This young, extremely clever, almost excessively clever young crowd, in their twenties, their early thirties, became our friends in varying degrees. They were at our house, and we were at their rooms. We really had a very full time. Life was gay, life was conversation late into the night, long teas. Very early we met through these fellows Elizabeth Bowen, and we became great friends with her so that when she came to our Cambridge she stayed with us.

It was a rich, stimulating, exciting, affectionate year. I say "affectionate." The English are terribly reticent and terribly withholding, but when you become friends with them they have a depth that we don't understand about friendship. They almost embarrass you with their candor. They talk about the intimate aspects of their lives in a way that we Americans don't. Whether we're too shy, or don't have intimate lives I don't know—I'm joshing. But when you make friendships they go very deep. There was also Sir Kenneth Clark, then director of the Ashmolean, a young fellow who was then already recognized as an important art critic, with his very handsome wife. Then Clark became whatever it was, director of the National Gallery. Then there was a very individualistic fellow who has since become Lord Pakenham. He was then an economics don and very interesting. As the memory is stimulated I think of lots more.

I belonged to two clubs. One was a radical club, the "young Turks" as it were, of which I remember that John Strachey was one. Cole was a member too. Then I belonged to a club of very eminent respectability. I remember the president of Magdalen, George Gordon, a distinguished critic of English literature called "Gentleman George," and Humphrey Milford, publisher of the finer books of the Oxford Press. You see his name on publications. What a lovely character he was! Then there was the librarian of the then King's Library, the librarian of Windsor Castle, a very considerable scholar.

The latter club met at lunch once a week at different colleges, and it came my turn to have them to lunch. Balliol College was famous for high thinking and poor living. You know, it gained the great reputation when Jowett was the master. Prime ministers came out of it, foreign secretaries, everything, and I said to myself, "It's not going to be any fun for them to just have the poor food of Balliol College and the meager wine that its cellar affords." I said to Basil Duke that I had a bright idea, what did he think of the idea and would it be possible. Most of my life I have operated on the principle of trying things out. I can't bear people who say, "It won't pass." Well, you know, how the hell do they know it won't pass! So I said to Basil Duke, "Is it feasible to rent a charabanc, chill a lot of good chicken salad, somehow or other get enough bottles of champagne and keep them cold, and have us all go to see the Derby and then lunch?"

He thought that it was an excellent idea, that it was perfectly feasible, and that he would carry out my wishes if that is what I wanted to do. All I had to do was pay the bill. When I put that to the members of this club they thought it was a wonderful idea because most of them had never been to the Derby although it was right around the corner from Oxford. Basil Duke arranged for hampers of stuff. We had early breakfast at Balliol—it was rather darkish—and then started off in this charabanc. Somebody tipped us off that Windsor Lad would win the Derby, and we put our money on Windsor Lad, and he did win the Derby. It was a most successful day, and my stock as a scholar simply reached astronomic heights. They said, "Well, at last we've got an American scholar!"

Really it was an extraordinarily happy occasion! It was one of those things that just broke right. I think two-thirds of them had never seen the Derby, just as I left Cambridge, Massachusetts never having seen the glass flowers, and I suppose that I will one of these days die never having been on the top of the Washington Monument. To this day I haven't been there. I should think that luncheon episode marked the highwater mark, the zenith of my scholarly career as a visiting professor at Oxford University.

People came to tea. Eastman House had a garden, and we'd sit out in the garden. Perhaps the best way to indicate the kind of a year it was, and I was recalling this the other day to Marion, is to say that again and again and again I would say to myself, "What do I have to do next?" The notion of the serenity of the atmosphere, the sense of living for the sake of life, the feeling that you were here to take in this wonderful thing called being alive and contribute your share to life, was something that I had never consciously experienced at Cambridge. It was partly the Puritan streak in me which is deeper than many persons suspect, the sense of duty, the sense of having to do something every minute, partly Puritan, partly engendered by the American hustle and bustle—you know, "We've got to do something," or "For God's sake, let's do something," but just to let life come in the way the air unconsciously comes in and sustains you, just sit in the garden and have a very good talk, pursue a conversation for its own sake, and have a contest just for the sake of seeing where you come out, or have somebody narrate something, it's a great experience, to tell you why this book is no good, or why it's very good, or to speculate idly. The endless Oxford talk was who will be what when—just as we talk about the next President. They talk about who will succeed "Sandy" as Master of Balliol. Then all sorts of intellectual games: "Who in England is most like Billy Graham, Nixon, Eisenhower, Dean Acheson, Chief Justice Warren?" Well, you know that can keep a crowd of eager, alert, fencing, imaginative minds busy for days. On many of these things we enjoyed it as spectators at a spectacle. The discussion among Austenites, the order of Jane Austen's novels and why, or a fellow who hates Austen, that rarity, who is nearly lynched—you know. Or they can be just as hot about, "No, the Second Philippic for these reasons is worse than the Third." Then have them rattle off or cite a paragraph of Latin as to why this rather than that.

I remember at our own table there were present Bowra, Isaiah

Berlin, Sylvester Gates and Freddie Ayer who is now Professor Ayer. This was a row between Sylvester and Ayer about Wittgenstein. He was a philosopher at Cambridge, a very original genius, a Viennese by origin who came to Cambridge and died about a year or so ago. Freddie Ayer said something about that wonderful remark of Wittgenstein speaking in German, "About what you do not know you should keep silent," and Sylvester Gates saying, "Yes, and he said it twice in his book." "Twice! No!" Well, they got into this wrangle about whether he said it twice in the book or not.

"In the course of his discussion in his book he twice used that phrase."

Freddie Ayer said, "No he didn't."

Then they appealed to me because I was the only lawyer there. I said, "Look, boys, you're now rowing about a fact. Freddie, have you got Wittgenstein in your room?"

"My room? It's my bed book."

I said, "You get on your bicycle and you go down and bring the book."

Something was in the wind. Somebody said, "Well, you be the arbitrator." They anticipated that I would be a judge, so the book was produced, and Sylvester with that absolutely sure thin lip of his pointed out that he said it just toward the end of the book—almost the last page, as I remember—and he said it in his preface before the table of contents. "That's not the text of the book!" Ayer was like an Arab steed. The debate was whether the preface was part of the text of the book. I said, "All right I'll hear argument on this: Is the preface part of the text?" Well, you can imagine what happened, but that gives you the kind of flavor and excitement we had with those men, particularly the two we've seen a great deal of because they've come here again and again—Isaiah Berlin and Maurice Bowra with whom we correspond. Bowra is a marvelous letter writer. It was a very rich year for us. Intimacies were formed that have remained intimate. It was a year that has continuing influence—deep associations that have continued to this day to our great pleasure.

25. *Students and Traditions*

I want to make some comments on the difference between the student body in England and American students. The place was full of Americans, and we saw a great many of them. We had a good many students and younger dons at the house at various functions—tea, that conventional standby English institution! We had them at tea, at lunch. We had an eggnog party on Thanksgiving Day. First and last we saw a good many of the young people, a good deal of the young life, and some generalizations I think are permitted.

Brain for brain the best Rhodes Scholars were as good as the men who get firsts at Oxford, but these two sets of equals aside, the English students were much more intellectual because they had read more. They were reading more, and they had the habit of reading, not snippets, "readings in," the conventional type of American textbook in studying economics, or political science. They really had read Hobbes and Locke, and they were ready to discourse and dispute on the books they had read, not read about, and they acquired the habit of reading. Courses, that curse of American non-intellectual university life, don't exist there. So much depends on a system that had its origin in the days when relatively few people went to the university, and you could afford that kind of system, but it became clear to me that intellectually, in the actual manifestation of intellectual power, the English lads were better than the Americans. Emotionally they were much more innocent. American boys were much more emotionally mature. They were freer, easier, fresher, more at home, but when it came to free discussion, taking you on and taking you on with capacity, the English boys were better, though of course there were exceptions. One of my young friends at Oxford was Sam Beer who is now one of the leading men in government at Harvard, but he was rather an outstanding exception. He was as good as his compeers, but that was not true on the whole. Our best in the mass were not as good as their best.

This observation about the reading habits disclosed itself in another aspect of our experience—reading as reflected in writing. No English lad who had enjoyed any kind of hospitality at our hands, whether it was tea, or lunch, or dinner, or whatnot—without exception my recollection is the next day there was a note addressed to my wife thanking her. They wouldn't send them by mail. They dropped them in the slit, and there they were without exception. So far as I can recall without exception not a single American lad ever wrote a letter.

Let me tell you another differentiation. I've told this so often that I may be merely repeating error, but it lies in my mind that no English student ever called me on the phone. If he wanted to ask me something, or he wanted to see me, or to invite me to speak at the numerous little clubs that grow up like mushrooms, some permanent, some ephemeral, and I spoke at a good number of them, they unfailingly wrote. I do not recall, and it lies in my memory very strongly, a single English undergraduate phoning me. The American lads phoned all the time. They never wrote. They just phoned, and I remember this episode very well because I think it tells its own tale. It was a standing order that while we were at dinner, telephone messages would be taken by Golder, and the dinner was not to be interrupted, but on one occasion Golder said, "There's a young man who says that it is very, very important for him to talk to you and would you talk to him?"

I went to the phone, and this was an American lad asking me one of those things that would hold until tomorrow, or could have been indicated to me by a note, or postcard, so when we got through our business I said, "Let me ask you a question. You know enough about our household to know this is about dinner time. Tell me why you phone about dinner time?"

"Oh well," he said, "because I thought I'd be sure to catch you."

That tells you a great deal, the insouciance of it! The charming impudence, the impudence of non-reflection, non-breeding, and also it shows the resourcefulness. Well, an English lad would rather die than do that, no matter how arrogant he may be as to other matters. He can be cocksure of how to run the empire, but he wouldn't phone.

I think that goes very deep. For instance—I came back so impressed—that's true not only of undergraduates, but true of young dons. They would write, not call me up. They'd write a note and ask me, or if they wanted to see me, they'd ask several days ahead so that ever since that experience I've been hoping to start a crusade in America, at least in my own life, of not having people just drop in, or knock at the door, things that happen to me all the time. An old student will phone, and my secretary will say, "Mr. Jones of the class of 1924 is on the phone."

"Yes, I'll talk to him. Hello! I'm delighted to hear from you."

"I call up because I've got just three hours before my train time, and I thought I'd like to visit with you."

I have said on occasion, "I'm so delighted. I was wondering what to do with my time, so come along."

They really think you sit here and twirl your thumbs waiting for the fellow whose train to Des Moines doesn't leave when he's through with his business at the Treasury at 2:30. His train doesn't leave until 5:30, and what better could he do with the time than to go call on Mr. Justice Frankfurter. This reticence about not breaking in on a Justice of the Supreme Court of the United States isn't something derived from a vainglorious regard for my lofty position. I know for a fact that I never phoned Mr. Justice Holmes. I wouldn't bring him to the phone. To be sure he was an elderly, young man, but I'm getting to be an elderly gentleman, but anyhow that wasn't the point. He was an elderly gentleman when I first came to know him. He was nearly seventy years old, the chipperest young thing I knew. I doubt that I ever phoned Mr. Justice Brandeis with whom my relations were of the utmost intimacy. I just had that kind of respect for his time, his own plans, and

I knew that if I brought him to the phone he was then doing something else. I wouldn't do that any more than I'd walk into his room without letting him know I was coming. All that's by the board. Indeed hardly ever does a fellow write me in advance, "I'm going to be in Washington next week, and I'll call up your secretary and by chance if you're free between four and six it will be a great pleasure to see you again." Not at all. Old and young they just drop right in so that for years now I've been up against these unhappy alternatives: either I must drop what I'm doing to see him, or if I just cannot do it I have to sit down and write him a note, how sorry I am to have missed him. I've told a number of people with whom I feel free to talk, "When next you come down, why don't you, unless you're caught in the last minute and you're suddenly brought to Washington by an emergency telephone call, which doesn't happen often, write me in advance."

The people who come to Washington on legal business, come here by pre-arrangement. Their business is pre-arranged, but they just think I sit there twirling my thumbs waiting for them to relieve me of my tedium. I can assure you that is never so.

Part of all this is the function of form in English life. We think form is effete—for non-democratic countries only. Form is just a heritage of feudalism, or monarchical institutions, or exploiting capitalism, or I don't know what, but for myself form and substance are inseparable. Cardozo has a lovely line somewhere about "form is liberating." He has some charming remarks about the compulsion of fourteen lines of a sonnet, to put all your thoughts within that framework, the compression it requires and the beauty that results from it. Punctuality is an aspect of English regard for form. I am an unpunctual fellow except where I have to be punctual, or with reference to people with whom my respect is so deep that they exact that kind of respect. I have nothing to say in defense of my unpunctuality except that I am aware that it is not a nice quality. My friend Croly used to say that he used to resent my being late with him because he knew that I would never be late with Holmes and Brandeis.

I always thought it would be helpful to introduce in this country an English institution at their formal functions, at their dinners, for instance at the Inns of Court called Grand Night. I was fortunate enough to be asked to several of those impressive functions. The invitation is for 7:45 for eight. That means that at 7:45 sherry will be served, and going on to the sixtieth minute the end of which is eight o'clock, the gong begins to sound, and they begin to walk into the hall—absolutely ruthlessly. That was true of the Supreme Court when Hughes was Chief Justice. He was like that. We started to ascend the bench at twelve sharp. We'd break up into divisions of three, and we'd begin to walk in, and by 12:01 we were all seated. We left sharply at 4:30. Hughes hoarded his time, the Court's time. If an argument was complete at 4:27, he didn't adjourn, but utilized that three minutes for the next case. The lawyer had to get up and start so that the next morning there were three minutes saved.

A John W. Davis story illustrates it all. Mr. Davis was as engaging a counsel as appeared before the Court in my years, and he was a tradition in the days before my time. He was an enchanting advocate with great grace, charm and distinction. Those were the days before the change which now prevails whereby counsel has to take care of his own time, except that five minutes before his time is supposed to be up a light at the lectern signals. When I came on the Court it had been the system, strangely enough, that the Chief Justice kept the time. Counsel would appeal to the Chief Justice, "How much time do I have left?" The Chief Justice would tell them, "Twelve minutes" or whatever it was, and they'd say, "I reserve that for rebuttal."

In a very, very important case that Mr. Davis was arguing, the time was running down, as he was aware. He stopped and said, "Mr. Chief Justice, may I trouble you to tell me how much time I have left?"

The Chief Justice, straightening out his bristles, looked at his watch and said, "Mr. Davis, you have a minute and a half left."

Davis stopped just for a second and with a distinguished, sort of Castilian bow to the Chief Justice and with a wonderful gesture with his right hand, an enormous wave, he said, "I present the Court with the minute and a half."

Everybody laughed except Hughes who immediately called the next case and took that minute and a half. The effect was that the atmosphere was taut throughout the session of the Court.

Everybody was on his toes, everybody was alert, no nonsense. It was exciting, quietly exciting, just as every member of the orchestra, I'm sure, was taut when Koussevitsky conducted and when Toscanini conducted—nothing easy going, nothing flabby, nothing relaxed any more than a runner at a marathon is relaxed, or are the Derby horses relaxed when they turn the bend at the Derby. That's what an argument before the Supreme Court of the United States should be, power applied to the very best that counsel are capable of. That means that they must bring their whole being into focus and the Court is engaged, alert, committed. That was a thrilling event—the voice, the handsome presence of Mr. Davis when he, absolutely poker-faced said, "I present the Court with a minute and a half," and Chief Justice Hughes grabbed it and was grateful to him for it.

That's what these English functions are, instead of straggling in—you know, the way you go to a dinner in the United States, come in in the middle and leave before the end, higgledy-piggledy. That's all right for children playing on the beach and making mud pies. Arguing a case before the Supreme Court of the United States isn't making mud pies. A stately dinner isn't children on the beach making mud pies and destroying them. Analyzing it to the bottom, it's the acknowledgement of a hospitality! There is the function of the appreciator, not merely the provider, the host.

I remember a brilliant letter in the *Times,* the London *Times.* The letter that has pride of place is regarded as important. A letter that had pride of place was by J. M. Keynes, written in his most powerfully caustic style protesting against the freedom of people calling up on the phone. He said, "Nobody would dream of walking unbidden into my study when I'm working. Well, one who calls me at his pleasure is walking in when I have to stop and answer the phone."

I think these observations, like all observations on national habits, or tendencies, or characteristics are subject to that wise observation by Lord Acton protesting against building a great deal on the differences among people. Somewhere or other he has a remark, "When short of argument rely on national characteristics." That is true, but there are such things as national habits, not biological differences, but habits, traditions of what is done and what isn't done. Some things aren't done in England. They just wouldn't be done. Certain things are done and if you don't do them, then you default. You're not doing what ought to be done.

26. *England as Source*

There's no doubt that English institutions became more vivid to me as a result of my Oxford year. They became first-hand experiences for my feeling and not merely something apprehended by my head. To have been there a year and to have seen the actors in the parliamentary drama, to have had lunch with them, as I did on occasion, made English institutions more vivid. I had some contact with MacDonald, the then Prime Minister, had some candid talks with him. English men when you talk with them assume that they are talking with a gentleman, that you're not going to leak to columnists. What struck me about the prime minister of Great Britain was the depth of his ignorance about the United States. Without going into particulars, America was a kind of a vague something. He had no sense of the conflicting regional and economic interests of the country, no sense even remotely of the kinds of problems that every President has to face, no sense of the vast difference between a prime minister commanding a majority in the House of Commons and a President with an independent Congress even though it may be of his own party, the kind of conciliations that had to be made on this, that or the other thing on this side of the ocean that a prime minister is free from. Not that even he doesn't have to make his conciliations and his adjustments, but America was a vague kind of a still more or less undiscovered continent.

That in a way reflected what was so striking to me about the ignorance not only about the United States, but about federalism and the federal systems on the part of the scholars concerned with history and government at Oxford. I told you that in all of Oxford I couldn't find a copy of the Constitution outside of the Bodleian Library. I tried to get the Oxford Press interested in reprinting a copy of the American Constitution for my seminar, but I didn't get much of a response. Finally, in Blackwell's, the big book shop in Oxford, I had them rummage around until they found a copy of the Constitution hidden in the back of a book designed to help immigrants into the United States, a kind of a manual to help them answer questions that they would be asked on landing.

What was startling about this was that here was what is now known as the Commonwealth, then the British Empire, and their Dominions, two of which were clear federalisms, one of them more or less based on the American scheme of things, namely, the Commonwealth of Australia. The British North America Act, which was passed shortly after the Civil War, emphasized the powers given to the Dominion, the central government. The Commonwealth of Australia Act passed in 1900 largely reversed the matter. There they were afraid of centralization, and so like unto the American Constitution the federal government had only those powers conferred, and the rest belonged to the states. But there was no interest in federalism; hardly anybody at Oxford knew about the federal systems.

In those days appeals went to the Privy Council from the High Court of Australia, and to some extent they still do. I was looking for, but I haven't got at hand, a recent judgment by Chief Justice Sir Owen Dixon, for whom I have the highest regard, who in a deft kind of way read a little lecture to the Privy Council on their unrealistic way of construing constitutional questions coming up from Australia. He rather envied people who aren't troubled by these intractable, complicated problems, but it was an awfully neat way of chiding English judges who are accustomed to a unitary form of government and who were dealing with problems that derive from the division of political power between the central government and the units within it called by us states, called in Australia states and provinces in Canada. Now of course India is another kind of a federation. The Union of South Africa is a little different, but has aspects of federalism, but nobody in 1933-1934 was concerned with those problems in Oxford. That was very striking both scholastically and politically, the little knowledge the prime minister of Great Britain and other public men with whom I talked had of this country, and I said to myself, "If that's true as between two people speaking so-called the same language" —was it Shaw who said, "Two nations having a kinship and separated by a common language"?—"if that's the lack of vividness of appreciation of the problems of the country you're closest to, or most friendly with, and eventually you'll be most dependent on, how much knowledge is there about other countries with whom you've had no intimate past, but with whom you've merely had a disdainful, going-to-the-continent summer experience?"

I saw something of Attlee who had impressed me through what he had said and what I read by him in Hansard. In personal contacts he impressed me as a very level-headed, uninteresting, able, not a warm-blooded fellow. That's my estimate of him today—sensible. He made a speech sometime ago on the functions of the prime minister in which he said that at times he has to be a ruthless fellow, cut people's throats, tell a minister who isn't doing what he ought to do, "I'm sorry, but I have to give your place to somebody else," and he did it with cold-bloodedness, unlike Asquith who couldn't do such a thing, certainly without groaning and agonizing. Thus English life became more vivid, part of my daily life, and to that extent intensified my feeling for the institutions, political and constitutional, antecedents of our own political and constitutional life and more particularly our legal life.

Naturally I was interested in the courts. I went to a trial that bears telling. There was a libel suit brought by Princess Yusupov against Metro Goldwyn for a movie which Metro Goldwyn had put on entitled "Rasputin." The movie told the story of that filthy, disgusting person who was such a baneful influence at the Russian court, particularly with the Czarina. He finally was killed. It was Prince Yusupov who, I believe, struck the final blow, and then they threw his body into the Neva River. Among other aspects of the Rasputin sordidness was the influence he had—I don't know the details, but certainly they were amorous, or romantic, or sexual influences with women in the upper crust of Russian society, not merely the upper crust, the aristocratic, but the Russian nobility, and his name was bandied about with the names of all sorts of women. One of the names mentioned was Princess Yusupov who was a leading lady, an important personage in the Russian nobility, with a suggestion that that's why the Prince, her husband, killed Rasputin rather than because of the evil political influence he exerted at the court. It so happened that my friend Sylvester Gates, a gifted creature, knew Russian. He was then a junior and was known at the bar, a limited circle in London as you know, and he was engaged as a junior by Sir William Jowitt, the senior who was leading for the defense of Metro Goldwyn. He was an ex-attorney general. Yusupov, the plaintiff, had retained as counsel another ex-attorney general, Sir Patrick Hastings, and these two ex-attorneys general faced each other. Sylvester Gates phoned down and said, "Would you like to come and hear when Prince Yusupov is put in the box?" I said, "I would be delighted." He said that the court was held in a very small court room, that each side had a few tickets, and that he would place one ticket at my disposal. I said to him, "Of course, I'll be glad to come up. It so happens that Francis Hackett is staying with me. Can you by any chance produce two tickets? I know it would excite him beyond words."

He thought he could, and so we went up. That was a very important experience as bearing on the way in which a trial is conducted on the two sides of the ocean. If that trial had taken place in New York, I'm sure the court would have been adjourned to Madison Square Garden so that ample room could be had for the thousand correspondents who would want to be there, the sob sisters and photographers, the everything, and the mob who would want to see it. Well, the English conduct of such a trial is just the opposite. Trials have to be public, but "public" doesn't mean that you must make a Roman circus out of a trial, and so instead of being held in the biggest court room, it was designedly held in the smallest court room. The presiding judge was one of the most experienced of judges nearer eighty than seventy at the time. I think Sylvester Gates told me there was room for I don't think more than twenty a side, so that when we went in this small room there was a judge, the jury, a clerk, counsel, junior counsel and each side had various solicitors who retained counsellors, a handful of reporters, very few, and there wasn't any room for any more. That's all, and we were there all day.

The witnesses stand in the box, and Prince Yusupov was immaculately dressed. He was examined by counsel for his wife, his English was perfect, his answers were clipped and short, clear and courteous. When Sir William Jowitt got up to cross-examine him, Prince Yusupov wouldn't be seen if he could avoid it, in the same room just as in the old days American employers wouldn't be seen with labor leaders because in their eyes that would involve "recognition." And so the Prince just wouldn't look at Jowitt. He turned away and answered out of his mouth, but not giving Jowitt his face. There were several questions without interruption. Patrick Hastings sat there, nonchalantly. Jowitt asked a series of questions and didn't get very far. Prince Yusupov held his own extremely well. Jowitt went on and asked the same question over and over again. Actually he told the story of what they did to Rasputin in great detail and then how they threw him into the icy river to make sure that he wouldn't survive. Patrick Hastings got up and instead of doing the conventional American thing, "Your honor, I object, immaterial, irrelevant, impertinent, calling for a conclusion and opinion" and all the other stuff, he just got up and before he said anything Jowitt said, "My Lord, it's the last question I'm putting to the witness."

Hastings didn't even put his objections saying, "My Lord, my learned brother has asked this witness the same question twelve times, and I think we can call a halt." He didn't even open his mouth. Jowitt saw and knew what objection he was going to make, and he bent before the storm, "My Lord, this is the very last question I'm going to put to the witness."

Well, they brought in a verdict of thirty-five thousand pounds against Metro Goldwyn. The judge charged the jury so that they couldn't have any doubt as to what the facts were and get off on foolishness, and that was that. Well, to see in the concrete the validity of it all! It helps to account for the impact of English history on me as an imperceptible process in the acquisition of understanding and feeling, intellectual feeling. Undoubtedly Dean

Ames must have had a great deal to do with it, and the influence of my own reading, but I can perhaps best illustrate my eagerness to become part of these institutions intellectually by a happening in 1940.

The President authorized Mr. Stimson to announce that we would protect—this is apropos of the battle of the Atlantic—the shipping half-way over, that the American fleet would protect shipping as against German submarines. That was a terrific thing for this country to do, a neutral nation, and it so happens that I knew that Mr. Stimson was going to deliver that speech on a particular night. We were dining at the Norwegian Embassy. Wilhelm Morgenstierne, the Ambassador, and I were old friends. He was a young fellow in the Norwegian Embassy when I was a young fellow in the War Department with Stimson in 1911, and that friendship continued. I said to Wilhelm as the men left the dinner table and went to have their coffee and smoke that there was this important speech of Mr. Stimson's coming at whenever it was, "Do you suppose we could turn the radio on and listen to it?"

He said, "By all means, naturally."

There was present that night Senator Gerry of Rhode Island, a direct descendant of Elbridge P. Gerry. He was very nice but not profoundly intellectual, the generous donor to the Supreme Court of one of the finest, perhaps the finest law collection in private hands, coming down from all the Gerrys, a beautiful collection. He was one of the guests, and as the speech of Stimson's went on about why we were giving this help to England—the menace to freedom—I could see Gerry's face. He was an isolationist, and I could see great disapproval on his face. I'd had pleasant relations with him because he was a friend of Justice Roberts, and I'd seen him at Justice Roberts' so that it was a perfectly easy, pleasant, non-intimate relation. When the speech was over, and as we started to go in to join the ladies I said, "Senator Gerry, one of these days I'd like to ask you a question."

He said, "Why don't you ask it now?"

I said, "It's likely to lead to some discussion. There isn't time, but if I can put it to you quickly, it was plain enough that you didn't approve of this speech of the Secretary of War. You don't like it, and so that leads me to put to you this question: How is it that I who, as far as I know, haven't remotely a drop of English blood in me, who never heard the English language spoken, certainly never spoke a word of it until I was twelve, who never saw England until I was past thirty, have such a deep feeling about the essential importance of the maintenance of England, have such a sense of kinship professionally speaking with English institutions and feel that our's are so deeply related to their history and therefore am profoundly engaged in this cause with Englishmen, whereas you who I believe have nothing but English ancestry would on the whole view with equanimity the destruction of England?"

He said, "The difference is that I have something you haven't got."

I said laughingly—he was a very rich man—"I suspect that you have a great many things I haven't got." I wanted to say how I envied his wine cellar. He had a famous wine cellar, "But what in particular is there that bears on the question that I put to you?"

"You see, you haven't got what I have—a memory of the red coats."

Was he really serious about this memory of the red coats' business?

Absolutely. That story and the way I put it to Gerry gives you the feeling that I took with me to England during the Oxford year, the kind of identification merely from the head, soaked in English legal history, so that I came to an intensive year in England with that kind of a professional interest, that kind of hospitality to what they had to offer and responsiveness to what I found there, so that the year was extremely congenial to me, and it has left very important influences. I cite English cases very often when I want to drive home a point about how we should conduct trials. I resent the third degree being called the "American practice," resent the defense of all the low forms of behavior by our American police and prosecutions as something essential to what is called the war against crime. Justice Murphy once said to me, "Why do you always cite English cases?"

I said, "Frank, I'll make a bargain with you. Whenever you

give me a good Irish case on the subject, I'll cite the Irish case instead of the English."

Life that year was rich, abundant and stimulating. It was very happy for both of us at Oxford. I should sum it all up by saying that it was the fullest year my wife and I spent—the amplest and most civilized.

27. *Supreme Court Appointment*

There's a good bit of speculation surrounding your appointment to the Supreme Court—part of the "New Deal" with emphasis on the latter word. What is the story?

Properly discarding infirmities of memory I think I can say that the thought of being named to the Supreme Court of the United States never crossed my mind, or was brought to my consciousness except, as I indicated to you in another connection, when Governor Ely named me to the Supreme Judicial Court of Massachusetts and FDR phoned me. He was flying out to Chicago to make his acceptance speech, that dramatic demonstration of the fact that being a cripple wasn't a handicap to an active life. He was much surprised that Ely should have named me to such a post, and he didn't suppose that I would have accepted, and then he said, "You ought to be on the Supreme Court of the United States." So far as I have any kind of recollection, that was the first time anybody ever said anything like that to me.

When I was a very young man, a young assistant attorney in Mr. Stimson's office, one of my heroes was the then District Judge Charles Hough, a powerful fellow, a heroic character, and I admired him enormously. I remember my utter surprise when he spoke adversely about some of his colleagues and then said, "I hope that one of these days you'll be a colleague of mine."

That was a great accolade, like a laurel placed on one's brow in the Olympic races. Later on in 1911, President Taft wanted to name me as a United States District Judge. I was then not yet thirty, and talking it over with Mr. Stimson I naturally was flabbergasted at this honor, but I didn't want to go on the bench at such a young age. It would be an interesting speculation, what would have happened to me had I then gone on the bench. By now I would have been a judge for forty-five years. Those things don't linger with me. They didn't seem to leave any deposit. They didn't lead to any speculation. They were like yesteryear's snow in my own feelings or thoughts. My wife says that one characteristic about me, psychologically speaking, is that I deeply live in the moment. Yesterday is gone and tomorrow hasn't happened. I tell her that that pictures a very shallow creature, but it wasn't until this remark of FDR's that anybody ever said something to me about the Supreme Court, and I just—well, I don't know how many minutes that lingered. I'm sure not many. I just thought that was a *façon de parler,* a very pleasant speech from a man who was accustomed to ply butter.

I should think FDR's talk with me about the Solicitor Generalship proves the opposite of hope, desire, or design in this world of reason. A President offers you that post which doesn't need any sweetening, and you refuse it, and then he plays his trump card and says, as he did say, "I'm now going to talk Dutch to you. I'm going to talk to you as friend to friend" and tells you that if you become Solicitor General then "I can put you on the Supreme Court." I think a fellow who was plotting would grab it instead of saying, "Thank you very much" and indeed said at the time that I didn't know whether I'd accept it if it came to me. "I'm not going to take one job I don't want on the chance or the expectation of having another job that I'm not sure I want." I should think that talk with FDR is decisive that there was nothing plotted, planned, or desired, or designed. I was very, very happy to be where I was, very happy to function as I was functioning.

Then Cardozo died in the summer of 1938—on July 9, 1938—at the home of his great friend, Judge Lehman of the New York Court of Appeals. Some time after Cardozo's death my wife and I had the usual invitation for a weekend at Hyde Park. I say "usual" because for several years preceding we were asked to go up to Hyde Park and spend a weekend there. This was the first week in October, 1938. We were at Dr. Alfred Cohn's in New Milford. We motored over for lunch, from New Milford to Hyde Park. I remember my wife saying to me, "There's something constrained about the President. There's evidently something on his mind. He isn't natural."

It was at lunch that this constraint of which my wife spoke manifested itself, and it was at the end of lunch that the President announced that he was going to carry me off in the afternoon. He took me into his study which was a little bit of a dinky hole really, a surprisingly small little cubby-hole at Hyde Park, his mother's house. To my great surprise he opened up and said, feeling a little awkward, a little ill at ease for a man who was so supremely at ease almost in every contingency, like a naughty boy almost, "I want to tell you why I can't appoint you to succeed Cardozo"—just like that.

I said, "Why heavens, you don't have to explain anything. You don't have to tell me that. There is no such thought in my mind, no reason why you should."

He was very insistent, "No, I want to tell you. I want you to know why, however much I'd like to appoint you to the Court because that's where you ought to be, I cannot possibly appoint you to the Court this time." He went on to say, "I have given very definite promises to"—he did not enumerate by name, but he indicated, "I've given very definite promises to Senators and party people that the next appointment to the Court would be someone west of the Mississippi. The West ought to have a representation, and I made a very solemn promise that I would appoint a fellow from west of the Mississippi. That's why"—very regretfully.

It was very embarrassing to me, and moreover I wanted to get through with it and relieve the President of the United States of something that evidently had been troubling to him. I said, "I perfectly understand. It never occurred to me that you should appoint me, and there is every reason in the world why you should appoint somebody west of the Mississippi."

He reiterated this feeling—that he couldn't appoint me. Anyhow that came to an end, and he said, "I want your opinion on some of the names that have been suggested. Let me read you a list of people who have been suggested, who are under consideration and who have been put to me by Attorney General Cummings and others."

They were all names of judges. About some of these judges I had an opinion. About some of them I said, "I don't know a thing about them. I know there is such a judge." I remember two of them were on the Court of Appeals of the Ninth Circuit on the West Coast, and I said, "I know that they are on the Ninth Circuit, but their opinions have left no impression to enable me to have a judgment about them. If you want me to read their opinions and write you a memorandum about the qualities their opinions show, I can do that."

He said, "I wish you would do that."

There must have been four or five judges apart from one or two state judges about whose work I was unprepared, but I undertook to study their opinions, what the printed page revealed and then wrote him an estimate about what justifiably their opinions manifested. He asked me if I would do that. It's difficult for me to believe that I didn't keep a copy, but I might not have. As you know, I'm not a very methodical fellow about such things, and unlike Mr. Wilson, that wonderful phrase of his, I do not "play for the verdict of history." I might not have copies of those memoranda, but they certainly went to the White House. After that talk, Marion said he was his old self again. He somehow or other had this weighing on his feeling, and it was betrayed in his action that he felt that he had to account to me for the fact that he wasn't naming me to succeed Cardozo.

I went back to Cambridge, worked on these memoranda, reported to FDR, and that was that. I awaited whom he would name from among the judges he canvassed with me. I attended to my knitting, and nothing further happened until during Christmas week. It was a day or two after Christmas, maybe two days after that I had a phone call. The phone rang, long distance, and there was the President of the United States, and he said that another suggestion had been made to him, and he wanted to know what I thought of it: Dean Wiley Rutledge of the Law School of the University of Iowa, what did I think of him? I said, "I do not know him. I've never met him, and therefore I have no opinion, but if you want me to find out from people in whose judgment I have confidence, what they think about it, it's very easy for me to do so because all the law professors are now meeting in Chicago."

It was the meeting of the American Association of Law Schools, and he said, "I wish you would."

I then got on the phone and got hold of T. R. Powell in Chicago, who was one of our delegation, (that is of the Harvard Law School) that year, and I told him absolutely nothing about the inquiry of FDR and the Supreme Court, but I put to him the questions on which I wanted light on Wiley Rutledge which would reveal the intellectual and moral content of the man. He knew Rutledge somewhat. I said, "You ask fellows like Lloyd Garrison and so on—just wrastle around and call me back collect and tell me what the results of your inquiries are."

He knew that it was something important. Men who had the kind of relations he and I had understood each other without spelling it out, and in due course Powell called me back and gave me a very detailed report, detailed estimate, assessment as to why he liked Rutledge's qualities and potentialities on the basis of which I wrote a memorandum to the President the upshot of which was that if I had to act on the information my net of inquiry had fished up I would think that Rutledge was qualified for the Court and would be a properly appointed man. This must have been not earlier than December 27. It may have been December 28. On Tuesday, January 4, seven or eight days later, while I was dressing, while I was in my B.V.D.'s, the door bell rang at 192 Brattle Street, and my wife was going down. We had a guest for dinner, Professor Robert Morse Lovett of the University of Chicago who is a very, very punctual man. It was seven o'clock. My wife all dressed was going down, and here I was in my B.V.D.'s. She said, "Please hurry! You're always late."

Just then while I had this conjugal injunction the telephone rang. I went to the telephone. My study was right across the hall, opposite our bed room. The telephone rang, and there was the ebullient, the exuberant, resilient warmth-enveloping voice of the President of the United States, "Hello. How are you?"

"I'm fine. How are you?"

"How's Marion?"

"Fine."

"You know, I told you I don't want to appoint you to the Supreme Court of the United States."

I said, "Yes." I no more expected the denouement of this conversation. You know, he was given to teasing. Some people said that it was an innocently sadistic streak in him. He just had to have an outlet for fun. "I told you I can't appoint you to the Supreme Court."

"Yes, you told me that."

"I mean this. I mean this. I don't want to appoint you to the Supreme Court."

Here I was in my B.V.D.'s, and I knew Marion would be as sore as she could be. She had said I'm always late which is indeed substantially true. "I mean it. I don't want to appoint you. I just don't want to appoint you."

I said, "Yes, you told me that. You've made that perfectly clear. I understand that."

I was getting bored, really, when he whipped around on the telephone and said, "But unless you give me an unsurmountable objection I'm going to send your name in for the Court tomorrow at twelve o'clock"—just like that, and I remember saying, and it is natural to remember this very vividly—"All I can say is that I wish my mother were alive."

I said nothing else. I probably stuttered and stammered. Then he said, "Where will you be tomorrow at twelve o'clock?"

I said, "I have no classes tomorrow, and I'll be right here at the same number to which you're now talking."

He said, "You stay there, be there at noon, and I'll call you up and tell you what kind of a reception your nomination's had on the Hill."

I said, "Very well," and went back and continued dressing. I went downstairs saying to myself, "Well, here is an event, something that has just happened which will change the course of the lives of Marion and me, and I can't tell her about it."

There was our guest, Bob Lovett, a charming, delightful and humorous creature, compassionate, humane, a really disinterested spirit, but said I to myself, "After all, the hours will pass soon," because he not only was punctual in coming, he was always punctual in leaving at ten o'clock. He came at seven and at ten to the dot he'd get up and leave, but for some strange reason—the way the unexpected happens in the world—that night he didn't leave at ten. He didn't leave at half-past ten, or even eleven. The world must be inhabited by a lot of lively gargoyles, and they were having a good time because it wasn't until finally at midnight that he said, "I suppose it's time for me to go."

When the door shut I said, "Marion, let me tell you what your fate and mine is."

Then we sat and looked at each other and faced this thing. I stayed home that morning, and at noon FDR did call and said that the nomination had had a pretty good reception. I had a very dear friend, Loring Christie, soon to be Canadian Minister in Washington who was to visit us on that Wednesday. He was a tall, handsome fellow. He came with a great big heavy, pink suitcase, one of these substantial things, and he arrived just as the place was mobbed by reporters. This nomination came like a bombshell. Here not so many years before I was this execrated character in Cambridge and Boston, and now newspaper people by the score and photographers were swarming around. We had to be as amiable as possible, and here was Loring Christie. He said that when he came through Grand Central Station on the way up from Washington there was a paper with great big headlines, and he said to himself, "Now, shall I go, or shan't I go."

Well, that's the story of the scheming and the long-headed plotting over the years to get myself on the Supreme Court of the United States. Then there was a committee hearing on my nomination, the Judiciary Committee. I asked Dean Acheson if he would attend and hold a watching brief, sit there and see what happened. I was charged with having despoiled the Cherokee Indians of ten thousand acres of land. Elizabeth Dilling and other crackpots came and testified. One day Steve Early called me, and he said, "Why don't you come down? You'd better come down to Washington."

They'd had these Senate hearings. I said, "Why should I? Did the Committee ask me to come?"

"No. You ought to come."

"Why should I?"

"Well," he said, "people are saying, 'Evidently he thinks it more important to be up there teaching at the Harvard Law School than to be in Washington while there's a hearing going on before a Senate Committee.' "

"I think it is more important."

"You're an impossible fellow to do anything with."

"I guess that's right. I just want you to know—I don't want you to be under any misapprehension—that if the committee of the Senate invites me to attend the hearing, of course I shall attend, but if they don't ask me, I shall stay right here and attend to my job."

He thought that was something! They finally did invite me. I did attend, but that's a matter of history, I had the time of my life with Senator Pat McCarran. Dean Acheson tells a story that I was really having a wonderful time, was misbehaving, playing tricks with the committee. I finally told Senator McCarran, in effect, "If I understand the philosophy of Communism and the scheme of society it represents, everything in my nature, all my views and convictions, life-long cares and concerns, are as opposed to it as anyone can possibly be. If I understand what Americanism is, I think I'm as good an American as you are," whereupon the whole place broke into terrific applause.

When I thought of going before the committee, I thought that it would be just a little room where we'd sit around. I found that this was Madison Square Garden. There were hundreds of photographers, movies, everything, the whole Senate Judiciary Committee, and I finally said to the chairman of the committee, that very nice Senator Neely of West Virginia, "Don't you think we'd better get through with this business?" In fact, I took charge. It was the only thing to do. Dean Acheson said to me that it was the only time he had a client who wouldn't let him do a thing, who just took control, and he just sat there. There were Borah, Norris, Wiley, etcetera, but when it came to McCarran's turn, he called me "Doctor." Well, the amount of poison he put into that term, as though "Doctor" was a contagious disease, and as for Harvard, that was a plague spot. This was in 1939. He did his damnedest by all sorts of devices and schemes to prevent my confirmation. I understand that Cummings fought like a Trojan against naming me because he thought that Roosevelt would have a great fight on his hands and I would open the sluices of the "Red" charges and everything else. The humor of the situation is that in the history of the Supreme Court, I'm one of the few people who was confirmed without a dissenting vote in the Senate. That was the funny thing about it.

At one point Dean Acheson had a terrible time because somebody tipped McCarran off that I really wasn't a citizen in that my father obtained his citizenship through fraud. Naturalization requires a residence of five years. McCarran was reportedly tipped off that my father took the necessary oaths in order to get his naturalization in New York a year before he was eligible. Therefore, I wasn't naturalized as a minor through him; therefore, I wasn't a citizen; and therefore, I couldn't go on the Supreme Court—you know the argument. It was an awful thing to get the documents, but I knew that what was essential was to dig out when my father came here. In my experience with the United States Attorney's Office I knew that the ship's manifest had to be at least in triplicate, so that one copy could be deposited at the Custom House in New York. I told this to Dean Acheson, but alas, the Custom House had burnt down years ago, so that all the documents prior to the burning were gone. Then I said that I knew they had another copy deposited in the Treasury. Henry Morgenthau got people busy in the mucky cellars of the Treasury Department, and sure enough they found the ship's manifest. This was 1939.

I never saw McCarran thereafter, never had another word with him until in May, or June of 1945, after the war with Europe was over. There hadn't been the formal surrender, but it was over. My secretary came in and said, "Senator McCarran of Nevada is on the phone."

I said, "Who?"

"Senator McCarran of Nevada would like to talk to you."

"Certainly. Put him on."

I went to the phone and said, "What gives me the pleasure of your call Senator?"

"Mr. Justice, I have a constituent right here in my office, a very important constituent, who has a son, a wonderful boy, been through the war, just demobilized. He has a wonderful war record, had a fine record at the University of Nevada, and he wants to go to the Harvard Law School."

I made one of the few remarks in my life I cherish. "He wants to go to the Harvard Law School? Senator, you're going to save him from that horrendous fate, aren't you?"

"No, no, no. I want you to help me to get him there."

I think it's the high point of triumph of my life. "You send me a note telling me about him, will you?" How unwittingly we become dishonest in the world of affairs! But I made things clear. I said, "You know, Senator, the one thing about the Harvard Law School is that kissage doesn't buy favors."

"I think you'll find that he satisfies all of the requirements."

Well, the fact of the matter is that he did. He was absolutely top notch, and so he got into the Harvard Law School on his merits, but McCarran thereafter always thought I did him a favor. There was on his desk when he died a memorandum, or telegram, or a message to me begging me to be the speaker at the Nevada Bar Association, that I would do him a great personal favor, and his office staff out of veneration for the great departed begged me to do this in memory of Senator McCarran, and one of my colleagues, Tom Clark, said that McCarran told him what a fine fellow I was. There are pleasurable experiences in my life, and Senator McCarran asking me to help him get the son of "an important constituent" into the Harvard Law School is certainly one of them.

Now I want to conclude about going on the Supreme Court. Why did I at once when the President said, "Unless you give me an unsurmountable reason" acquiesce, I haven't any idea. I just haven't. I'm not implying one way or the other, but I don't know what I would have done if I had been asked to go on the Supreme Court in January 1939, had the world remained at peace as it was before Hitler changed its face for a time. The quick, negative response indicated that I could not give him an unsurmountable objection. Retrospectively, not rationalizing it, but framing it—rationalize implies a fake reason, a surface, intellectually good but not real reason—but what spoke through me, I'm confident, was that in the context of world affairs in 1939, with all the brutal, barbaric behavior of Germany and generally the infection that was caused thereby elsewhere in the spread of anti-Semitism, and not least in this country, for the President of the United States to appoint a Jew to the Supreme Court had such significance for me to make it impossible to have said "no." It would have been quixotism to the nth degree, and the reason I speak with such confidence in saying this is that within forty-eight hours—news of the appointment was cabled all over the world—I had a telegram from my friend Francis Hackett, who had a Danish wife and was then living in Denmark, saying, "The leading Danish newspaper has front-page streamer headline: ROOSEVELT APPOINTS JEW TO SUPREME COURT." I think that was the historic significance of the appointment.

It wasn't merely the difference between the Supreme Judicial Court of Massachusetts and the Supreme Court of the United States. I think I told you T. R. Powell's remark, "Why would you ever think of going on the Supreme Court?" I said, "After all I'm not disdainful of a post that was occupied by Lemuel Shaw or Wendell Holmes."

It wasn't merely the difference in significance between the Supreme Court of the United States and the Supreme Judicial Court of Massachusetts. I was six years older, and that made a difference. I'd passed my fifty-sixth year. You do a thing at fifty-six that you don't do at fifty. That's the story.

As you were packing up I was glancing in my mind as to what I said, and I realize I have left out the most important part of President Roosevelt's communication to me when he called me and told me that he was going to name me to the Court, and I leave it to you Freudians to decide what it signifies that I should have left it out: to wit, after he said repeatedly so, as I indicated, it nearly bored me to have him say, "I told you that I can't name you," he said, "But wherever I turn, wherever I turn"—I remember his repeating that—"and to whomever I talk that matters to me, I am made to realize that you're the only person fit to succeed Holmes and Cardozo," and then he said, "Unless you give me some unsurmountable" etcetera.

Well, isn't it amazing that I should tell that story and leave that out because otherwise it makes no sense as to why he changed his mind.

28. "Religion"

I suppose we've talked about religion in the broad sense of that word, but we have not treated religion in its narrow, formal, organizational sense. What is the story?

There was a time as a boy when I was religiously observant. I wouldn't eat breakfast until I had done the religious devotions in the morning. As time went on, to no small extent influenced by the Victorians and more particularly, I think, by John Morley's *On Compromise,* the Victorian agnostics, I was more and more confirmed in my own slow feelings of disharmony between myself and Jewish rituals and the synagogue. At home we were an observant, not an orthodox, but observant Jewish family as a kind of a family institution, a kind of emotional habit. It had for me the warmth of the familiar, the warmth of the past and of the association at family festivals.

I didn't go to the synagogue even as a young man except on holy days and particularly on Yom Kippur which, as you know, is the day of atonement on which you're in the synagogue all day long. I felt more and more weaned from the rituals and more and more alien to those to whom Yom Kippur was a matter of the utmost significance and importance. Certainly it was not later than my junior year in college, I think, while I was in the midst of a Yom Kippur service that I looked around as pious Jews were beating their breasts with intensity of feeling and anguishing sincerity, and I remember with the greatest vividness thinking that it was unfair of me, a kind of desecration for me to be in the room with these people to whom these things had the meaning they had for them when for me they had no other meaning than adhering to a creed that meant something to my parents but had ceased to have meaning for me. I no longer had roots in that kind of relation to the mysteries of the universe, and I remember leaving the synagogue in the middle of the service saying to myself, "It's a wrong thing for me to be present in a room in a holy service, to share these ceremonies, these prayers, these chants, with people for whom they have inner meaning as against me for whom they have ceased to have inner meaning."

I left the service in the middle of it, never to return to this day. By leaving the synagogue I did not, of course, cease to be a Jew or cease to be concerned with whatever affects the fate of Jews.

I happen to be greatly interested in theological matters. I have a great interest in the history of religion and theological controversies. I don't believe in spiritual Messiahs, I don't believe in economic Messiahs, I don't believe in political Messiahs. I don't believe that poor fallible man, however great, wise and deep his insight, is endowed with ultimate wisdom, any more than I think that Karl Marx has discovered the eternal laws of social arrangement. Harold Laski was a Marxian, and I was not. Apart from that great difference between Harold Laski and me, there are only two matters, two specific things on which we had real difference of opinion. One concerned the function of federalism, and the other was the Revised Prayer Book, that great controversy in English political life. We had a very hot controversy when Parliament was confronted with the requirement, since the Episcopal Church is an established state church, of approving or disapproving the revision of the Prayer Book. Laski had very strong feelings that it was none of Parliament's business to reject the Prayer Book, the revisions. The great controversy was that the revision had been in the direction of high church as against low church. I was strongly of the view that if you have an established church and if government is concerned with religion as part of the political structure of society, so long as there is an established church and Parliament must pass on it, then the church does not have an independent function. It is open to Parliament to reject. Well, it was rather amusing to have these two Jews have this fight across the Atlantic that so divided English opinion. It didn't divide us, except intellectually.

Two small items epitomize my attitude toward the essential problems that are called religion. I'm very much interested in theological discussions, theological problems, and one of my close friends, one of my most esteemed friends, is Dr. Reinhold Niebuhr, and he and I have had talks on this subject from time to time. We summered together for some years up in Heath, a small town in western Massachusetts. Once, a few summers ago, I went to a community church there, a non-denominational church to which the people of the community except the Catholics go, because I heard that Reinhold Niebuhr was going to deliver the sermon. He did deliver a sermon, a non-denominational sermon, and after the service I said to him, "Reinie, may a believing unbeliever thank you for your sermon?"

He said, "May an unbelieving believer thank you for appreciating it?"

The other remark was a response that was awakened in me the other day apropos of the alleged return of Gilbert Murray during his fatal illness to the Church of his baptism. He was baptized a Catholic, and it was rumored that he had received extreme unction. His son, Stephen Murray, said that his father had died as he had lived, a reverent agnostic, and if one has to put a label on complicated processes, or complicated beliefs, or feelings about complicated aspects of life, I suppose that's a good label for me. I'm a reverent agnostic.

29. *Function of a Judge*

You could not mention many themes more enticing for talk than T. R. Powell. He's not an easy man to talk about, but I should say that one of the finest and best things about him was his wife who was one of the most exquisite spirits that my wife and I ever knew, Molly Powell. She was a dear and a darling, a luminous, radiating creature.

Tom Powell had an acute critical mind, a very questioning mind, and he was also witty. He could dash off happy doggerels. He was a general-store debater, smart, puncturing the other fellow, delighting in repartee, but very much better than that. I think this faculty in him, this critical faculty, this surgical talent, this master of autopsies that he was, tended to reinforce a natural vein of negativism, a natural destructive vein. Powell was a great exposer, and he loved exposing. Indeed, he once told me—let me digress a bit. Saying nice things about people wasn't a specialty of his, and it was the least of his specialties to say nice things about me, though we were warm friends. Speaking of students he once told me, indeed, more than once he told me this because he was a great repeater, "I clear the students' minds of rubbish, take away all their bum furniture, but you furnish their minds."

Whether that remark is true of me, I think it is very considerably true about him. In the period during which he was functioning that was a very important need to meet. He came to the teaching of Constitutional Law in the era of great, big, sterile absolutes—you know, "liberty of contract" was riding high. On the whole, courts were looked to as our saviors from undesirable—at least "undesirable" to powerful economic interests—legislation. It was the era in which the pretensions of the courts in enforcing absolutes, which too often were dogmas, regarding arrangements that were familiar in the judges' minds and lay warm in their assumptions, were put out of their heads, out of their assumptions, and into the Constitution as though the Philadelphia Convention had placed them there. And therefore, to strip legal decisions of their pretensions was an important function. You had to make clearings before you could build. Somehow or other Powell never got around to building, partly because clearing fitted in with his temperament, and it was fun. He speared his victims. He had their scalps on his belt. Besides clearing—necessary clearing—is constructive. Without it, there can be no building, certainly none that lasts.

The burden of proof was on the Court to prove that they were not morons.

There's no doubt about that. McReynolds, Butler, Sutherland and Van Devanter were setups for him—clay pigeons! They are a perfect illustration of that against which de Tocqueville warned us, not to confuse the familiar with the necessary. And of course, the warm feeling with which T. R. Powell could show up their inadequacies and deficiencies and therefore was superior to them all was not outside of his ego satisfactions.

He did great service in connection with this in his vigorous analysis of language, in his exposure of the emptiness in and beneath phrases, the illogicalities. He had a very good, tough, dialectical mind. This was wonderful training for students who came, as most students did come, with all the uncritical, half- or quarter-education most lads brought from even the best of colleges, or even the best of lads brought from the worst of colleges. A lot of things were taken for granted. Powell was the fellow who pierced them. He lanced all these pretensions. He encouraged the habit of questions, of inquiry, of logicalities—not formal logicalities, though he was a master of that. He was very effective in utilizing formal logic as a destructive instrument. It was tonical, but I should think that it is not unfair to say that he played most of his variations on that theme.

Let me give an instance which illustrates the deep negativism that was in him, this showing-up tendency. He was a truth-seeker in exposing, in taking away pretensions, falsities, fronts, and facades, but truth-seeking with a view, however hopeless the endeavor, to find some germinating idea interested him less. At all events, he manifested it less. He came into my room one day, fresh from his class, and with delight in his voice—I wish I could reproduce the unmistakable southern Vermont tang, sharp, very un-like Oxford English—"I showed up your hero just now!"

"What did you do?"

"I just showed up what a question-begger Holmes is."

I said, "Tell me about it," and then he told me they were discussing the *Pipeline* cases, and at this point I must state what the *Pipeline* case was and what it was about. Perhaps the most powerful factor, certainly one of the most powerful factors in the economic control that Standard Oil had built up over the oil industry was its ownership of vast networks of pipelines built near the wells in the oil regions of the southwest. These pipelines, thousands of miles, came near the wells where the crude oil came out of the ground. That is where the oil was brought, and it would then go through the pipelines to the refineries and then to various parts of the country. Transportation through pipelines was very much cheaper than transportation by oil tank cars, and the possession of the pipelines by Standard Oil gave it an advantage over those who didn't have or couldn't ship by pipelines. Possession of them also enabled Standard Oil to buy the oil cheaper. Not only could the oil be transported cheaper by pipeline, but by virtue of the cheaper transport cost, the owners of the oil wells were under economic coercion to sell the oil at Standard Oil prices, for the alternative was to sell through the more expensive transportation.

That was an evil that had been much bruited about for years and years, and finally President Theodore Roosevelt got through Congress in 1906, over the powerful opposition of oil interests led by the then vigorous Senator Joseph B. Foraker of Ohio, the Hepburn Act, subjecting the pipelines to regulation by the Interstate Commerce Commission so that these pipelines which were owned and built by the Standard, were built by them with great care that they should remain private, non-common carrier carriers, were available on fair terms to all shippers of oil. By "great care" I mean they never invoked the power of eminent domain in the states through which the pipelines ran which would give some basis for saying, "You got a public charter. You got an exercise of governmental power, and therefore, you are amenable to governmental control." Their very able lawyers in the Eighties, Nineties and in the 1900s carefully sought to provide against this. Along came Congress and said, "Hereafter you must carry oil from whoever offers you the carriage of oil and not merely oil that you own by having purchased it."

In other words, Congress subjected what were private pipelines to the easement, the servitude, the duty of carriage, to which the railroads had been subjected because the railroads were common carriers. That legislation was fought not only by those economically interested, but it was opposed by people who honestly thought that there was no constitutional power to subject such private business to public control any more than the government can tell me to whom I can and to whom I cannot sell my private house. Not that government in some circumstances hasn't been telling us something like that for reasons fundamentally similar to those that led Congress in 1906 to subject these so-called private pipelines to control. The then prevailing argument was that the government couldn't take them away. It couldn't despoil me of my property. The government couldn't take the pipelines away, or if it could, it would have to pay for them. By this legislation Standard Oil was told that you can continue the ownership, but you must carry other people's oil as well as your own at a fair charge for carriage and not merely give them the alternatives of selling to you at your price, or not being able to send it through the pipelines.

The case finally came before the Supreme Court. It took some time before the litigation got under way and before it got through the lower courts. In the Supreme Court it hung fire for a whole year. The case was argued for the government by the then Solicitor General, John W. Davis, and for the pipelines by some of the most eminent, towering figures of the bar. Finally, on the last day of Court sitting in 1914, down came the opinion by Holmes with one dissenting voice, Mr. Justice McKenna. Holmes said, in effect, in a very unsatisfactory opinion—on its face an extremely unsatisfactory opinion and everybody found it unsatisfactory who thought about those things—except that the statute was sustained . . . But the reasoning by which the statute was sustained was meager and inadequate because Holmes said that these pipelines were in fact common carriers in all but form, and Congress just made them common carriers in form. Some aid was given to that mode of explaining the legislation by the form of the statute which said, "shall be deemed to be common carriers"—in other words as though this was a declaratory statement instead of a creative pronouncement. Instead of saying, "We make them common carriers," this was legislation which said, "We recognize them to be common carriers." And that, in substance, was almost all Holmes said with a hint here and there. Well, that is the background of this episode of Powell—his room was next to mine in the old Langdell Hall at Cambridge—bursting into my room with his books, saying, "I showed up your hero! Showed them what a question-begger Holmes was in the *Pipeline* cases!"

"That is not an unfair characterization of Holmes's opinion," I said, "but, Tom, don't you think you might have done a better service to your students than showing up Holmes, to tell them, as you no doubt did, powerfully and wittily, how Holmes begged the question, to say it is a bald question-begging."

"So it is!" Powell insisted.

"Don't you think," I went on, "it might have been more helpful, more stimulating to the thought of your students to say, 'This is, to be sure, question-begging. But Holmes is no fool. He's probably as bright as you are, even as bright as I am, and why would he indulge in and not see a simple *petitio principii?*' And then invite your students to speculate on why he did beg the question instead of demonstrating the obvious that he did beg the question. This would raise the whole problem of the considerations that lead a court to write an opinion one way rather than another, or the considerations that lead a court to have an opinion written for it one way rather than another.

"On the face of things the *Pipeline* cases were argued at the very beginning of the term in October, and they weren't decided until the last day of the term on June 22, 1914. It is a matter of common knowledge—you and I know it—that Holmes dashes off his opinions within a few days after a case is assigned to him, and for him to take even a week for the writing of an opinion, even the most complicated case, is rare. The *Pipeline* case was an important case, but not complicated on its facts, and it didn't require a vast amount of what we call legal research, certainly not for Holmes. One thing is incontestable, and that is that it took all this time to get the case out not because Holmes took a lot of time to write the opinion. Considering the nature of the legislation and the make-up of the Court, one can be sure that there were differences within the Court. The ground that seems to you and to me obvious on which to sustain the constitutionality of the statute, namely, that under the Commerce Clause Congress has power to deal with the more or less economic monopoly as much as it has in dealing with a legal monopoly such as a franchise implies, that ground which, I have no doubt, would commend itself to Holmes in the light of his past opinions and might commend itself to one or two other people on the Court might be a little frightening to others on the Court to whom 'liberty of contract' and the distinction between private carrier and common carrier is almost as deep and immutable as the differences between the sexes. Therefore, the problem was to get out an opinion that is not disturbing for the future, which sustains this legislation, and gives little further encouragement to the underlying economic impulse behind the legislation which some of the boys certainly feared. This is all speculation, Tom, but I should think that that course of speculation might have been a more profitable thing for you to give your students than to make them feel that this poor slob Holmes begs questions without knowing it."

Well, time passes. After Holmes's death there became available to me the volumes in which he year by year collected the opinions he wrote, his original circulation of printed opinions—he didn't keep any working papers. He wrote and then sent it to the printer, and that's all there was to it. But, in the cases in which he wrote, either for the Court, or in dissent or concurring, he did keep and had bound the opinions that he circulated and the returns he had, the comments from each of the Justices. When I came into possession of the papers, the opinion as originally circulated in the *Pipeline* case and the opinion that finally became the opinion of the Court, the documents revealed that Holmes did go on this essentially economic justification for Congressional interference, but the boys wouldn't stand for it. In all the years Holmes was on the Court, from 1902 to 1932, in no other case did he write and rewrite and circulate and re-circulate with a view to getting an agreement on the part of the Court, and the opinion that now appears is an eviscerated document—a castration really, not an evisceration, a castration of his original opinion. And in his own annotation on his copy of the opinion that Powell dealt with in class as "question-begging," Holmes wrote in his own handwriting, "This is a wholly unsatisfactory opinion," and then stated why it was unsatisfactory. I don't think there's another instance—well, I can't say that, but I should be greatly surprised—yes, I don't believe that there is another instance in which a member of the Supreme Court, or for that matter any court, analyzed and characterized with such naked candor an opinion of his own as "unsatisfactory" and gave the reasons why it was and why he yielded to having his name put to such an opinion; namely, that if he hadn't done that, the case would not have been decided that Term with the risk of being adversely decided later. It would have gone over, and the important point was to get an adjudication which would sustain the statute. The vital fact is that the statute was sustained. When you have to have at least five people to agree on something, they can't have that comprehensive completeness of candor which is open to a single man, giving his own reasons untrammeled by what anybody else may do or not do if he put that out.

That is a perfect illustration of the kind of thing Tom Powell would do which was the weakness of his quality. Of course, it was his duty to expose the inadequacy of Holmes's opinion. Holmes did it himself, but exposure is not enough.

You may be interested in a story I got from John W. Davis on the *Pipeline* case, the first case he argued as Solicitor General. As he put it, he jumped into the stream as it flowed by, and he waited all year for the opinion. After it came down, he had occasion to visit Justice Holmes, and he made some comment to the effect that he was glad the government won, but that he was not entirely happy with the opinion. Mr. Davis reported that Holmes said, "Well, that's the trouble. I write out my opinions, and I send them around to my brethren. One of them picks out a plum here, and the other picks out a plum there, and they send it back to me with nothing but a shapeless mass of dough to father!"

When I got Holmes's annotation on his copy of the opinion—it was sometime after I saw John Davis, and he had referred to the case—I sent him a copy of Holmes's self-condemnation of the ground of his own opinion.

Some people might say, "Well, why didn't Holmes tell them to go to hell!" Imagine him thinking, "Let the statute be declared unconstitutional. I'll satisfy my vanity to have Powell know that I am as bright as he is." That was cheap at the price—to have it declared constitutional.

Powell was a sharp, smart, stimulating critic. I don't mean to depreciate his talent because he undoubtedly inculcated in his students, and therefore generations unborn to whom these students will pass on the tradition, a sense of the joy as well as the duty of clear, tough thinking. Well, that's a terribly important thing in a teacher.

If one is to compare Powell with the great figure in constitutional law at the Harvard Law School, James Bradley Thayer, I think William D. Guthrie and those fellows who wanted the courts to declare everything unconstitutional that mainly reflected the new re-adjustment, the new conflicts and interrelationships of interests, the new emerging economic forces, they were quite right in saying that James Bradley Thayer was the mischief maker. He influenced Holmes, Brandeis, the Hands, Mr. Stimson, Joseph Cotton, and so forth. I am of the view that if I were to name one piece of writing on American Constitutional Law—a silly test maybe—I would pick an essay by James Bradley Thayer in the *Harvard Law Review,* consisting of 26 pages, published in October, 1893, called "The Origin and Scope of the American Doctrine of Constitutional Law" which he read at the Congress on Jurisprudence and Law Reform in Chicago on August 9, 1893. I would pick that essay written 67 years ago. Why would I do that? Because from my point of view it's the great guide for judges and therefore, the great guide for understanding by non-judges of what the place of the judiciary is in relation to constitutional questions.

> The view which has thus been presented seems to me highly important. I am not stating a new doctrine, but attempting to restate more exactly and truly an admitted one. . . . It has been often remarked that private rights are more respected by the legislatures of some countries which have no written constitution, than by ours. No doubt our doctrine of constitutional law has had a tendency to drive out questions of justice and right, and to fill the mind of legislators with thought of mere legality, of what the constitution allows. And moreover, even in the matter of legality, they have felt little responsibility; if we are wrong, they say, the courts will correct it. Meantime they and the people whom they represent, not being thrown back on themselves, on the responsible exercise of their own prudence, moral sense, and honor, lose much of what is best in the political experience of any nation; and they are belittled, as well as demoralized. If what I have been saying is true, the safe and permanent road towards reform is that of impressing upon our people a far stronger sense than they have of the great range of possible mischief that our system leaves open, and must leave open, to the legislatures, and of the clear limits of judicial power; so that responsibility may be brought sharply home where it belongs. The checking and cutting down of legislative power, by numerous detailed prohibitions in the constitution, cannot be accomplished without making the government petty and incompetent. This process has already been carried much too far in some of our States. Under no system can the power of courts go far to save a people from ruin; our chief protection lies elsewhere. If this be true, it is the greatest public importance to put the matter in its true light.

You know, that's saying something, but that, of course, isn't popular because now many of my friends want me to save them the effort to prevent bad legislation from being passed, and if it is passed even more effort to get it repealed. "What are you there for? You've got the power. Why don't you declare it unconstitutional?" Meaning by "power" that nobody can overrule me except God by cutting me off and Congress by impeaching me. I regard Thayer's essay as the most important single essay. "This leaves to our courts a great and stately jurisdiction." Lovely touch! He was a very great man.

Index